DUNS SCOTUS LIBRARY
LOURDES COLLEGE
SYLVANIA, OHIO

LOURDES COLLEGE LIBRARY

3 0379 1002 2028 6

820.996
C 44

▲▲▲▲▲
**Toward the
Decolonization of
African Literature**

▼▼▼▼▼

D0145532

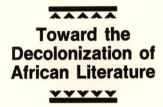

Toward the Decolonization of African Literature

Volume I

African Fiction and Poetry
and Their Critics

by

Chinweizu
Onwuchekwa Jemie
Ihechukwu Madubuike

HOWARD UNIVERSITY PRESS
Washington, D.C.
1983

93-1321

Copyright © 1983 by Chinweizu, Onwuchekwa Jemie and Ihechukwu
Madubuike. First published in the United States in 1983 by Howard
University Press. Published in 1980 by Fourth Dimension Publishing
Co. Ltd., Enugu, Nigeria.

Printed in the United States of America
Second Printing

All rights reserved. No part of this book may be reproduced or utilized
in any form without permission in writing from the publisher. Inquiries
should be addressed to Howard University Press, 2900 Van Ness Street,
N.W., Washington, D.C. 20008.

Library of Congress Cataloging in Publication Data

Chinweizu.
    Toward the decolonization of African literature.

    No more published.
    Bibliography: p.
    Includes index.
    Contents: v. 1. African fiction and poetry and their
critics.
    1. African literature (English)—20th century—
History and criticism.   2. Criticism—Africa.   I. Jemie,
Onwuchekwa, 1940–   II. Madubuike, Ihechukwu.
III. Title.
PR9340.C48   1983   820'.9'96   82–23357
ISBN 0–88258–122–8
ISBN 0–88258–123–6 (pbk.)

To

These giant voices of the Black World calling us to liberation

These exemplary inciters against toleration of our oppressed condition

These husbanders of our memory, raisers of consciousness who through long centuries have nursed our Pan-African will to freedom

These reminders to our needless despair that it is morning yet on creation day

This Work is Dedicated:

Chinua Achebe
Amiri Baraka
Edward Wilmot Blyden
Amilcar Cabral
Aimé Césaire
Leon Damas
Martin Delaney
Cheikh Anta Diop
Frederick Douglass
W. E. B. DuBois
Olaudah Equiano
Frantz Fanon
E. Franklin Frazier
Marcus Garvey
Nicolas Guillen
Langston Hughes
C. L. R. James

George Jackson
Martin Luther King, Jr.
Malcolm X
René Maran
Thomas Mofolo
Kwame Nkrumah
Julius Nyerere
George Padmore
Walter Rodney
Jacques Roumain
Leopold Sedar Senghor
Absalom Vilakazi
David Walker
Chancellor Williams
Eric Williams
Richard Wright

Epigraphs

"Black duty
Or the bacchanal of white night . . . ?"
(Chinweizu)

"Flow then spirit streams . . . .
that ikenga in its return
might purge the infected hearth . . . ."
(Menkiyi)

"Night breezes drum on the plantain leaf:
Let the plantain leaf take over the dance . . . ."
(Okigbo)

Contents

About the Authors

CHINWEIZU is an occidentalist, poet and critic. Born in Isuikwuato in Imo State, Nigeria, he was educated at Government College, Afikpo. He studied Mathematics and Philosophy at the Massachusetts Institute of Technology in the United States, and received his M.A. in American Studies and Ph.D. in History at the State University of New York at Buffalo. In 1976 he was a Rockfeller Research Fellow in Environmental Economics at M.I.T., and in 1978–79 he was Associate Professor of Afro-American Studies at San Jose State University. Since 1973 he has served as associate editor of *Okike*.

Chinweizu's essays, poems, polemics and satires have appeared in various journals in Africa, Europe and the United States. He is the author of the acclaimed historical study, *The West and the Rest of Us* (Random House, 1975; Nok Publishers, 1978), and of *Energy Crisis and Other Poems* (Nok, 1978). Two other books, "The Footrace and Other Satires" and "Towards a Liberated Pan-African Culture: Selected Essays" (1969–1978), are awaiting publication.

ONWUCHEKWA JEMIE is Head of Department of Communication and Languages at the Institute of Management and Technology, Enugu, Nigeria. Born in Item in Imo State, Nigeria, he was educated at the Hope Waddell Training Institution, Calabar, and in the United States at Columbia and Harvard universities. He holds a Ph.D. in English and Comparative Literature from Columbia.

Before returning to Nigeria in 1977, Dr. Jemie taught at Columbia University and at the University of Minnesota where he was Associate Professor of Afro-American Studies and English.

His publications include a critical study, *Langston Hughes: An Introduction to the Poetry* (Columbia University Press, 1976), and two books of poems, *Biafra Requiem* (1970) and *Voyage and Other Poems* (1971). He is currently completing an anthology of previously unpublished versions of Afro-American orature.

IHECHUKWU MADUBUIKE is the Minister of Education of the Federal Republic of Nigeria. Born in Isuochi in Imo State, he was educated at the Duke Town Secondary School, Calabar, and at the Alvan Ikoku College of Education, Owerri. He studied in Canada at Laval University, in France at the Sorbonne, and in the United States at the State University of New York at Buffalo, where he obtained his Ph.D. in French and Comparative Literature.

Dr. Madubuike was Assistant Professor of African Studies and French at the State University of New York at Buffalo and at the Ohio State University before returning to Nigeria in 1976. He then served as Principal Lecturer at Alvan Ikoku College of Education, Owerri. In 1979 he was elected into the Imo State House of Assembly and subsequently appointed Federal Minister of Education.

His publications include critical essays and poems in various journals, plus three books: *A Handbook of African Names* (Washington, D.C.: Three Continents Press, 1976); "The Sociology of the Senegalese Novel," due from Three Continents Press in 1980; and "Ighota Abu Igbo," due from Oxford University Press in 1980.

Preface

We are three Nigerian writers and critics who are intensely concerned for the health of African culture. In undertaking this work we set ourselves the limited task of probing the ways and means whereby Western imperialism has maintained its hegemony over African literature, and the effect of that hegemony upon the literary arts of contemporary Africa. We do realize that there are vaster issues to be examined and rectified if African literature is to cure itself of its colonial hangover, but we have merely tried to follow the sensible rule of one thing at a time. We hope that other African writers and critics, and, indeed, all the participants in African literary culture, will join in this endeavour and extend the range of our work. We would like to stress that nothing in our discussion is a definitive judgment on the *oeuvre* of any writer or critic mentioned; rather, we have chosen to highlight faults and excellences because our primary concern is for practitioners of both the literary craft and the critical craft, and especially for the younger ones among them. We hope that the positions we have taken will provoke efforts, whether out of agreement or flat disagreement, to investigate African literature and its traditions, and to formulate critical canons and procedures adequate for our times. Let controversy rage; may it stimulate creative discussion.

This work was begun in 1971 with attention to African poetry and its criticism. The result of that effort was embodied in an essay completed in mid-1972 and first published in 1974–75 in the African journals *Okike,* Nos. 6 and 7, and *Transition,* No. 48. The rest of the work was begun in December, 1975 after Roscoe, Larson, Palmer and Company had conveniently gathered and published in their books the prejudices and errors about African literature which have long been floating freely in their various groves of academe. That first essay has been incorporated into this larger work.

Contrary to some impressions voiced in some quarters following the appearance of the earlier essay, quarters where we were thought to be "pretenders" to some unheard of and, as far as we know, non-existent and quite undesirable "crown of Pontifex Maximus of African poetics" (a designation predictably borrowed from an alien Greco-Roman experience by a eurocentric African mind), we would like to make it quite clear that, if anything, we are *bolekaja** critics, outraged touts for the passenger lorries of African literature and that we are administering a timely and healthy dose of much needed public ridicule to the reams of pompous nonsense which has been floating out of the stale, sterile, stifling covens of academia and smothering the sprouting vitality of Africa's literary landscape. There comes a time, we believe, in the affairs of men and of nations, when it becomes necessary for them to engage in *bolekaja* criticism, for them to drag the stiflers of their life down to earth for a corrective tussle. A little wrestle on the sands never killed a sturdy youth. We expect Africa's sprouting modern literature to thrive, as its traditional oratures and literatures have done for millenia.

We would like to thank all those, too numerous to name here, whose reactions, of all kinds, spurred us to continue and complete this work.

We are grateful to the Graduate School of the University of Minnesota, and to the Ohio State University, for faculty research grants which enabled us to travel to collaborate on

---

*Bolekaja: "Come down let's fight!"—a term applied in Western Nigeria to passenger lorries ("mammy wagons") from the outrageous behavior of their touts.

this work. We would also like to thank the Departments of Afro-American Studies and English of the University of Minnesota, and the Department of Black Studies of Ohio State University, for their supportive clerical help.

Chinweizu
Onwuchekwa Jemie
Ihechukwu Madubuike

Acknowledgments

Grateful acknowledgment is made to the following for permission to reprint previously published material:

OKIKE Magazine for parts of this book previously published in its pages under the titles "Towards the Decolonization of African Literature," "The Hopkins Disease," and "The Leeds-Ibadan Connection."

Faber and Faber, Ltd. and Harcourt Brace Jovanovich for selections from "The Waste Land" by T. S. Eliot, from *The Collected Poems 1909–1962* by T. S. Eliot and for selections from *Feather Woman of the Jungle* by Amos Tutuola, published 1962.

New Directions Publishing Corp. and Faber and Faber, Ltd. for selections from Canto XX of *The Cantos of Ezra Pound,* copyright © 1934 by Ezra Pound.

Editions du Seuil for selections from "Nuit de Sine" and "Femme Noire" by Leopold Senghor, from *Poèmes* by Leopold Senghor.

Alfred A. Knopf, Inc. for "The Negro Speaks of Rivers," "Suicide's Note," and "Harlem" from *Selected Poems of Langston Hughes,* copyright © 1959 by Langston Hughes; and for selections from *The Autobiography of Malcolm X,* by Malcolm X, with the assistance of Alex Haley, copyright © 1964 by Alex Haley and Malcolm X.

Doubleday & Co., Inc. and Harold Ober Associates for selections from "I Heard a Bird Cry," which appeared in *Night of My Blood* by Kofi Awoonor. Copyright © 1971 by Kofi Awoonor.

Frank A. Aig-Imoukhuede for selections from his poems "Negritude" and "Life in the Country . . . Life in the Town."

Ethiope Publishing Corp. for selections from *The Novels of D. O. Fagunwa* by Ayo Bamgbose.

Eyre Methuen Ltd. for selections from *Idanre and Other Poems* by Wole Soyinka.

University of California Press for selections from *Hero and Chief* by Daniel Biebuyck, and for selections from *The Mwindo Epic* by Daniel Biebuyck and Kohombo Mateene.

Richard M. Dorson for selections from "The Epic as a Genre in Congo Oral Literature" by Daniel Biebuyck, and for "Description in Gbaya Literary Art" by Philip A. Noss, both of which appeared in *African Folklore,* ed. Richard M. Dorson, Anchor Books, 1972.

Matei Markwei for his poem "Life in Our Village."

Wande Abimbola for selections from "The Second Odu of Ifa" from *Sixteen Great Poems of Ifa* by Wande Abimbola.

Ifeanyi Menkiti for selections from "The Pagans Sat Still" from *Affirmations* by Ifeanyi Menkiti. Chicago: Third World Press, 1971.

Ulli Beier for "New Yam" and "Alajire" from *Yoruba Poetry,* ed. Ulli Beier, Cambridge University Press, 1970, and for "Prayer to the Dead Father" from *Python,* ed. Ulli Beier, Papua Pocket Poets, 1967.

M. J. C. Echeruo for "Sophia" and for selections from "Ure Igne," from *Mortality* by M. J. C. Echeruo.

Okogbule Wonodi for his poem "Moonlight Play."

Presence Africaine for selections from "Monzon and the King of Kore," transcribed by Amadou Hampate-Ba in *Presence Africaine* No. 66 (1966).

Romanus Egudu for his poem "The First Yam of the Year."

Dr. Pius Okigbo, Heinemann Educational Books, and Holmes and Meier Publishers (parent company of Africana Publishing Corp.) for selections from "Distances," "Heavensgate," "Elegy for Slit-Drum," "Elegy for Alto" and "Lament of the Masks" by Christopher Okigbo.

Cambridge University Press for "The Dog and the Tortoise" from *Limba Stories and Story-Telling* by Ruth Finnegan, © Oxford University Press 1967; and for selections from "A Judgment" from *Tales of Amadou Koumba* by Birago Diop, translated by Dorothy S. Blair, © Oxford University Press 1966.

Chinua Achebe for selections from *Things Fall Apart* by Chinua Achebe, and from Foreword by Chinua Achebe to *A Selection of African Prose,* I, ed. W. H. Whiteley.

Donatus Nwoga for selections from "Obscurity and Commitment in Modern African Poetry" by Donatus Nwoga, and from Preface by Donatus Nwoga to *West African Verse: An Anthology,* ed. Donatus Nwoga.

Twayne Publishers, Inc. for selections from *Wole Soyinka* by Eldred Jones. Copyright 1973 by Twayne Publishers, Inc. and reprinted with permissions of Twayne Publishers, a division of G. K. Hall and Co., Boston.

University of Texas Press for selections from "*The Horn*: What It Was and What It Did," by W. H. Stevenson in *Research in African Literatures,* Vol. 6, No. 1 (Spring, 1975), pp. 17–19.

Minnie Postma for selections from *Tales from the Basotho* by Minnie Postma, published by University of Texas Press, 1979.

Longman Group Ltd. for selections from *Sundiata; An Epic of Old Mali* by Niane, translated by G. D. Pickett, published 1965 by Longman.

Holmes and Meier Publishers, Inc., parent company of Africana Publishing Corp. for selections from *An Introduction to the African Novel* by Eustace Palmer (Africana Publishing Corp., 1972), and from "Thought on June 26" and the poem "A Farewell" both from *Zulu Poems* by Mazisi Kunene (Africana Publishing Corp., 1970).

African Universities Press for "Hunger" from "Salutations to the Gut" by Wole Soyinka.

* * *

Anchor Books for selections from "Description in Gbaya Literary Art" by Philip Noss, in *African Folklore,* ed. by Richard Dorson, published 1972 by Anchor Books.

T. S. Dennison Co. for "The Great Race" from *Folk Tales of Liberia* by J. Luke Creel, published 1960 by T. S. Dennison Co.

* * *

Numerous requests have been made to obtain permission to reprint the following materials:

Selections from the poem "Insomnia" by Abiola Irele.

"The Race" from *African Myths and Tales* by Susan Feldmann (Dell Publishing Co., New York, 1963).

Selections from *Batouala* by René Maran, translated by Alexandre Mboukou (New Perspectives, Rockville, Md., 1973).

Selections from the poem "Ibadan Dawn" by J. P. Clark.

Selections from *Song of Lawino* by Okot p'Bitek (East African Publishing House, Nairobi, 1966).

Selections from *The Songs of Seydou Camara, Volume I: Kambili* by Charles S. Bird (Indiana University Press, 1974).

* * *

Permission was denied to quote from *The Emergence of African Fiction* by Charles R. Larson, © 1975 by Charles R. Larson. However, we believe that our quotations from his book fall within the conventions of "fair use."

Introduction

At this point in history it is Africa's mission to intensify its decolonization and pursue it into liberation. How is this to be done? How, in particular, shall Africa's literary culture be decolonized and liberated?

The cultural task in hand is to end all foreign domination of African culture, to systematically destroy all encrustations of colonial and slave mentality, to clear the bushes and stake out new foundations for a liberated African modernity. This is a process that must take place in all spheres of African life—in government, industry, family and social life, education, city planning, architecture, arts, entertainment, etc. This book is intended as a contribution to this process in the realm of African letters.

Given the task in hand, and the necessity for rooting out imperialist rot and planting fresh African seeds, this book is unabashedly polemical and pedagogical. In Africa's present situation, Africa's prose literature is under attack from a dominant and malicious eurocentric criticism. Africa's poetry is being crippled by malicious praise by that same school, and Africa's orature is under a blanket obloquy spread by the same school. Let us pause and define some of our terms.

Our conception of literature is perhaps a little broader than is conventionally allowed. In our view, literature must include all the genres of publicly communicated written matter of a society. Thus, in addition to prose fiction, poetry and drama, we consider essays, biographies, addresses and orations a vital part of literature. Now, it should be borne in mind that poems, plays, stories, essays, speeches, etc. do exist in two modes—the written and the oral. Bearing this fact in mind, we find it useful to follow Pio Zirimu and Ngugi Wa Thiong'o's seminal example in using the term *orature* to denote poems, plays, stories, etc. in oral form, and in reserving the term *literature* for the same things in their written forms. Because obloquy has been routinely heaped upon African orature by eurocentric critics of African literature, we have, in discussing African literature, found it necessary to examine at some length the qualities of African orature. Furthermore, African orature is important to this enterprise of decolonizing African literature, for the important reason that it is the incontestable reservoir of the values, sensibilities, esthetics, and achievements of traditional African thought and imagination outside the plastic arts. Thus, it must serve as the ultimate foundation, guidepost, and point of departure for a modern liberated African literature. It is the root from which modern African literature must draw sustenance.

This work is presented in two volumes. Volume I is a diagnostic analysis of the state of African writing. It is an afrocentric criticism of African poetry, fiction and criticism during the period 1950–1975. It demonstrates the mutilations which these genres of African writing have suffered under the euromodernist dispensation. Since much of Africa's essays and addresses have thankfully been spared the attention of euromodernist criticism, they have escaped these mutilations and therefore have required no diagnostic analysis. Drama and its allied arts have been left out of consideration for the basic reason that they rely heavily upon means other than the word for their effect.

Volume II is an anthology of exemplary works in prose and verse, fiction and non-fiction, from both the literature and orature of the pan-African world. It is a collection of works which, in all their grand variety of themes and techniques, are models of memorable thoughts and utterances from the entire pan-African world. These examples of the achievements of the African peoples, in the homeland and in the diaspora, have been gathered to show what the literatures of African peoples have been, and what the literature of the African homeland cannot afford to cast aside in the perverted fascination with and emulation of Western literature.

In examining the criticism of African writing we find that a significant number of African critics are eurocentric in their orientation, whereas they ought to be afrocentric. Such critics habitually view African literature through European eyes. If at all they are aware that African culture is under foreign domination, they seem to think that it ought to remain so—with minor adjustments; or they may perceive a need for a restorative cultural enterprise but fail to see its implications for literary criticism. Most of them would be ashamed to admit it, but the fact of the matter is that these African critics view African literature as an overseas department of European literatures, as a literature with no traditions of its own to build upon, no models of its own to imitate, no audience or constituency separate and apart from the European, and, above all, no norms of its own (none, at any rate, that would be applicable to contemporary writings) for the proper, the beautiful, or the well done. As a result, these critics have followed their European colleagues in charging African novels with various technical, thematic and ideological inadequacies—charges which might conceivably make sense if African novels were intended to be replicas or approximations of European ones, employing the same techniques and in approximately the same ways, treating the same themes with approximately the same emphases, and urging the same values. In addition, these critics have encouraged the manufacture of a stiff, pale, anemic, academic poetry, slavishly imitative of 20th-century European modernism, with its weak preciosity, ostentatious erudition, and dunghill piles of esoterica and obscure allusions, all totally cut off from the vital nourishment of our African traditions and home soil—a poetry in such sorry contrast to the vibrancy, gusto and absolute energy of the African oral poetry which is so firmly and deeply rooted in the African home soil.

But African literature *is* an autonomous entity separate and apart from all other literatures. It has its own traditions, models and norms. Its constituency is separate and radically different from that of the European or other literatures. And its historical and cultural imperatives impose upon it concerns and constraints quite different, sometimes altogether anti-thetical to the European. These facts hold true even for those portions of African literature which continue to be written in European languages.

In our essay we have examined the eurocentric prejudices, showing them for what they are, that is, not the "universal" values which their adherents, African as well as European, habitually pretend that they are, but rather as quite provin-cial, time-and-place-bound *European preferences,* with little or no relevance or validity for African peoples. In addition, we have attempted to define the proper constituency for African literature, explored some of the traditions into which modern African writing should seek to insert itself, displayed some models from those traditions, and itemized some of the qualities and norms which we believe to be transferable from traditional African orature to contemporary African literature.

The anthology may thus readily be seen as a continuation of the diagnostic analysis. It is a display, on a wider field, of traditional models as well as modern examples. The selections are such as engage, probe, assess and reveal the black experience in all its rich diversity. In their thematic range they represent a cross-section of life in the Pan-African world, with the attitudes of members of that world to their lives and conditions, in magnificent variety. The aim of the anthology is to present the community to itself, a community discussing its experiences with itself, commenting, for its own entertainment and enlightenment, upon the world in which it finds itself—the physical world, the social world, the esthetic world, the moral/political world, the private life—but all communicated as part of a dialogue *within* the community, a dialogue of the community with its traditions, its present, and its future.

The essays and speeches, in their African cultural nationalism and anti-universalism, are included to provide some general direction and a controlling consciousness within which African writers, critics, disseminators and consumers of African literature need to work. The task of decolonization cannot be carried out in a vacuum. It requires an atmosphere of *active nationalist consciousness*. It must be conducted within the guiding parameters set by those intellectuals who have upheld black consciousness through the centuries. It is by constantly keeping in touch with such African nationalist thinking that we all, and our writers and critics especially, can avoid being conned into pseudo-universalism. We must keep touch with the intellectual tradition of African cultural nationalism lest we forget or be led astray from the central purposes of African intellectual life.

Our primary obligation, within the above terms, has been to excellence. Only distinct and consummate voices have been considered. Materials with engaging themes, but indifferently or ineptly handled, have been excluded. Examples of different treatments of the same theme have been included. Each author is represented by what he does better than other authors, and it is for this reason that several eminent writers with well-earned reputations have not been included. We have also attempted to represent as fully as possible, first, our women writers, and secondly, all regions of Africa and of the diaspora—but always with an eye to excellence, not to geographical, sexual or ethnic balance.

Needless to say, we have excluded poetry of the ivory tower, poetry of the disoriented modernisms of English Departments squinting at life from overspecialized sensibilities dominated by edicts of alien scholars. We have also sought to exclude the off-track utterances of "orphic messengers to the West" whose words are directed either to no community at all, or to the wrong one.

On works by members of the African diaspora our rule has been: that one drop of black blood makes you one of us—unless you object (for living writers), or unless there are overriding reasons of cultural commitment on a writer's part, especially in the case of dead writers (such as Aesop, Pushkin, and the elder and younger Dumas), who can no longer be consulted for their opinion.

We have also attempted to represent the very wide variety of genres that there are in African literature and orature. This is especially important in view of the many genres which have been overlooked by contemporary African writers. Among the genres included are: essays, speeches, letters, epics, novels, shorter narratives, religious texts, jokes, boasts, bombast, praises and abuses, songs and satires.

This book is intended for readers of all ages throughout the black world. But insofar as, in its polemical and pedagogical intent, it might be said to be directed at writers, it is directed, first and foremost, at aspiring and younger writers, who need good models to imitate; but it is also directed at those older writers who do not feel too old or set in their ways to learn from good examples. To repeat, the general aim of this work is to help release African culture from the death-grip of the West; and the particular aim of the anthology is to help scotch the modernist infection, with its narrowness of themes and genres, its anemic treatment, and its general lack of robustness and gusto. Gathered here are some pieces of memorable utterance to show what African literature cannot afford not to be!

CHAPTER 1

The African Novel and Its Critics (1950-1975)

▼▼▼▼▼

EUROCENTRIC CHARGES AGAINST THE AFRICAN NOVEL

There is a long list of charges usually levelled against the African novel by its Western critics, and authoritatively echoed by their African adherents. Where these charges do not emanate from the importation into the African literary scene of problems and pseudo-problems within the Western tradition, they are either the expression of a literary tourist mentality addicted to a nouveaumania whose easily jaded sensibilities cry out for new supplies of exotica or they are underhanded efforts to defend the Western imperialist, pro-bourgeois status quo in the cultural domain. For instance, with respect to *technique,* some African novels are said to suffer from inadequate description or inadequate characterization, motivation, psychology and depth, or from unrealistic and awkward dialogue, or from alleged problems in the conception and handling of time and space. Others are faulted for being too short or for having thin plots or no plots at all. With respect to their *themes,* some novels are denounced as "situational," and the critical literature is filled with reprimanding laments that too many African novels are autobiographical or preoccupied with culture conflict or unnecessarily fascinated with the African past. With respect to *ideological* matters, some critics claim that there is too much didacticism or not enough of the right kind. Some cry out for what they consider a "consistent moral attitude," and others denounce what they call "protest literature," "topicality," anthropological or journalistic documentation, and "local color."

In levelling these charges, these critics usually ignore several important facts: (1) The African novel is a hybrid out of the African oral tradition and the imported literary forms of Europe, and it is precisely this hybrid origin which needs most to be considered when determining what technical charges could legitimately be made against African novels. (2) The African novel's primary constituency is different from that of the European or other regional novels, and it would be foolhardy to try to impose upon it expectations from other constituencies. (3) The colonial situation imposes a different set of concerns and constraints upon the African novel than upon novels of the imperialist nations. The African novel therefore has every cause to be concerned with issues antithetical to those which the imperialist countries would prefer to see treated in their literatures.

Eurocentric criticism of African fiction stems from colonialist attitudes whereby these critics see the African as an apprentice European whose literary production has no other canons to adhere to but those of whichever part of the Western tradition the critics happen to subscribe to. These critics do not concede the autonomy of African literature. They do not grant it the elementary right to have its own rules and standards, but insist rather on viewing it as an overseas department of European literature. Adrian Roscoe puts it quite bluntly in his *Mother is Gold: A Study in West African Literature:*

> If an African writes in English his work must be considered as belonging to English letters as a whole, and can be scrutinised accordingly.
>
> (Roscoe 1971:x)

He and his publishers reiterate this position even more categorically on the jacket blurb advertising the book:

> *Mother is Gold* expresses a basic critical viewpoint: if an African writes in English his work must be considered as belonging to English literature as a whole, and it must be judged by the same critical standards as any other work written in English.

John Povey goes even further than Roscoe in supplying grounds for this expropriative claim when he says:

> When one can so readily make cross-comparisons with the work of Achebe and, say, Thomas Hardy or Joseph Conrad, one has the satisfying sense that the African writer can be conveniently set within the context of the much wider field of English language writing: the whole "Great Tradition" of which F. R. Leavis so persuasively writes.
>
> (Povey 1972: 97)

These statements articulate a basic premise of eurocentric criticism of African literature, i.e., the refusal to draw a distinction between European national literatures and non-European literatures in European languages; between English as a language used in literature by many outside the British nation, and English letters as a body of works of the British nation. It is by ignoring or glossing over this crucial distinction that eurocentric critics are able to perform the imperialist trick of justifying the application of British literary standards to African works written in English. There are therefore various preliminary issues which need to be clarified before the specific charges can be properly examined.

9

PRELIMINARY ISSUES: AFRICA'S LITERATURE AND ORATURE

What is African Literature?

The central issue is: (1) by what criteria should African literature be judged? In attempting to answer this question, it is important to investigate two underlying matters: (2) what is African literature?—that is, what works, and for what reasons, fall within the body of African literature? (3) what is the proper relationship between this body of works and the other national or regional literatures in the world?

It is important to begin by declaring the separate and autonomous status of African literature, however defined, from all others. By this we mean that genuinely autonomous criteria would have to be applied in judging African literature. As we indicated earlier, eurocentric critics usually answer question 3 by asserting, as Roscoe and his publishers do, that African literature in English, French or Portuguese are appendages of British, French or Portuguese national literatures. In essence, they would like to appropriate African literature as part of European national literatures, and as necessarily inferior parts thereof.

Problems about the definition of African literature (question 2), or about the proper criteria for judging it (question 1), which arise out of this imperialist hegemonic intention, should be dismissed out of hand as spurious, and as problems for the imperialists, not for Africans. However, some African critics, partly because they have been nurtured on and have internalized the prejudices of imperialist criticism, display genuine confusion in defining African literature, and in choosing the criteria by which to judge it. To such critics we would like, first, to point out that, no matter what disclaimers are proffered, to insist on judging African literature by European criteria, or by criteria allegedly universal which on closer scrutiny turn out to be European, is indeed to define African literature as an appendage of European literature, and to deny its separateness and autonomy.

Now, in order to bring a more judicious attitude to the business of defining African literature, it is necessary to examine the classificatory criteria and how to apply them. We must take cognizance of the following situation in world literature: There are *regional literatures,* for instance the European regional literature, which includes many *national literatures* in different languages, or the American regional literature which includes the literatures of the United States (in English), Canada (in English and French), the Caribbean and South America (in English, French, Spanish and Portuguese). There are also *language literatures,* some of which include many national literatures. English language literature, for instance, includes (a) British national literature; (b) the national literatures of those countries where an exported English population is in control, e.g., Canada, the United States, Australia and New Zealand; (c) the national literatures of those countries where English, though neither indigenous nor the mother-tongue of the politically dominant population or group, has become, as a legacy of colonialism, the official language or one of the official languages, e.g., Nigeria, Kenya, South Africa, India, Jamaica, Trinidad and Malaysia. A similar classification can be made for literatures in the languages of other imperialist nations.

The hegemonic attempt to annex African literature for European literatures has usually been made for such African works as are written in non-African languages. The main instrument of such annexations has been the fact that the language used in writing them is non-African. Those concerned with shaking off these encroachments and annexations would need to (1) examine how much such language-based claims are worth; (2) come to an understanding of what works indubitably constitute African literature; and (3) find a procedure for deciding the doubtful cases.

It seems to us quite clear that works done for African audiences, by Africans, and in African languages, whether these works are oral or written, constitute the historically indisputable core of African literature. Works done by Africans but in non-African languages, and works done by non-Africans in African languages, would be those for which some legitimate doubt might be raised about their inclusion or exclusion from the canon of works of African literature, and it is for them that some decision procedure would have to be established.

Though cultural imperialists have used the language criterion as a subterfuge for appropriating to their national literatures works done by persons from outside their nation, language is not the crucial factor in determining the national or regional literature to which a particular work belongs. Inclusion within a national literature is something to be determined by shared values and assumptions, world outlook, and other fundamental elements of culture—ethos, in short. Although language does embody and is a vehicle for expressing cultural values, it is not the crucial generator of those values and cannot *alone* be relied upon to supply literary criteria.

Given the fundamental differences in values and experiences which often appear between two nations who use the same language, it should be obvious that the fact that two works are written in the same language is far less than sufficient grounds for judging them by identical criteria. For example, British, United States, Canadian, Australian, and New Zealand national literatures share the English language, and German and Austrian national literatures share the German language. In addition, there are multilingual national literatures, e.g., Swiss national literature in German, French and Italian; Canadian in English and French; Belgian in French and Flemish. And in both kinds of cases, it is elements of national ethos, not the languages, which supply the decisive criteria used in evaluating them.

Coming to the African situation, then, that Achebe's works may be written in the English language and may therefore be considered part of *English-language literature,* does not mean that they can be criticized with British national values. Indeed, the basic differences between British and Igbo experience and values are what make it necessary for Achebe to have to bend the English language in order to express Igbo experience and values in it.

In brief, then, it is such considerations that make it quite clear that, contrary to the emphatic but confused assertions of Adrian Roscoe and his publishers, it is not the case that if an African writes in English his work must be judged by the same critical standards as any other work in English. In short, attempts at annexation based on language claims are worthless. Language and nation are not the same, and language criteria are not the same as national criteria. The two should never be confused. And in particular, *national criteria* are more important in determining critical standards than mere *language criteria*. While we do not deny that a work written, say, in English, must meet some minimal English language criteria our point is that it does not have to conform to other non-language criteria derived from the English national experience and values. Confusing English-language criteria with non-language criteria derived from the English national experience and values is what allows Roscoe and his publishers to extend their hegemonic claims over African literature written in English. We should not allow ourselves to be taken in by such subterfuges.*

As stated before, works done for African audiences, by Africans and in African languages, whether these works are oral or written, constitute the historically indisputable core of the canon of African literature. In a pragmatic application of family resemblances in order to decide what other works should be included in this evolving canon, the following are some of the most important considerations: (1) the primary audience for whom the work is done; (2) the cultural and national consciousness expressed in the work, whether through

*See Appendix.

the author's voice or through the characters and their consciousness, habits, comportment and diction; (3) the nation-
ality of the writer, whether by birth or naturalization—a
matter that a passport can decide; and (4) the language in
which the work is done.

These considerations are ranked in an order that reflects
the relative importance of the primary audience, and the
treatment required to make the work conform to the values
and taste of that audience, by a writer who is conscious of
working within and for the purpose of furthering the traditions
of that audience, in any language that the circumstances
require. Clearly, in this view of things, the instrumental
medium, that is, the language employed to carry out larger
and more important cultural functions, is hardly by itself to
be considered sufficient, let alone exclusive grounds for
assigning a work to one tradition or one body of literature
rather than another. That Tutuola, Armah, Efua Sutherland,
Ama Ata Aidoo, Flora Nwapa, p'Bitek, Brutus, Peter Abrahams, Nicol, Ngugi, Achebe, Mphahlele, or Menkiti, for
example, speak or write in English, however perfectly or
imperfectly, does not make them Englanders, and their works
belong to them and, through them, to African literature—
certainly not to England's literature. And the point is not
so much their passports as the consciousness they project
in their works, and the primary audience to which their
works are directed. The grounds for the place accorded
language in our ordering of considerations is perhaps best
brought out by an example from the other arts. Just because
an African or Afro-American plays a piano—a European
invention—does not at all mean that the highlife or jazz he
produces on it is European music, which therefore should
be judged by the same standards as European music.

Another example of the pragmatic application of the above
criteria would be Joyce Cary's *Mister Johnson*. It is set in
Africa, and most of its characters, and indeed its central
character, are African. While these might incline some to

include it among the body of African literature in English, we would reject such a classification on the grounds that the writer is an English-born English national describing African characters in an African setting but with a decidedly British consciousness and with prejudices calculated to appeal to his British audience. Similarly, Joseph Conrad's *Heart of Darkness,* though written by a Pole, in English, and set in Africa, with an "all-European" protagonist in Belgian employ, is nevertheless rightly considered a British novel because Conrad is British by naturalization and by assimilation into British culture and its values, and wrote for a British audience. Furthermore, since the body of his works belongs to the central British tradition, one finds no reason to treat *Heart of Darkness* eccentrically by classifying it as anything but a British novel. It is by such judicious examination, combining principle, precedent and pragmatic considerations, that we believe such classifications can usefully be made.

In addition to the problem of defining specific works into or out of African literature, there is the other problem of how to classify expatriate African writers, i.e., African writers living abroad and working away from Africa, as well as works set in places outside Africa, Mars and fantasyland not excluded. Perhaps the best way to tackle this problem is to ask a few questions: Do the novels of Ernest Hemingway set in Europe with a mixture of Americans and Europeans as characters cease to be American novels? Does Gertrude Stein cease to be an American writer because she lived a good part of her career in France, or James Baldwin because he has lived a good part of his in France and Turkey? Does Ezra Pound's poetry cease to be American because of his long sojourn in Britain, France and Italy and the tremendous influence he exerted upon the national literatures of some of those countries? Is it impossible for a writer to belong to two or more national or regional or language literatures. If so, is Samuel Beckett to be read out of English or Irish literature because he has lived much of his life in France, has written some of his works in French, and has been appropriated by the French into their national literature? And what would be said of Pound who was appropriated into British literature (at least by F. R. Leavis in his *New Bearings in English Poetry*) even without his being naturalized? What would be said of American-born Henry James and T. S. Eliot who became naturalized British citizens and who are claimed by both British and United States national literatures? Or of British-born W. H. Auden who became a naturalized U.S. citizen in mid-career? Or, again, of Russian-born Vladimir Nabokov who became a naturalized U.S. citizen in mid-career and thereafter wrote in English. With these perspectives on the matter, questions of classification raised about expatriate African writers can be seen to belong to those borderline situations where a judicious exercise of commonsense is what is mostly called for.

In conclusion, we must remind critics and readers alike, and especially the Adrian Roscoes and John Poveys, that there are none but imperialist grounds for insisting that non-British literatures, whether or not written in English, be judged by technical norms and moral values that are specifically British. Efforts to smuggle these British norms and values into the discourse by disguising them as English language criteria, or as criteria of the so-called Great Tradition, shall not be tolerated.

*Tutuola and the Distinction Between the African Novel
and the European Novel*

The eurocentric view of African literature as an appendage of European literatures manifests itself most forcefully in the preoccupation of eurocentric critics with meticulously documenting the European pedigree of African novels. They spend an inordinate amount of time and effort insisting that a work by an African is patterned on some novel or other by

Conrad, Dostoevsky, or Kafka, and when they cannot find a suitable European ancestry for a work, as in the case of Tutuola, they generate elaborate puzzles as to how the work should be classified. Some invent fanciful antecedents for subsuming the work into some kind of European category; others throw up their hands and declare the work not a novel at all but some curious deadend in the evolution of the African novel (Moore 1962: 57; Abraham 1962: 98; Tibble 1965: 95). What is important in and common to these various positions adopted by eurocentric critics is the unwarranted presumption that in order to qualify for inclusion in one category or another, an African work must conform to rules or criteria developed within the European tradition. If it does not, it is claimed to be problematic.

The eurocentric criticism of Tutuola's writing provides perhaps the best available battleground for examining the question of the autonomy of African literature. What is at stake here is: what is the proper conception of the novel— is it the eurocentrically-derived conception, or should it be one that brings to the fore characteristics specific in the cultural traditions into which the European novel has been imported? In any development from hybrid cultural strains it is normal to expect differences between the new growth and any of its parent forms. It is therefore pernicious, and a manifestation of cultural imperialism, to try to constrain fresh developments by demanding strict and exclusive adherence to the characteristics of one of the parent strains. In their efforts to legislate conformity with European models, these critics might be said to operate like a compulsive murderer licensed to perform surgery. They perceive as malignant growth something which is not, and proceed frantically to cauterize or excise it. (If the patient's life should be endangered, no matter; if he should die, all the better: a threat to Western cultural hegemony will have been squelched!)

Rather than being considered novels pure and simple,

17

Tutuola's works are usually dismissively classified as ghost novels, romances, quest romances, fantasies, allegories, etc., "written in young English" (rather than grown-up English?), and are considered problematic on the grounds that they introduce into human affairs supernatural beings and occurrences which European academics officially regard as superstition worthy of belief only by the "primitive" or "infantile" mind. To argue for the inclusion of Tutuola's works among novels would require that the eurocentric conception of the novel be disestablished in Africa, and that African criteria be established for the African novel. Let us therefore consider the European novel and why its canons are untenable in Africa.

The novel is usually defined as an extended fictional prose narrative whose subject matter is "man in society." There are some misleading terms in this usage which need to be rectified if an intelligent and fruitful discussion of the matter is to take place. First, what is misleadingly called "the novel" is really the European or Western novel. This is implicit in the practice of referring to the European or Western novel as "the novel," whereas other regional novels are routinely qualified as "African novel," "Chinese novel," etc. This behavior has the same misleading and disorienting effect as that which is produced when Western culture insists on calling itself "civilization" instead of "Western civilization," conveying the undeserved impression that it had attained a unique situation called "civilization," and that no other culture in the world had.

Secondly, the term "man in society" is strictly speaking, used to mean man in European or Western bourgeois society. It is not used to refer, for instance, to man in Western feudal society, let alone to man in Celtic Britain, Viking Scandinavia, Ainu Japan, or in any African societies before the European incursion.

To correct these misusages, the term "the novel" should, strictly speaking, be used to stand generically for all extended fictional prose narratives treating of any bourgeois reality (i.e., whose subject matter is man in any bourgeois society), and the term "European novel" or "Western novel" should be routinely applied to novels which treat of European or Western bourgeois reality. In this way they can be properly distinguished from their counterparts in other regions which treat of Japanese, Chinese, or African bourgeois realities. Historically, the European bourgeoisie was the first to emerge and so the first to accumulate a substantial body of written extended fictional prose narratives treating of a bourgeois reality. But this historical precedence ought not to be used to make the European novel stand for the worldwide genre of which it is only a regional version.

The European novel is said to have evolved in the 18th century, its ancestors being the prose and verse narratives, epics and romances, of the Greco-Roman and medieval eras of Europe. The evolution of the European novel from these forms roughly coincided with the developments in European society usually known as the Renaissance—a process which involved the decline of religion, the rise of science and the secular state, the rise of the notion of man as the center of his universe, the rise of protestantism and its stress on individualism, and the conquest of political power by the European bourgeois class, with a concomitant transition in European governments from feudal monarchies to bourgeois constitutional governments. These changes are reflected in European narrative literature in the decline of kingly, aristocratic, and divine heroes, and in the rise of bourgeois protagonists. Secularization was reflected in the narrowing of the view of human society—the world of the novel—to exclude ghosts, the supernatural, and other fantastic beings. But since bourgeois Europe still adhered to the Christian faith, this secularization did not go so far as to eliminate the Christian God, angels, devils and saints from the world of the European novel. The European novel therefore focussed on the interaction of European bourgeois man with his

19

immediate physical environment, human society, and Christian divinities.

Admittedly, in the central tradition of the European bourgeois novel, divinities do not usually appear in their own persons as they did in Greco-Roman and medieval European epics, dramas, romances and tales. Rather, they figure indirectly through their human intermediaries; their presence is transmitted by the priests through baptisms, marriages, communions, confessions and other rites and rituals, and through the fear these priests instill and the influence they exert on the society's ethical opinions and (sometimes) behavior.

Significantly enough, even when African divinities do not appear in their own persons in African novels but, like the official European gods, manifest themselves through their institutions, priests, rites and rituals, the eurocentric critics nevertheless rail against them as an unwelcome intrusion of what they consider "primitivism" into the enlightened secular court of the novel. Clearly, given the retention of Christian spiritual beings in the European bourgeois view of man in society, there is certainly nothing in a bourgeois world view, other perhaps than European prejudice, that would call for the exclusion of spiritual beings from the world of the novel. European academics may choose to banish ghosts, goblins, fantastic beings, etc., from the world of the European novel; that is their prerogative. But it is not their prerogative to seek to banish them from the world of any non-European novel. In particular, it is not their prerogative to seek to banish them from the world of the African novel when the African bourgeoisie have not banished such beings from their reality. Indeed, it is not the prerogative of any European to banish from or introduce anything into Africa.

It is a commonly and easily observed fact that even the most "detribalized" and "modernized" Christians, scholars, scientists and entrepreneurs among the African bourgeoisie today still consult African divinities, diviners and healers when their health or other affairs are in serious trouble. Many have been known to sneak away from their church pews, discard their three-piece suits, steal away by night to some healer in his forest shrine, and carry out all manner of ritual sacrifices when these are demanded. In fact, even among those with a Ph.D., D.Sc., LL.D., and assorted strings of other Western bourgeois academic degrees, the going attitude is still that Western medicines and the Western Christian God are fine in their place; but when things get tough, you run back to your roots and ancestral ways. Nothing could be more revealing of the fundamental loyalties and cosmographic beliefs of the African bourgeoisie. The view of "man in society" involved in this behavior of the African bourgeoisie is one that incorporates the world of Tutuola's novels.

In comparison with this cosmography of the African bourgeoisie, the official cosmography of post-Renaissance Europe, which eurocentric academics attempt to impose upon Africa, is a deviant one, at odds with the cosmography that has historically been common to most of the world, including pre-Renaissance Europe. And what is more, even in the West today, that larger cosmography has merely been driven underground by the official cosmography of post-Renaissance European bourgeois man. Anyone who knows anything about the secret cults and superstitions prevalent today among Europeans and Westerners, knows that the official European cosmography demanded in the novel by European critics is a minority and eccentric one. Consider, for instance, the obsession of the Western public with psychic phenomena; their fascination with exorcism as represented, for example, in their widespread interest in "The Exorcist" sequence of movies and in the performance of exorcisms by their priests, bishops and archbishops. Consider also underground cults like that of Charles Manson in California which periodically come to light, or the belief in haunted houses upon which gothic novels still thrive, or the widespread regard of Friday the 13th of any month as a day of ill omen. Perhaps the most monumentally revealing of these Western superstitions is the fact that in many modern skyscrapers in shiny glass and steel, financed, built, owned, managed and occupied by the cream of the Western bourgeoisie, there are no 13th floors! Of course, the 13th floors are simply numbered 14th to deceive the witches, ghosts and other evil spirits!

The fact that the official Western cosmography is a deviant one subscribed to by a minority of Westerners is of supreme importance in appraising some of the requirements which eurocentric academics would like to impose upon the African novel. In contrast to the deviant cosmography officially upheld in the West, the African world is a world defined by the common, received cosmographies which embrace in their conception of human society the spirit world of the dead and the unborn as well as the world of the living. It is a cosmography which takes for granted interpenetration by these realms and intimate interaction between their human and spirit inhabitants. In short, the African human universe is more inclusive than the revised and attenuated official universe of post-Renaissance Europe. It therefore follows that the realities admissible in the African novel will be more diverse.

Given these differences between the African and the official European notions of human society, it would be surprising if there were no significant divergences in the elements, characters and techniques used in the African and European novels. Specifically, Tutuola's longer narratives are not to be downgraded and dismissed as ghost novels, quest romances, fantasies and the like, but must be accepted as legitimate African novels—as extended written fictional prose narratives whose subject is African man in African society, rendered in accordance with the social realities and cosmography of the African bourgeoisie. They are indeed continuations in English of the African genre of heroic epics. Like the hero in *The Mwindo Epic,* for example, Tutuola's heroes pass through the various spheres of the African cosmography. The action takes place on earth, in the underworld or land of the dead, and in the remote sky, and the heroes interact with human and superhuman characters, divinities and mythical beings. These extraordinary adventures of his heroes, written in prose, make Tutuola's longer works prose epics, i.e., a sub-genre of the novel. In other words, the universe of the African novel is broad enough to include encounters of humans and spirits, transformations of humans into animals and vegetables, and of inorganic matter into organic matter, and vice versa, as in Tutuola, as well as the more narrowly realistic portrayals in Achebe, Ngugi, Peter Abrahams, Mphahlele, Armah, Ouologuem, Beti, Oyono, Sembene, Camara Laye and others. It is a vast, almost limitless universe, and African novelists therefore need make no special effort to "make believable" to eurocentric readers accounts involving the spirit realms which are a legitimate part of their African view of the universe. Specifically, Tutuola, contrary to Gerald Moore's advice, has no need to "banish the goblins and gnomes back to the Northern forests where they belong [in order to] become a short story writer of great interest" (Moore 1962: 56). By the way, which Northern forests? Those of Europe? And of great interest to whom?

Those critics who consider primitive a belief in a world of spirits, of the unborn and the dead, and who dismiss as dangerous hangovers from the "childhood of civilization" a belief in magic, in the possibility of human communication with the dead, and in transmogrification and other supernatural occurrences, might well be told to do themselves the favor of keeping out of the way of novels in which supernatural events take place. After all, it is not an author's job to dissuade them from their basic cosmographic skepticism. For those whose cosmography is broad enough to accept these so-called weird elements, and for those skeptics willing to suspend their disbelief in order to enjoy a well-told tale, a legitimate concern might be expressed if the presentation of supernatural characters and occurrences is botched. Therefore those writers who choose to write novels which incorporate divination, witchcraft, the benevolent and malevolent intervention of gods and spirits in human affairs, etc., would do well to go to the various African folk traditions to learn the traditional conventions for handling such characters, incidents and settings. Examples of what conventions might be learned and adapted are as follows:

(1) Those spirit beings which can be seen or felt usually have some characteristic which gives them away: they may walk backwards only, or their feet don't touch the ground, or their speech is extraordinarily nasal. When they cannot be seen or felt, their presence is described in terms of the usually fearful effects they produce on their surroundings.

(2) Journeys by humans to spiritland involve in some conventions, a hazardous crossing of seven rivers, or a boatride with a ferryman or pilot from the land of the dead. In any case there usually is a hazardous crossing of the boundary between the land of the living and the land of the dead.

(3) Intervention by spirits in human affairs is usually effected through the agency of humans, animals, trees, the elements—when the spirits do not directly enter into and possess individuals. When a spirit possesses a human being, it affects his character and observable behavior.

(4) Spiritland, like dreamland, tends to be surreal. Terrestrial conventions of space and time do not apply there; hence, a tree, for instance, could hold within its trunk a palace or even a vast city.

What is important in all this is not which particular convention is followed, one with some traditional sanction or one invented by the author; it is rather that the reader and the critic should be sufficiently made aware that they are reading a work in which the conventions of the narrowly realistic novel have been suspended. It is up to the reader or critic to acquiesce in the suspension or not, but it is not up to him to insist that no conventions other than the narrowly realistic be followed.

In particular, it should be pointed out that there is no necessary connection between the mere presence of supernatural beings and occurrences in a novel, and its artistic quality. Just as a narrowly realistic novel can be botched, even so can one with a wider cosmography be botched. And just as the one can be very well done, so can the other. The view that all incidents and characters in a novel must have a sufficient explanation of the narrowly naturalistic kind, and the view that the presence of supernatural beings and "weird" occurrences necessarily diminish the artistic quality of a work, are pure prejudices of a narrowly scientific world view. In short, since many Africans believed and still do believe in the kinds of supernatural occurrences associated with the wider African cosmography, African writers, if they choose to represent African realities, and to write for their African audience, cannot allow themselves to be inhibited by official European prejudice from exploring matters of this sort in their novels. It is an inescapable implication of African cosmography that such characters, themes and techniques of presentation which are absent from European novels have a place in the African novel.

Africa's Oral Antecedents to the Novel

In their attacks on Tutuola, eurocentric critics not only fail to admit implications for the African novel of African cosmography, but they also fail to give due weight to influences from Africa's oral antecedents to the African novel. Their usual position is as follows: (1) that there were no African novels prior to the European cultural invasion; (2) that there was nothing in Africa comparable to the novel

93-1321

out of which the African novel might evolve; (3) that whatever there was in the African oral narrative tradition has had a negative influence on the African novel because of the limitations of the oral medium; and (4) they therefore insist that the only "legitimate" model for the African novel is and ought to be European.

Even if the first of the above claims were conceded, the rest cannot. The facts are otherwise. There are both oral and written African antecedents to the African novel, and they are comparable and in no way inferior to the European novel. It should be borne in mind (a) that written literature has a long tradition in parts of Africa; (b) that Africa was not totally unliterate when Europeans arrived there; and (c) that some parts of Africa had written literatures long before many parts of Western Europe. Long before Caesar led his Roman legions to bring civilization to barbarian Gaul, to Celtic Britain, and to the Druidic German tribes of Vercingetorix in the 1st century B.C., the African Nile Valley civilizations of Pharaohnic Egypt, Nubia, Kush, Meroë and Ethiopia had literate cultures—in territories where Sudan, Ethiopia and Egypt are today located. And long before these Johnny-Come-Latelies to civilization—England, France, Germany and all of non-Mediterranean Europe—were taught the literary arts, these same literate African cultures of the Nile Valley had taught writing to the Mediterranean cultures of Crete, Greece, and Judaea, had given them their religions and gods, and schooled them in mathematics, astronomy, architecture, and philosophy, and in the other arts and sciences. (By the way, for anyone unaware of and startled by these facts, please read, among other works, Book Two of *The Persian Wars* by Herodotus, a Greek historian who visited ancient Egypt in the 5th century B.C., and who had no reason either to flatter or disparage blacks and their achievements; and read the Old Testament Judaeic accounts of the arrival, 400-year sojourn, and exodus of the Israelites from ancient Egypt. Other works which the reader ought to consult are Cheikh Anta Diop's *The African Origin of*

Civilization; the appendix, pp. 199–208, to Diop's *The Cultural Unity of Black Africa*; *Stolen Legacy*, by George G. M. James; and *The Destruction of Black Civilization,* by Chancellor Williams.) Besides extended narratives in Egyptian hieroglyphs, there are pre-colonial African extended narratives written in Amharic, Hausa and Swahili, among others.

In addition to extended written narratives in African languages, there was in pre-colonial Africa an abundance of oral narratives which are in no way inferior to European novels. It might be noted that some of these, especially the epics and epic cycles, when written down, are comparable in length to quite a few European novels. These narratives have made thematic, technical and formal contributions to the African novel. Among the formal are contributions in the area of length, structural complexity, and textural complexity. In their themes and techniques, African novelists have utilized material from African tales, fables, epigrams, proverbs, etc. The structural and textural complexity of their narration have counterparts in short as well as extended oral narratives. And as for the question of sheer length, upon which the Adrian Roscoes harp so much, it is not part of the concept of the novel that it must be of the same length as *War and Peace.*

Since there are these pre-European African narratives, both oral and written, some of which are comparable to European novels, and others of which have contributed to the development of the African novel, there is no reason why they should not be considered African antecedents to the African novel, antecedents out of which the African novel might entirely have evolved, without hybridization by the European novel.

In order to forestall those anxious to deny this, it would be useful to make clear the place of the novel in the long tradition of extended narrative in each society. The fact that the novel, an extended fictional narrative, treats of bourgeois reality is not sufficient to take it out of the general category to which belong extended fictional narratives that treat of

27

feudal society, slave society, socialist society, or other social formations. In other words, far from being a unique and unprecedented achievement, the novel is merely the bourgeois counterpart of the romances and epics of the feudal and pre-feudal eras. The romance, the heroic epic, and the novel are *equivalent forms* in their respective social formations. Specifically, their equivalence consists in the fact that they are extended, narrated, imaginative constructs which handle or treat of the social reality of the dominant stratum of their respective social formations. Being equivalent forms, the novels of a given nation or region would stand in similar relationships to the romances and epics from earlier eras of that given nation or region.

Thus, for instance, the Chinese or Japanese novel of their respective bourgeois eras would bear the same relationship to the Chinese or Japanese romance or epic of their respective feudal and pre-feudal eras as the European bourgeois novel would bear to the romance and epic of Europe's pre-bourgeois times. By the same token, the pre-colonial equivalents of Africa's bourgeois novel would be found in the extended narratives of pre-colonial Africa, particularly in the epics and romances of that era. By the way, it should be noted that the terms "epic," "romance," and "novel" are merely European terms for some European versions of extended narratives which have their counterparts throughout the world in analogous social formations. One therefore shouldn't, strictly speaking, look for Japanese "epics" or African "romances" (that is, not in the European sense of these terms), but rather for the dominant and functionally equivalent forms of extended narrative in feudal Japan or pre-colonial Africa.

These equivalent forms from earlier eras of a given society are the proper antecedents or prototypes of the novel in each society. Wherever a bourgeois class has come into prominence, and has produced novels to reflect its own social realities, such indigenous antecedents have helped to shape the development of its novel. Therefore in the case of the African novel it is important to realize that its indigenous antecedents should be sought in the continent's traditions of extended narrative.

However, even those critics who recognize, in the case of the European tradition, that Europe's extended narratives, both the oral and the written, whether in prose or verse, were the antecedents or prototypes of the European novel, seem reluctant to search in the analogously appropriate area for whatever African antecedents to the African novel there are. Part of their problem in this regard might well derive from the fact that they are unaware of, or turn a blind eye to, Africa's pre-colonial, written, longer narratives. To further compound their blindness, they have, out of various cultural biases, constructed a grand mountain that separates oral and written literatures, and are unable to look beyond that divide. They are therefore unwilling to even entertain the notion that some extended narrative antecedents to the African novel might exist in Africa's oral traditions. If at such moments they had managed to cure themselves of their parochial formal fixation upon the writtenness of narrative texts, they might have remembered that the earliest of their own European narratives, some of them still unsurpassed, were oral long before they were written down, and they might then have been better disposed to look into Africa's oral traditions for some of the African antecedents to the African novel. But in a situation bedevilled by imperialist arrogance, racist bias, a formalist bias against orature, and the unexamined assumption that Africa had no pre-colonial written texts, these glib scholars and critics quite contentedly turn their eyes away from where they ought to look, and in their pompous ignorance roundly declare, as does Roscoe, that

> the novel, *as it is known in the West,* precisely *because it is a written form,* has no history whatever in Africa.

> ... It is a literary import. ... from Europe. ... It
> is not, in its nature, an African form. ... It is not a
> fact of the African past.
>
> (Roscoe 1971: 75. Italics added)

Roscoe again misperceives the matter. That the novel, a
bourgeois form of extended fictional narrative, has no history
in pre-colonial Africa, is not at all because it is a written
form. As we have said, there were written literatures in pre-
colonial Africa. It is rather because there was no African
bourgeoisie in pre-colonial Africa. And even if there had
been such a bourgeoisie, its novel would hardly be expected
to conform to the characteristics of the Western novel. Africa
is simply not the West.

In order to buttress their entrenched prejudices, these
scholars and critics seem compelled to make more of the
written form itself than is warranted, and seem concomitantly
compelled to disparage, without the warrant of examination,
the capabilities of the entire oral medium in order to attribute
to the influence of that medium whatever features in the
African novel they find not to the liking of their European
or Europeanized tastes. In examining these mutually supportive and formalist prejudices, that is, their prejudice in
favor of the written form and their prejudice against the oral
form, let us begin with their prejudice in favor of the written
form and evaluate some of the claims that have been made
for that form.

Roscoe's view on the written form is not unrepresentative.
What is remarkable is that such views are shared by oth-
erwise good African scholars and critics. For example,
Emmanuel Obiechina tells us:

> Literacy is crucial to the emergence of the novel,
> because the novel is meant to be read by the individual
> in quiet isolation, and complex narrative is more easily
> sustained and followed by reading it than by hearing it.
>
> (Obiechina 1975: 3)

Although it is true that the novel historically has been a written form it is doubtful that some claims made for it on that account cannot also be made for non-written extended narratives. For instance, some epics display all the complexities of character, situation, plot, theme, technique, etc., that are found in the novel. Since these epics were generally written down from the fully developed oral form, it follows that all the complexity found in them was sustained and followed by narrating and listening, during the centuries when they were handed down by word of mouth. Specifically, such epics as the *Iliad,* the *Odyssey, Beowulf,* the *Nibelungenlied,* the prose and verse *Eddas, Sundiata, Mwindo, Monzon and the King of Kore,* and *Kambili,* which were orally delivered long before they were written down, all display the complexity of plot, theme, situation, technique, character development, etc. of both the consciously written epics such as the *Divine Comedy,* the *Aeneid,* and *Paradise Lost* (which incidentally were modelled on the oral ones), and of the novel at its most complex and extended, as in *War and Peace, Ulysses, Remembrance of Things Past,* and *Don Quixote.* These examples would conclusively demonstrate that any claim that a work has to be written in order to be as complex as a novel is at best a prejudice, however fashionable or accepted. In other words, literacy or writing, as such, is not a condition for satisfying those supposedly distinguishing characteristics of the novel. An oral epic or an extended oral narrative, insofar as it has those characteristics which are said to distinguish the novel, and especially those that are alleged to derive from the fact that the novel is a written form, could be designated if not an *oral novel,* then at least a *prototype* of the novel.

It would follow, therefore, that even though it might be demonstrated that the novel, a written bourgeois form, did not exist in Africa before the European invasion, its oral antecedents or prototypes did. And since African novelists have utilized and modelled themselves upon these prototypes, the African novel cannot rightly be regarded as a purely borrowed narrative form without African antecedents. There are these African antecedents, and critics who assert or argue otherwise thereby place themselves in fundamental opposition to those African writers who are developing a new form out of contributions levied from both the European and the African traditions.

The Alleged Deficiencies of African Orature and Its Allegedly Negative Influence on the African Novel

The prejudice against the oral form manifests itself most strongly in the claim that whatever there was in the African narrative tradition has had a negative influence on the African novel by contaminating the African novel with the "deficiencies" of the oral medium. This prejudice is inculcated and employed by eurocentric critics to shore up the eminence and authority they would like permanently to confer upon European literature over the minds of Africans. The schema of their argument is as follows: oral is bad, written is good. African narrative is oral, therefore bad; European narrative is written, therefore good. If Africans desire to progress from bad to good they must ape European narrative. Furthermore, they must not allow their apery of European narrative to be marred by influences from African narrative which, being oral, is of course indelibly bad, or beyond redemption. As examples of what they consider characteristically faulty in oral narrative, these idolators of Europeana allege that African oral narratives have thin plots, thin narrative textures, and undeveloped characters.

Those among them who set out to be charitable towards the African novel further allege that when similar characteristics appear in the African novel, it is the fault of the African oral tradition. Dan Izevbaye, for instance, tells us:

> The view that undeveloped characters are typical of
> African fiction has been a popular one and was prob-
> ably first expressed by Professor Abraham of Ghana,
> who also attributed the phenomenon to the traditional
> African conception of the individual and society but
> thought it a shortcoming in written fiction. There is of
> course a danger in applying to written forms concepts
> abstracted from the oral tradition. Apart from the
> communal character of traditional societies, the imme-
> diacy of oral communication, which contrasts with the
> opportunity for mediation that writing offers, must
> have severely limited the chances of character devel-
> opment in the oral tale. Besides, the oral tale made
> up for its narrative texture with a dramatic vitality,
> and it is now usually accepted that dramatic characters
> are not as fully "rounded" as fictional ones.
>
> (Izevbaye 1975: 4–5)

Whether these characteristics attributed to the African novel
are to be considered shortcomings or not, it would seem
crucial to determine, first of all, whether the charges are
indeed substantiable; and when they are, whether they are
indeed attributable to the alleged causes.

If an examination of African orature should show that it
cannot be regarded as characterized by these "shortcomings," then it would be unwarranted to regard it as bad, as
characteristically faulty, or as inferior. And insofar as it has
influenced African novels, it cannot be blamed for the
shortcomings of those novels. Secondly, if the "faults" in
the novels are not attributable to the African narrative
tradition, the oral as well as the written, there then will be
no room for the remedy, usually envisaged, which encourages
the African novelist to look exclusively to European models
for how to develop character, complicate plot, make his
narrative texture dense, and handle all other aspects of his
novel.

As a fine specimen of this eurocentric impulse now under
consideration, the passage quoted above from Izevbaye

demands careful scrutiny: (1) How seriously should the speculation be taken that "the immediacy of oral communication . . . must have severely limited the chances of character development in the oral tale?" (2) Is it true that the oral tale necessarily has a "thin narrative texture?" (3) How seriously should the speculation be taken that "the communal character of traditional societies . . . must have severely limited the chances of character development in the oral tale?" (4) However popular the view, in what sense, if any, of the term "developed" could it be true that "undeveloped characters are typical of African fiction?" (5) Are "undeveloped characters," however defined, a shortcoming in written fiction, and if so, why? (6) Is it true that characters in drama are not as fully "rounded" as characters in narrative fiction?

Before we proceed to investigate the above issues, it is necessary that, as part of an important bush-clearing work, we examine one further matter raised by Izevbaye's passage, namely (7) an assumption of non-parity and non-reciprocity between oral and written fictional forms. Given that concepts abstracted from the written forms are widely and routinely applied to oral forms, in baldly declaring that there is a danger in applying to written forms concepts abstracted from the oral tradition, Izevbaye implies an absence of parity between them, and a non-reciprocity in the matter of considering one form with concepts abstracted from the other. He implies, thereby, that the oral form is inferior to the written form. If this is anything more than a prejudice we would very much like to know the grounds for it, especially since they are both narrative forms, and as we have shown earlier in our discussion, there are genres in the one equivalent to genres in the other, e.g., oral epics and written epics; oral extended narratives and novels. Given these equivalencies, Izevbaye needs to supply good reasons why concepts abstracted from the oral may not be applied to written forms.

This issue of parity and reciprocity has implications for the matter of making comparisons between the oral and written modes. Cognizance ought to be taken of the diversity of genres within the oral and the written forms, so that only comparable forms are compared. From our earlier argument, the oral epic is comparable to the written novel; the oral counterparts of the written short story would be tales and fables; and common to both oral and written media would be drama, proverbs, aphorisms, plus all the various genres of poetry except perhaps concrete poetry, which depends to an unusual degree upon the pictographic aspect of its display of letters. If the parity between the oral mode and the written mode of narrative is acknowledged, and if the reciprocity between oral and written fictional forms is acknowledged, we see no danger in applying to written forms concepts abstracted from the oral tradition, provided that this is done between comparable forms.

The importance of the requirement that comparison be made between comparable forms lies in this: it makes it harder for critics to indulge in vague, misleading or inappropriately grounded claims in favour of either the written or oral mode and their forms. Such misleading or inappropriately grounded claims are regular grist for those critics who churn out disparagements on the head of the oral mode. Quite often, their rationalizations for their prejudices appear to have an air of validity only because they are, at least in part, based upon cavalier comparisons of non-comparable forms. For example. Adrian Roscoe attributes the shortness of African novels to the influence of African oral tales, all of which he regards as short. He says:

> The oral story, then, has been Africa's dominant form. As Borges points out, a piece of the length and complexity of a novel could never be related by word of mouth. In Africa's oral past, and present, texts as long as *Things Fall Apart* or *The Interpreters* are not normally found. Africa has been brought up on much

shorter narratives; epics like *Sundiata* being special, occasional, exceptions . . . and in any case of fairly short length. . . . Important results stem from this. The African child . . . may acquire a taste for the novel; but his home life, his society's history—in a word, his culture—predispose him to the story. It also means that, for the moment, the African reader is a short distance performer. And curiously enough, so, too, are many of the writers. Notice the brevity of many of their texts, whether they are traditionalists like Tutuola or moderns like Soyinka and Clark.

(Roscoe 1971: 75–76)

Roscoe is comparing the novel, not with the epic which would be its comparable oral form, but rather with the shorter oral narrative. He perfunctorily dismisses the epic, which would have been the right kind of evidence, and instead focusses on the short narrative, which is the wrong kind of evidence. So long as he manages to block oral epics from consideration, thereby suppressing the evidence, it becomes possible for his claim to acquire an air of validity which it could not otherwise. Gerrymandering the evidence enables him to get away with comparing non-comparable forms, a process whereby he enables himself to suit his prejudices by turning into a fault, allegedly derived from African orature, some features of the African novel.

In comparing comparable forms, there is a further question of what kind of transcript of an oral narrative would be appropriate for comparison with a written text. That the choice of an appropriate transcript is a serious matter can be seen from the fact that most of what has so far been published read like bare-boned, truncated texts shorn of most of their narrative texture. They tend to read more like plot summaries then fleshed-out narratives. Persons familiar with masterly performances of oral narratives, or with good transcripts of masterly performances, know that most of the available transcripts have as much relationship to their oral originals as a plot outline of *Tom Jones* has to the narrative artistry displayed in that novel by Henry Fielding. Usually missing from these bare-boned plot summaries are such elements of narrative texture as: narrative formulas, arresting images, alliterations, ideophones and onomatopoeia, repetitions, exclamations, puns, allusions, proverbs and aphorisms, digressions explaining this natural phenomenon or that historical fact or custom, dialogue, songs, chants, audience responses, description or invocation used again and again and again, gnomic pronouncements, etc. In short, narrative texture is a matter of the quality of the telling; it includes all those things with which a story outline is embroidered into an accomplished tale. Most of the transcriptions presently available read like tales shorn of their narrative texture. They give the impression of story outlines as remembered and sketchily fleshed out by indifferent artists or even by non-artists.

Such losses of narrative texture as result from transcribing performances by indifferent artists are quite often compounded and aggravated by losses due to (a) incompetent transcription from tapes and oral performances; (b) the impatience of some scholarly transcribers with elements of the narrative which they consider boorish, boring, irrelevant or peripheral to their notion of the "main story line;" (c) sloppy and incompetent translation; and (d) the fact that much of the theatrical dimension to the performance of an oral narrative cannot be captured in writing. These sources of transcription loss make it imperative that if the judgments made on oral tales by scholars are to have much value, they should be shown to have been made either on performances of the tales by master story-tellers, or on the best possible transcripts of performances by such master story-tellers. Until scholars show that they have proceeded in this manner in arriving at their judgments, they should hold their peace; otherwise they are justifiably open to the suspicion that they purvey unexamined popular prejudices, racist as well as imperialist, with professorial authority. The onus of showing that they have taken these matters into consideration lies with them. Furthermore, those especially who feel called upon to disparage a whole tradition should, in fairness to their own integrity, show that they are not comparing the best works of the European tradition with average or less-than-best works from the African tradition. Considerations of fair comparison require that the best of the one tradition be compared with the best of the other—at all times, but especially before white supremacist impulses are indulged.

When it is clear that observations are being based upon proper evidence, the standard features of an African oral tale may be construed as faults only by ignoring the purposes of its genre and the impositions made upon its form by the context of its delivery. The appropriate conventions and narrative aims which determine its form and techniques should first be ascertained, for it is only against these that they can be judged adequate or inadequate, and certainly not by inappropriate narrative conventions, nor by conventions from other genres.

Bearing these caveats in mind, let us go on to discuss the issues raised by Izevbaye's passage, starting with the first two: (1) How seriously should the speculation be taken that "the immediacy of oral communication . . . must have severely limited the chances of character development in the oral tale?" (2) Is it true that the oral tale necessarily has a "thin narrative texture?"

Let us consider the evidence, first from the shorter oral narratives. Such stories can broadly be divided into those that are *parabolic* and those that are not. For those that are parabolic, it should be borne in mind by reckless critics that it is part of the convention of parables that they are expected to utilize easily recognizable characters—that is, stock characters—in conventional or stock contexts, using narrative devices which do not divert attention from the moral lessons of the story to extraneous considerations or titillations, such as an overly dense narrative texture, or subtle character development, or an unnecessarily complicated plot would be. It is not surprising, therefore, that parables are short, bald, and to their point. To fault them for these characteristics would be to announce one's ignorance of the requirements and conventions of the genre.

The charges of thin narrative texture, undeveloped characters, or uncomplicated plots, which Izevbaye and others make, cannot be sustained against *non-parabolic* African tales when good transcripts from performances by masters of the verbal art are examined. For instance, consider the following three transcripts of the same oral tale—the well known story of a race between an animal renowned for its speed and one notorious for its slowness, in which the slow-footed but sure-witted triumphs. First a version collected among the Igbo and published by Susan Feldmann:

THE RACE

A frog challenged a deer to a race. Before the day appointed for the contest, the frog entered into a league with all his companions and arranged that they should station themselves at regular intervals along the course, and that each should wait in readiness to answer the calls of the deer as he raced along toward the goal. The race started. The deer thought to outstrip the frog with ease, and soon called back in mocking tones to ask where the frog was. To his surprise the answer, "Here I am," came from the opposite direction to what he expected. He raced along once more and repeated the challenge. Again a voice answered from in front of him, and once more he was deceived and thought he was being left behind in the race. The strategy was repeated all along the course until the deer fell down exhausted and died.

(Feldmann 1963: 140–41)

Clearly, although masquerading as something better, the above version of this classic tale is no more than a bare-boned plot summary, either collected from an indifferent artist or non-artist, or set down by a scholar who had no interest in the story as a specimen of oral art, or both. It contains nothing at all indicative of Igbo narrative style, not even the obligatory formulas with which such stories begin and end.

Now, here is a Limba version of the same story performed by Mrs. Mase Gbawuru and transcribed and translated by Ruth Finnegan:

THE DOG AND THE TORTOISE

Excuse me, you chiefs . . .[1] I have come, I Mase, Mrs. Gbawuru II.

A dog once competed with a tortoise. They said they were seeking the chiefship. Then the tortoise said—the dog said, 'Let us go to Freetown to seek the chiefship.' When they went to Freetown, they went and did—they went and said, 'All right.' They set a date, saying that at that time, at that time they were to come about the chiefship.

When they went, the dog, the dog said, 'Let us go and get ready.' As they came to get ready, then the dog said, 'Oh! Look at the one who is thinking he is to beat me for the chiefship—[going] kɔkɔrɔ kɔkɔrɔ kɔkɔrɔ kɔkɔrɔ.'[2]

Behold, cleverness is more than anything in the world. The tortoise had many children. He took them; all the way from here to Freetown, he came and placed them on the roads.

Now the dog, he trusted to his ability to run. When the dog came and stood ready, he said, 'Now I, the time has come—let us go. You go first. You are not able to go [fast].' The tortoise said, 'All right. I accept. Well, all right, I will go first.'

---

[1] She asks the chief and elders for silence so that she can begin.
[2] The dog is referring contemptuously to the tortoise's gait.

When he set out, then he said,[3] 'Kombo kɔmbɔ o kɔkɔrɔ tɔ, mba kɔkɔrɔ tɔ. Kombo kɔmbɔ o kɔkɔrɔ tɔ, mba kɔkɔrɔ tɔ. Kombo kɔmbɔ o kɔkɔrɔ tɔ, mba kɔkɔrɔ tɔ . . .' Then he did—he sat down to rest.

Then the dog got up. 'Walaahi,[4] I and the tortoise we are competing. Walaahi. I and the tortoise are competing. See the one who is beating me for the chiefship, the one who goes kɔkɔrɔ kɔkɔrɔ as he walks. Ha!'

Then he got up, 'Pampaŋ, kanthapande,[5] pampaŋ, kanthapande, saŋsaŋ, kanthapande, saŋsaŋ nuwɛke pande ni wo. Pampaŋ kanthapande, pampaŋ kanthapande, saŋsaŋ nuwɛke pande ni wo. Pampaŋ kanthapande, pampaŋ kanthapande, saŋsaŋ nuwɛke pande ni wo. . . '

Then the tortoise sang 'Kombo kɔmbɔ o kɔkɔrɔ tɔ, mba kɔkɔrɔ tɔ . . .' Then he went and he rested.

Then the dog got up. 'Hŋ! Walaahi, see the kɔkɔrɔ kɔkɔrɔ who is beating me for the chiefship! I will go and sit on the [chief's] hammock. Just wait!' He urinated. 'Pampaŋ kanthapande, pampaŋ kanthapande, saŋsaŋ nuwɛke pande ni wo . . .'

The tortoise—wherever he rested, there another [tortoise] answered him in the distance. A [tortoise] child answered there again, 'Kombo kɔmbɔ o kɔkɔrɔ tɔ, mba kɔkɔrɔ tɔ . . .' He sat down and rested.

Then the dog said 'Walaahi, see the tortoise, the kɔkɔrɔ kɔkɔrɔ he is beating me, we are competing for it now. Just wait! Walaahi, pampaŋ kanthapande, pampaŋ kanthapande, saŋsaŋ nuwɛke pande ni wo . . .'[6]

---

[3]The song represents the way the tortoise walks, and Mase sang it in a rather slow but sharply rhythmic way to make this more vivid. The chorus on each occasion sang mba kɔkɔrɔ tɔ. The whole was, here and later, repeated many times over.

[4]An exclamation of surprise or determination, here also representing the sound made by dogs.

[5]The song of the dog's running, sung more quickly than the tortoise's song, the succession of quick short syllables showing his speed.

[6]The dog's song is now very breathless and weak. The teller does not need to describe his exhaustion, showing it instead by the way the dog sings.

> Well, when they reached there now, they came
> now right to here, the tortoise was now here in this
> house!
>
> The tortoise answered now from where he was
> sitting in the chair. 'Hŋ, kombo kɔmbɔ o kɔkɔrɔ tɔ,
> mba kɔkɔrɔ tɔ . . .'
>
> The tortoise took the chiefship. If you see now
> that he has the property—the dog failed. If you see
> now that the dog always goes 'Walaahi'—if you see
> the dog sitting, ha! it is the surprise he had when he
> competed with the tortoise. Behold, the tortoise was
> now sitting in power(?). The tortoise was now sitting
> there, doing—saying 'I am here now, see!'
>
> Since I heard that, and Yenkeni came, I had to
> tell it to her. It is finished.
>
> (Finnegan 1967: 323–25)

Finnegan's headnotes confirm what the reader may already
suspect, namely, that this version, though a considerable
improvement upon the first, was performed by an undistin-
guished story-teller rather than by a master of the oral art.
Finnegan reports that

> There were a number of hesitations and slips by the
> teller, filled in by such words as "something," some-
> one" (*wanini*): the emphasis was very much on the
> *singing* rather than the narration.

Such would hardly have been the case with a master
performer.

Though this version captures the ideophones and dramatic
voices in the story, and includes the opening and closing
formulas, it was, on the whole, transcribed with the conventional scholar's aversion to repetitions and indifference
to narrative structure. Finnegan has relegated these aspects
of the narration to her headnotes and footnotes. For instance,
her headnotes inform us that

> The songs were sometimes repeated as many as ten
> or fifteen times and took about as long as the narrative
> parts of the story, or longer.

In her rendition of the singing, she fails to arrange the words on the page in such a way as to suggest even something so elementary and conventional as the leader-choral antiphony but confines it all entirely to a single mention in her footnotes where she says:

> The chorus on each occasion sang mba kɔkɔrɔ tɔ. The whole was, here and later, repeated many times over.

It just so happens that the very things she chose to leave out are among the crucial elements of narrative texture which would have enabled the reader to experience with some fullness the drama of the story.

With the next version of this story we come into the presence of the master, Bai Gai Kiahon, and of a good transcriber and translator, J. Luke Creel:

THE GREAT RACE

One time the animals decided to hold a big contest—a racing contest. The king—the lion, of course—in his unquestioned wisdom had for a long time been observing that the animals, all of them, liked nothing better than running, and prized nothing more than speed. Speed was of prime importance to animals, whether they were running from something, or running to something or whether they were just running.

For all of them, as the king in his undisputed wisdom had observed, often ran just for fun. They were not going anywhere. They were just running. And that was the best running of all. So carefree. So delightfully without destination. So purposeless. Seemingly without purpose and yet there was a purpose. And that purpose, though not one of the animals would admit it, was to show off oneself before all the other animals, to let all others see with their own eyes just how good he was, how expert, how nimble, how swift! And each dreamed ambitiously of showing himself off so well, he could see the eyes of all others, from king to skunk, turn green from envy. Thus they leaped, ran, cavorted when they were going nowhere.

The king observed this and he proclaimed a great racing meet in which everybody was permitted to take part. Nobody was barred, and the aspiring racers were numerous. And still the numbers grew, a sure forecast of a tremendously big day and a successful tournament until the deer, the swiftest of his kind, appeared and entered his name in the race. That discouraged everybody, for the deer was known as the swiftest of animals and this one was the swiftest of all deer.

Thus nobody expected the deer, with so much reputation already established, to enter the race. They told him he should not enter, that he could add no glory to his glory, and for three days, in united action, they used every persuasive reason and force that united action can muster. But the deer went around all the time with a faint smile on his face, happily self-satisfied, and looking wiser than wise. And at the end of the three days of concerted persuasion, he announced calmly again that his name was there to stay; he *would not* withdraw from the race.

Then all the others, with their heads together, said, "What's the use?" and they began fast to withdraw. It was like a panic caused by an epidemic when everybody withdraws from an area to insure his health; and soon there was nobody intending to race except the deer, who went around still with a faint smile on his face and looking more self-pleased than ever. A good prize had been offered for the winner, and with no challenger, the deer would have the prize without even having to run for it. It was easy money. It would have been difficult for the deer to say with which he was the more pleased—with his enviable reputation or with the prospect of an easy prize. But anyway, his was a double pleasure, and he walked around all the time with that pleased smile on his face.

But the king pleaded with the animals not to let the prize go by default. Yet still nobody budged an inch. Then he roared out another proclamation to the effect that if anybody would volunteer to race the deer, the king would give a small prize to the one who came in second. He felt certain that many would now re-enter the race. But he was mistaken, for the animals are proud creatures and nobody wanted voluntarily to accept second place. That would be to acknowledge one's satisfaction with second place, and though one be actually second, or third or fourth, it is shameful to be satisfied with less than first. Satisfied, aspiration is dead, and that is a sad state of being, for one should aspire always to first place though he be lowest. And so out of pride everybody was silent and motionless, and the king frowned with disappointment.

Then finally in this tense moment, everybody heard the silence punctured by a low, squeaky voice squeaking up from the ground, and looking suddenly downwards they all beheld the turtle, the leader of his tribe, standing high on his front toes, as high as a turtle can possibly stand on his front toes, and in his squeaky voice-tones offering to race the deer for the prize. There was surprised silence for a moment, and then the animals broke loose with spontaneous uproarious laughter. They sat back on their haunches, lifted their heads and laughed to the sky, and the sound rose over the treetops and was borne for miles around.

But when they had finished and could laugh no more the turtle was still standing there in the same position, high on his toe points. He had not cracked a smile and he looked deadly serious. And so the king set down his name and solicited more volunteers, but no others came. Then the animals waited gleefully for the day of the race. "This is the joke of the century," they said, "this is going to be good."

Meantime the turtle called his healthy tribesmen together and said to them: Not I alone, but we together are going to win this race. And not the second prize, but the first, for it is shameful to aspire to less than first place. Over-confidence is a fatal disease, and the deer is eaten up with that disease. I know his habits of the race. He stops and eats grass; he munches on tender leaves along the way; he stops and chats if he sees somebody he likes; and he even takes naps, and yet he has always won.

"But we must take advantage of these habits, and I'll tell you how. You know that we turtles all look so much alike nobody can tell us apart without minute examination. Now listen well. The race will be run, as you know, along the long valley between bookando and boolendo. I will conceal myself beneath a shrub near the end of the valley not far from the goal. And all along the way each of you will conceal himself beneath a shrub certain distances apart. One of you whom I shall name shall take his place with the deer at the starting point. Each time the deer stops to eat grass, munch leaves, chat with a passerby, or take a nap, the one of you just far enough ahead to see him must creep quietly out and, unperceived by him, jog stealthily onward down the valley. The one left behind will creep under the nearest shrub and lie there concealed until the race is over. Now the deer will probably take a nap this time about a mile from the goal, thinking to dash in afterwards well rested and looking fresh as morning. And he will know, that I, slow-pacing Mr. Turtle, will be still far behind, and that much waiting must be endured by him and the king and spectators before I finally arrive, dusty, sore-toed and wind-broken, to receive second prize. But trust me, humble friends, I shall not keep him waiting one moment." As he ended, Mr. Turtle's solemn face for the first time broke into a smile that was somewhat like the smile of the deer, only more cunning, and the turtles danced an applause on the green, on the soft, cool green where the secret meeting was held.

On the opening day of the race every turtle was

at his appointed place. Only a few spectators came to see the start-off. The great crowd had gathered around the king at the far, far end of the valley, not to see a contest but just to joke together about the great joke of the century and to have many a good laugh, for animals like to laugh and will go distances to get a good laugh. So eager are they to laugh, they often start laughing at nothing and end with thinking they have laughed at something. Thus it is easy for an ordinary wise cracker among them to pass for a real wit, and his unsuccessful wise cracks are never unsuccessful. The animals roar each time he opens his mouth. On this day everybody was ready to laugh at the ludicrous crowning of the turtle with second prize. Already their smiles were so broad they almost cracked into sound, and the smile-exposed beautiful white teeth looked like a harvest of pearls.

The start-off took place at sunrise with but slight incident. The few spectators who had gathered there at that early hour had to laugh when they saw the turtle start bravely jogging off, looking happy, they thought, because second prize was his—and without competition. And their laughter increased when, after two bounds which put him much ahead, the deer looked back to the turtle and bleated softly, "Good-bye-e-e," in a make-fun tone of voice. Then they all left, for the deer disappeared from view and nobody cared to watch the turtle jog slowly and tediously out of sight.

Soon the deer, grown weary, not of running, but of running without necessity, called on his nimble feet to halt the speedy nonsense and take him out to a tender green plot of grass. He had not taken breakfast before the race. He had risen only in time for the start-off, because he had slept very little since he announced himself for the race. Indeed he had had little time for sleeping because his attentions had been in great demand by the admiring does, doting and fawning constantly upon him, not one of them ever quite able to admire enough the charms of his fast, athletic fellow. But now separated from their calling, he heard again the call of his stomach, and that tender grassy plot was the answer to his need. He took his time. He ate at leisure. Why not? He had done so before when he had had contestants in the race. Now he had none.

Meantime, the turtle who had started the race had by this time disappeared beneath a shrub as had been directed. He knew that wherever the deer stopped, a turtle up ahead would see him and glide stealthily out and away. After a long while had passed—the deer himself could never say how much time had passed— he returned to the race-way and started bounding lightly, but casually still, down the valley. He wondered if the turtle could possible have passed while he was away, and he hoped he had done so, for then he would soon pass him up and thereby keep a check upon him, although in this race a check was scarcely necessary. "It is a boring race," he said to himself.

But about the time he said that, he spied the turtle down ahead of him moving incredibly slowly along with his four-pace hop. He chuckled to himself and said aloud, "What a ludicrous creature! Every move-ment, every motion a hop. Each kick a hop: four kicks, four hops." Then he laughed again and as he passed the hopping creature he whinnied out a giggle into the sad face of the turtle, and then with a kind of kick unnecessary for the bound he knocked dust into the turtle's eyes, giggled again and disappeared from sight. Soon this turtle moved out to a nearby shrub where, with the help of another turtle concealed there, he relieved as best he could the painful smarting of his eyes by pouring into them drops of dew-water still clinging to the lower leaves of the shrub.

Next for the deer there was the munching of delicate young leaves, then the chatting with a pas-serby. He could not resist chatting with each one, for he seldom saw anybody because nearly everybody, as you know, was with the king at the goal-end of the valley. And each time he passed the turtle he kicked dust just as he did with the first passing, and giggled just as before, think how sore and how red the turtle's eyes would be by the time he had arrived for his measly and inglorious second prize.

Finally the deer decided to take a nap while he was far enough away, yet safely enough near the goal. But he slept longer, much longer than he had thought possible, for he had not realized how much of his strength he had given to the doting of the does. Simply expressed, he had indulged in too much night life. Had he been before the race as temperate as a turtle he could have been now as wide awake as a hoot owl. But so long he slept that the few turtles left had time to report from station to station, and the last was the station of the leader who moved out and trotted for the goal line, which, as you know, was very near, so that soon the king and spectators who were now looking intently up the green valley, expecting any moment to see the deer appear, were surprised to see the turtle instead bobbing up and down and moving with greater energy and excitement than a turtle had ever been known before to do.

But the laughter began, because everyone thought the deer had smartly decided to give them a good show, and so would encourage the simple turtle to the very end, then come dashing by only just in time to kill the poor turtle with grief. But finally the turtle drew dangerously near, and at last crossed the goal line before the eyes of everybody, whereupon the king opened both lungs and let out a roar that shook the leaves of the forest, reverberated for miles around and fell like a crash of thunder upon the ears of the sleeping deer.

"Ah! Kambam bao!" he exclaimed. "Was that thunder? Anyway it's time for me to overtake the turtle, unless the poke-along is still behind." And with that he bounded swiftly the rest of the way down the valley and broke into a broad grin to the spectators as he neared the goal line, pleased to think that he could dawdle so much along the way and still leave the turtle so far behind he could not even give a report of him. He crossed the goal line still grinning and wiggle-waving his tail, only to hear and to behold the awful truth! He fainted, and was brought back by the elephant who dashed a trunkful of cold water onto him, but each time he was brought back to consciousness of lost face and lost reputation he promptly fainted again, until the elephant, tired of monotonous repetition, lifted him, body and soul, immersed him in the pool, lifted him carefully out again and supported him against a grassy bank until he could stand.

He started to faint again a few moments later when the king bestowed the prize and the medal upon the turtle. But the elephant had anticipated this weak moment and he promptly dashed another trunkful of water over him. His knees had already buckled under him but the reviving water halted the downward trend. His legs hesitated for a moment and then slowly, gradually straightened into position, but looked uncertain. This interrupted leave-taking and gradual return looked very comical, and the spectators almost split with suppressed laughter, which is always more humiliating than honest, outright laughter. The poor fellow seemed scarcely conscious when the king hung upon him the badge of second prize and placed before him the insignificant money prize.

That night in the light of the moon the entire turtle tribe held a celebration dance on the broad grassy plot in the valley where the deer had fallen asleep. The deer might as well have joined them, for he, too, slept not a wink that night. And since that time the deer has been timid and self-conscious. The turtle still carries a high head.

(Creel 1960: 41–52)

Would Izevbaye and Co. accuse this version of thin narrative texture, undeveloped characters, or uncomplicated plot? To forestall any such judgment which they just might be rash enough to make, let us briefly analyse the text. Though sparse in its use of ideophones, narrative formulas and repetitions, the texture of this tale is rich with narrative embroidery. It has arresting images, explanatory digressions, philosophical reflections on life, on social existence and the nature of things, and a variety of moods and tones—including humor, doubt, surprise, and dramatic suspense. This is a controlled rendition whose artistry can hold the interest of listeners and readers who already know the story. It contains deft character studies: the deer is portrayed as a smug, over-confident, arrogant, insolent character, a spoilsport who insists on having his way by running in a race which has nothing to contribute to his already established reputation as a runner. By entering the race, the deer all at once, and with sadistic relish, takes both the fun and the challenge out of it for the other animals.

The turtle comes across as a serious, cunning fellow with tremendous imagination and dare, who knows his opponent's psychology and how to take advantage of it. The turtle community is shown to be a cooperative one which hangs together. The other animals are portrayed as beings who love a good time, who enjoy the thrill of running and showing off their athletic form. They are too proud to compete for second place, yet sane enough not to attempt to compete with the deer for first place. And the lion is presented in his appropriate kingly aloofness as initiator and organizer of events for the pleasure and well-being of his kingdom. The society of animals is rendered as, on the whole, a fun-loving, proud, realistic and happy one.

Now, what more could any reasonable person ask for by way of characterization?

As for its plot, it is clearly not as linear and uncomplicated as the two preceding renditions of the same story, but it is also obviously and appropriately less complicated than the plot of a longer narrative would be. The plot is studded with details—such details as the deer's nightlife and its after-effects, and his lackadaisical running habits. It has subplots of activities woven into the basic plot: there is, for instance, the three-day delegation to the deer to pull out of the race; the elephant's thoughtful, timely, and repeated first aid to revive the fainted deer; and the victory celebration of the turtle tribe out on the green. On the whole, the plot in this masterly version is no less complicated than plots in a great number of excellent short stories, oral or written. Are Izevbaye and Co. satisfied? Would they be willing now to withdraw their rash charges?

Now, how is such a difference in quality of rendition possible? In particular, by what methods is such an excellent rendition achieved when unsatisfactory versions seem to be the norm? There are two basic steps involved in converting an oral tale in one language into a written tale in another— a transcription and a translation. Of the various ways in which these steps could be combined, let us consider that which has the most to recommend it, i.e., that in which the oral performance is first transcribed into its language and then is translated.

To obtain a good translation of an oral tale, it is crucial to have a good transcript. There are, in the main, two ways to do this. (1) The first, as mentioned before, is to find and tape a master story-teller's performance of the tale, and then to transcribe that performance in the correct manner, as outlined earlier. This, we believe, was the case with *Folk Tales of Liberia,* set down by J. Luke Creel in collaboration with Vai master storyteller Bai Gai Kiahon, from which the preceding example was taken. (2) The second is for a master story-teller in the oral tradition to, himself, set down his own version in writing. In a transcript obtained in either of these ways, the narrative style and linguistic flavor of the tale's culture is captured. When such a transcript is translated into any other language, care must be taken to carry across into that language the narrative style and linguistic flavor of the original. In this regard, the example of Achebe's success in his novels in capturing in English the style and flavor of Igbo rhetoric, could serve as an example.

In order for African scholars and writers to become oral master story-tellers so that they could set down traditional stories properly, they would have to immerse themselves in the story-telling tradition, undergo the appropriate apprenticeship, master the verbal art, and then write down their own retellings of traditional stories. This may be a difficult procedure for most scholars, but it certainly is not impossible, as is illustrated in the example of Birago Diop, a Western-trained scholar and writer who became a master of the verbal narrative art, and has given us his retellings of Amadou Koumba's master versions in the remarkable *Tales of Amadou Koumba*. Indeed, there is a further example, one where even a non-African, Minnie Postma, having trained herself in the Basotho story-telling tradition, has rendered in writing her own retellings of Basotho tales in her *Tales from the Basotho*. To achieve this feat, she took full advantage of her bicultural and bilingual upbringing in an Afrikaans household by parents fluent in Sesotho and with Basotho house servants in the British Dominion of South Africa. She then went on to become

> so familiar with the manner in which the Basotho tell a story that she, too, could take a five-line jingle and embroider it into a *tsomo,* with the required length and all the poetic phraseology and repetitions and emphases that the Basotho use. Usually the tables were turned, and it was Mrs. Postma who told stories to Basotho audiences, who were amazed and amused that a white woman could make a "*tsomo* of the old people."
>
> (McDermid 1974: xx–xxi)

Clearly, what was possible for Postma, a non-African, should not be impossible for an African who takes the trouble.

The above examples illustrate the following: (1) You don't have to be an African to master an African oral story-telling art. (2) As is well known, the fact that you are an African does not make you automatically a master at traditional oral story-telling. Diop's training in the oral story-telling tradition would appear to have been far greater than that which most Western-educated Africans get, on the basis of which they fancy themselves to be somehow innate experts in African oral art. Still, Diop had the commendable wisdom to base his versions on those of Amadou Koumba, a master story-teller. Clearly, the notion that every African is somehow an innately accomplished African artist is preposterous. Just like other arts, good story-telling, whether oral or written, requires a rigorous and successful apprenticeship. (3) Even where, as with Diop and Postma, the master story-teller is bilingual and is writing down in one language a story that comes from the culture of his other language, care would still be required to convey the narrative style and linguistic flavor of the language of the story's origin.

Just to illustrate the accomplishment of good bilingual retellers, consider the following selections from Diop and Postma:

JACKAL AND HEN

This is a story that the old people tell. They say that Hen flew to the top of a stack of wheat one day to find food. From where she stood on the stack she could see far out over the fields. She could see far, and she saw Jackal coming from afar. She saw him coming toward her, she saw him out of the corner of her eye, but when he came closer she did not look up at all. She went on hunting for food.

"Good morning, mother of mine," Jackal greeted her.

"Yes, I greet you," she replied.

"Are you still living?" he asked, according to the correct way in which one person greets another.

"Yes, I am still living. And you? Are you still living also?"

"Yes, I too am still living, Mother," he replied. And then he asked, as the custom was, "Did you wake well this morning?"

And she answered, as it is proper, "Yes, I woke well."

And all the while he was talking, talking, talking, Jackal was looking closely at Hen, and he saw that she was young and that her flesh would be tender and that she would taste sweet if only he could get at her. But now she was standing on top of that stack of wheat, where he could not reach her. He could not get hold of her at all, not while she was top of the stack of wheat, and he would have to think of a way to get her down.

Jackal had many plans. He was a man who was not just a little bit clever. No, he was very clever. Very clever. He asked her: "Mother, have you heard that there is peace among everybody on earth? One animal may not catch another animal any more, because of that peace."

"Peace?" she asked.

"Yes. Mother, peace. The chiefs called together a big meeting, and at that *pitso* they decided this business of peace on all the earth."

"Oh yes," said Hen. But she wondered about it. She wondered whether this Jackal could be telling the truth. He was a man with many clever stories, and many times those clever stories were nothing but lies.

"You say there is peace now?"

"Yes, Mother. The big peace. There has never been such a big peace. You can safely come down from that stack of wheat. Then we can talk about the matter nicely. We shall take snuff together. Come down. Mother! Remember the peace!"

But Hen was not quite as stupid as Jackal thought she was. She wanted to make quite sure first that Jackal was telling the truth and that he was not telling her lies again. She turned around and looked far out over the fields behind her. Then she went to stand on the highest point of the stack and kept staring out over the fields until Jackal asked: "What is it that you see from up there that you stare so. *Me?*"

"What do I see? Why do you want to know what I see? It does not matter what I see, for there is no danger anymore for any animal on earth. Is it not peace among the animals? It is only a pack of dogs that are running towards us."

"Dogs! A pack of dogs!" he cried. And his fear was very great. "Then I shall have to greet you, Mother. I am a man who has a lot of work waiting."

"Kêkêkêkê!" Hen laughed. "I thought it was peace among all animals on earth? Have you forgotten it? The dogs will do nothing to harm you! Why do you want to run away, Grandfather?"

"I don't think that this pack of dogs came to the meeting of the peace!" And Jackal ran so fast that the dust rose in great clouds from the road behind him.

"Kêkêkêkê!" laughed Hen, for then she knew that the story of the peace was just a big lie. And she knew that if she had taken snuff with that fellow he would have caught her, so she made up a story herself and with it she had caught him beautifully.

"Kêkêkêkêkê!" she laughed. "I caught the story-teller with another story!"

And this is the end of this story.

(Postma 1974: 115–17)

From A JUDGMENT

Golo, the chief of the monkey tribe, really went a bit too far that night, when he paid a visit to Demba's water-melon field. He must have summoned all his subjects, every single one of them, and they had not simply queued up in an orderly fashion and passed the water-melons down the line, from one to another. Whole gangs of them had leapt over the euphorbia hedge. Euphorbia bushes are the stupidest of plants;

the only thing they are capable of doing is weeping; but to make them weep you have to touch them. Golo had touched them and he had laid his hands on other things as well. He and his tribe had ransacked the whole field. They had behaved like common jackals; and everyone knows that if the jackal is supposed to be the greatest water-melon fancier ever born on this earth, there has also never been a more ill-bred creature under the sun—or rather under the moon—to this day.

Golo and his tribe had behaved like real sons of jackals for they knew full well that these were not the water-melons of old Medjembe, who had once given the great-grandfather of all the monkeys such a hiding that it had taken the skin off his bottom. The trace of this, as well as the memory, has remained with his posterity for ever.

Demba would certainly have done the same thing as old Medjembe, since Golo had behaved like Thile-the-jackal, who had also had some dealings in the past with the very first water-melon farmer, but neither Golo nor any of his subjects had waited for Demba's arrival on the scene.

Golo had gone too far, we agree, and Demba had been far from pleased the next morning, when he discovered the extent of the damage done to his field; but to pass on his annoyance to his wife Koumba was quite another thing. But that is exactly what Demba did, the moment he stepped into his hut.

He complained that the water, which Koumba knelt down to offer him as she greeted him, was not cold enough. He complained that the *couscous* was too hot and not salt enough, and that the meat was too hard. He complained that that was this and this was that, for the fact is that when the hyena wants to eat his own young he complains that it smells of goat . . .

When he was tired of shouting, Demba began to beat Koumba, and when he was tired of beating her he said, "Go back to your mother, I repudiate you."

Without a word Koumba began to collect up her goods and chattels, washed herself, and put on her best clothes. Her breasts were sharp beneath her embroidered camisole, her buttocks rounded beneath her *pagne* from N'*galam*. Her beaded belts tinkled at each graceful movement and her persistent odour teased Demba's nostrils.

Koumba put her bundle on her head and crossed the threshold. Demba made as if to call her back, but he stopped and said to himself, "Her parents will bring her back to me."

Two days, three days, ten days passed without Koumba's return, but Koumba's parents showed no signs of life.

You only know what use your bottom is when the time comes to sit down. So Demba began to realize what use a woman was about the house.

Roasted pea-nuts are very good, but all gourmets, and even those who only eat to keep themselves alive, agree that they are better made into a sweet sauce to help down the millet porridge, or else salted and seasoned as an accompaniment to *couscous* and beans. Demba saw the time not far off when he would be forced to this point of view. His midday meal was no longer brought out to him in the fields, and in the evening he had to light his own fire to roast pea-nuts or sweet potatoes.

A grown man is forbidden to touch a broom, yet what is a man to do when dust, ashes, pea-nut shells, and sweet-potato skins pile up more and more on the floor of the hut every day?

A man can really only work well when stripped to the waist; but when the day's work is done and he slips on a *boubou,* he would like this garment not to be as filthy as a dog's liver; but is it in keeping with the dignity of anyone who deserves the name of man to take calabash, soap, and dirty linen and go down to the river or the well to do the washing?

Demba began to ask himself these questions and

many more besides. His wisdom, which was somewhat slow to get going, kept on telling him, "You only know what use your bottom is when the time comes to sit down."

Continence is a very noble virtue, to be sure, but it is a very wretched companion. It is too slender to fill a couch, and Demba now found his bed too wide for him alone.

Koumba, on the other hand, found with every passing day that to be a repudiated wife, if one is young and comely, in a village full of enterprising young men, was by no means unpleasant—quite the contrary.

(Diop 1966: 8–10)

Such examples of excellent transcription and translation show that Izevbaye's charges cannot be upheld against nonparabolic, shorter, oral narratives from Africa.

In the case of the longer oral narratives, and especially of the oral epics, an examination of the proper evidence does not at all substantiate the characteristics which Izevbaye and others attribute to African oral narrative. Our examination of several epics show that their plots are as complicated as in the best epics and novels from any place or period in the world. They employ all the familiar elements of characterization, from physical description to interior monologue and other devices of psychological probing of character, and they do not omit exploration of character by action, dialogue, or observation through the minds and comments of other characters. In the matter of narrative texture, like all oral traditions they display precise and deft use of detail as well as summations, variations in perceptual distance, and montage. Their presentations of their stories also employ philosophical reflections on human life, on death, fate, destiny, and the paradoxes of social existence, whether in the narrator's voice or in the voice of characters within the tale. And proverbs, aphorisms, and judicious allusions are not at all lacking. From a close reading of, say, *The*

Mwindo Epic, Sundiata, Monzon and the King of Kore, and *Kambili,* one wonders from what evidence these disparagers of African oral tradition draw their conclusions. At some risk of providing what should be obvious, we submit a few passages from the above works for the reader's scrutiny.

From SUNDIATA

Sogolon's son was now ten. The name Sogolon Djata in the rapid Mandingo language became Sundiata or Sondjata. He was a lad full of strength; his arms had the strength of ten and his biceps inspired fear in his companions. He had already that authoritative way of speaking which belongs to those who are destined to command. His brother Manding Bory, became his best friend, and whenever Djata was seen, Manding Bory appeared too. They were like a man and his shadow. . . .

Every man to his own land! If it is foretold that your destiny should be fulfilled in such and such a land, men can do nothing against it. Mansa Tounkara could not keep Sundiata back because the destiny of Sogolon's son was bound up with that of Mali. Neither the jealousy of a cruel stepmother, nor her wickedness, could alter for a moment the course of great destiny.

The snake, man's enemy, is not long-lived, yet the serpent that lives hidden will surely die old. Djata was strong enough now to face his enemies. At the age of eighteen he had the stateliness of the lion and the strength of the buffalo. His voice carried authority, his eyes were live coals, his arm was iron, he was the husband of power.

(Niane 1965: 23, 47)

From MONZON AND THE KING OF KORE

Douga's wife looked at Da Monzon.
She was overwhelmed by his manly splendour;
the immediate love and desire she experienced
took away all control over her action.

She spent a restless night and
her body was wracked with a desire difficult to satisfy.
Her head was full of wicked ideas.
She forgot all Douga's generosity;
she forgot that she was first queen
of a country famous for the courage of its warriors
and the wealth of its people.
One idea obsessed her:
to possess Da, hold him in her arms; to give herself
to him entirely.
She was lost without realizing it.
Her frantic mind plunged into the darkness and
she forgot the rest of the world.
She had to have Da at any price.
She was prepared to commit any folly
and would even betray
the man who had never refused her anything.
She began to wonder how
she could declare her love to Da and convince him
that she was ready to leave everything, give up
everything,
as long as she could be his.

She called her seven house servants,
her trusted confidantes, the keepers of the secrets of
her soul who were ready to make any sacrifice for her.
She said to them: "I am dangerously ill,
and I shall not survive my sickness."
"How can you, mistress, since yesterday
have caught such an illness that you are afraid you will
die?"
"The illness penetrated my eyes.

It has taken root in my heart
and has drained away the waters of tranquility
in which my soul bathed.
My heart is as dry as a *balanza* in winter;
the *balanza* which withers in spite of the rains
and becomes white, dead wood.

In spite of my gold and silver, servants and slaves,
in spite of the fields full of cattle,
the granaries full of corn,
in spite of the greatness of my husband
the hawk who pounces on the enemy
and takes him as if he were a chicken—yes, alas!
I am unhappy amidst all this!
and I shall die if no remedy can be found for the
illness!''

"What can this strange sickness be which makes you
so unhappy, oh beautiful and kind mistress?'' exclaimed
one of the servants.
"I am suffering from a love which burns more than
fire,
which wounds more than an arrow,
which cuts more than a razor-edge.''

"You! in love!
You, who only had to jump over
a sick horse to cure it of its colic;
You, the precious pearl whom only the eyes of Douga
alone have beheld?
No, mistress, you cannot make us believe
that you have ever loved any other than Douga
and never will you love anybody else.''

"If you do not believe my words
and will not help me to quench my desire,
then make ready to warm the water
which you will use to wash my corpse.
If tomorrow at sunrise
I have no hope of possessing my loved one
who kept me from sleep last night,
I shall die before the day is out, I swear it!''

The seven servants opened wide their eyes
and looked at each other in silence.
"Has not a wicked spirit,'' they asked themselves,

"entered the soul of our queen
and taken away all control and reason?"
One said: "Our duty must be
to try to cure our mistress
and do everything to perserve her health."
Kounadi, the eldest of the servants,
said to the queen, going against the rule
forbidding anyone to pronounce her name: "Saran,
good, kind Saran, with whom are you in love?
with a spirit of the palace of King Solomon
or an heir to the throne of the Pharaohs of Misra?"

"No," replied Saran. "The one I love
is not a spirit of the elements, nor a prince of Misra.
He is born of a Bambara woman.
He grew up on the banks of the Dioliba
and played under the *balanzas* of Ségou.
I am in love with the prince Da."

"Da Monzon! He who has come to besiege Koré
Douga?"

"Yes, him. I cannot prevent myself loving him.
It is something too powerful for me.
I am ashamed of myself, but I can neither resist it
nor remain silent.
That is why I am telling you this mortal secret.
The choice is yours: either you help me to reach Da
or you go and denounce me to Koré Douga.
If you choose the second solution
Know then that Douga will have my head shaved;
he will dress me in rough bark and
will weigh me down with ignoble chains
as before he weighed me down with gold and silver
and pearls.
You will see me collapse under the whip
and then my head will be cut off and thrown to the
crows.
But before the end, when my mouth is bleeding, my

teeth broken, when I am dying of thirst,
I shall refuse the water offered me by a kind soul.
Give me Da, I shall say, I am thirsting for him;
water cannot quench my soul!''

Kounadi looked at her companions:
they were all weeping sincere tears . . .

The morning of the battle, even before
the two armies had taken up position,
Douga heard a shot to the East.
He thought it was his soldier
as he had given orders for this to be done
and he did not worry about it unduly.
He waited quietly for the second soldier
to come back with the plucked hen.
A fire was already burning to roast the bird
which Douga had to eat before going into battle.
But Da had posted at every bend of the road
a sharpshooter with instructions to fire
on any horseman riding past plucking a live hen.
Just then, the Koré soldier appeared
with the hen in his hand. He spurred his horse on
and began to pluck the bird
while his horse galloped forward at full speed.
When he got to where the first soldier was hidden,
suspecting nothing, he felt a violent blow.
Something burnt his flesh
and a deafening sound stunned him.
He had been wounded in the leg
by the first soldier who had fired at him.
His horse was galloping so fast
that the soldier had not been able to take aim well
and had not killed him outright
but mortally wounded him.
The rider lost strength rapidly
and could not control his horse
which galloped on wildly.
It got as far as the second solider who,

alerted by the other's shot,
took his time to aim more carefully, pulled the trigger,
and the bullets struck the poor Koré soldier full in
the chest.
He lost his balance and fell from his horse,
clutching the half-plucked hen to him.
He fell to the ground head first
and crushed the hen under the weight of his body.
His horse galloped on towards the entrance to the
Tata, but alas for the poor animal,
the third soldier had already seen it
and fired a shot through its brain.
The horse fell just in front of the main gate.
Only then did Douga and the patriarch
realize that they had been betrayed. Their secret had
been revealed
but they were far from suspecting
that the traitor was Saran, Queen of Koré.

In spite of this set-back, Douga's men
set out to attack with their ruler leading them.
It was a terrible day and a bloody night.
The soldiers of Koré had their powder-horns full
for two days' fighting.
They accomplished many feats of bravery
and pushed Da far from their town.
Da saw the field of battle littered
with his best marksmen and archers.
At one time he thought that he himself
was going to be taken prisoner.
He had lost two-thirds of his soldiers.
he sent word to his father that Koré
was not a cold cake to be eaten in comfort
but a hot fortress burning
the tongue and the palate of whoever tried to swallow
it.
He asked his father to send reinforcements.

(Hampate-Ba 1966: 103–5, 116–17)

From THE MWINDO EPIC

When many days had passed that his wives had remained pregnant, one day six of his wives pulled through; they gave birth merely to female children. One among them, the preferred-one, remained dragging herself along because of her pregnancy. When the preferred-one realized that her companions had already given birth, and that she remained with her pregnancy, she kept on complaining: "How terrible this is! It is only I who am persecuted by this pregnancy. What then shall I do? My companions, together with whom I carried the pregnancy at the same time, have already pulled through, and it is I who remain with it. What will come out of this pregnancy?" After she had finished making these sad reflections, reawakening from her thoughts, at the door then there was already a bunch of firewood; she did not know from where it had come; lo! it was her child, the one that was inside the womb, who had just brought it. After some time had passed, looking around in the house, there was already a jar of water; she did not know whence it had come; all by itself it had brought itself into the house. After some time had passed, raw isusa vegetables also arrived there at the house. When the preferred-one saw it, she was much astonished; lo! it was the child in her womb who was performing all those wonderful things . . .

After they had looked at him, the councillors went to the forest to cut a piece of wood for the husk of the drum. They arrived in the forest; they cut it; they returned with it to the village. Arriving in the village, they carved the wood; they hollowed it out so that it became a husk. When the husk was finished, they went again to fetch Mwindo; they carried him; they stuck him into the husk of the drum. Mwindo said: "This time, my father has no mercy; what! a small baby is willingly maltreated!" The Banashemwindo went to get the hide for the drum; they glued it on top of the drum, they covered the drum with it. When Shemwindo had seen how his son had been laid in the drum, he declared to all his people that he wanted two expert divers, swimmers, to go the next day and throw this drum into the pool where nothing moves. After the divers, swimmers, had been found, they picked up the drum; all the people abandoned the village; they went to throw Mwindo. When they arrived at the pool where nothing moves, the swimmers with the drum entered the pool, swimming in the river. When they arrived in the middle of the pool, they asked in a loud voice, "Shall we drop him here?" All those who were sitting on the edge of the river answered "Yes," all saying together: "It is there, so that you will not be the cause of his return." They released the drum in the middle of the pool; it sank into the depths. The waves made rings above the place where the drum had entered. After the swimmers had thrown him into the pool, they returned to the shore. Shemwindo was very pleased with them, "You have performed good work!" He gave each swimmer a maiden; thus those two got married because of receiving a gift for their labor. That day, when Mwindo was thrown away, earth and heaven joined together because of the heavy rain; it rained for seven days; hailing left the earth no more; that rain brought much famine in Tubondo.

(Biebuyck 1975: 326–27, 329)

From KAMBILI

She said all there was to be said.
That's better than saying nothing at all.
Ah! To each slave his reason for coming,
To each slave his reason for awakening!
The omen for staying here is not good.
Ah! Namu-sayers!
Ah! The child affair has started to heat up!
The favored wife said, "If he doesn't come out a goat child,
    child,
I'll sweep the courtyard with my buttocks."

A little old lady come forward, gwiligigwologo,
And like a liar who has missed the market,
Said that she went and saw the despised wife there.
"Ah, Toure ni Manjun," she said.
"I saw it myself.
The ram mounted her before my very eyes.
If he doesn't become a goatchild,
You can trim a bit off my height."
The little old woman was setting up an evil plot.
Ah! Namu-sayers!
The favored wife went on to the market,
And went and bought some rice,
And bought some choice meat,
And bought some things for the sauce,
And came and cooked Kanji some rice in oil.
She cooked the rice for Kanji,
And cooked the meat till it was done,
And put it on the rice in oil,
And then who did she give it to?
She gave it to Kanji.
Ah! the brave ate it all up.
When he had filled himself with the rice,
The favored wife let down the mosquito net,
And sprayed perfume about the room,
And filled the room with incense,
Saying that she would become the chosen one.
Ah! Namu-sayers!
The favored wife has beaten all the other women out!
The favored wife spent the night with Kanji.
When the day had lightened,
She announced, "Ah! People, I have something to tell
    you.
As for me, I am going to spend the next four nights
    here."
Kanji said that that would never ever be for the best.
"It is better that you come one after another.
After all, no one knows who will have this child."
She then said, "If I don't spend four nights here,
    Kanji,

You won't get me out without killing me."
And so the favored wife spent four nights with Kanji.
After the fourth, in the morning,
She took a seeding stone,
And took some charcoal and a little oil
And crushed the charcoal with the stone,
And poured the oil over it,
And rubbed it over her nipples,
And puffed out her belly before Kanji,
There beside the fire.
"Ah!" he exclaimed, "People, my favored wife is
      pregnant!
Many thanks, Bari of the Omens!
The pot that Bari prepared has turned out well.
My favored wife has come out of it pregnant."
To this she replied: "I am somewhat sure."
Ah! Namu-sayers! . . .

The favored wife went to find the despised Dugo.
She said, "Despised Dugo!" "Yes," the reply.
    "It was the king who told me
    that I should mash up Kambili,
    And give him to the horses.
    Kambili is a child of evil sign."
Despised Dugo left herself in the hands of Allah,
And took Kambili and gave him to the favored wife.
She put him down inside a mortar
    And raised the pestle high overhead,
    Saying she would pound Kambili up,
    It was then that Kanji arrived.
    Nothing happens without Allah's will.
Ah! Jealousy is evil!
The woman's evil jealousy can't succeed.
Kanji came, pulling up the reins behind the favored
    wife.
"What kind of thing is that in the mortar,
Making a noise like that?"

She replied, "I was just playing a game with the little
    man.
I wasn't doing anything to him."
"With the pestle raised up like that,
You call it a game?"
And he struck with both barrels,
    Yes, fired both barrels at the favored wife,
    Putting one ball right in her ear,
    Putting the other ball in her chest,
    Laying the butt to her head, smash!
"Ah! Favored wife, pick up your tail,
And get out of this child affair.
You have always made me feel dirty!"
Namu-sayers!
Then he dragged off the favored wife,
    And threw her off at the edge of town,
    And threw her into a ditch,
    Then called to the despised wife.
    "Get out of the goat pen,
    And come take my favored wife's hut."
    There's no way to say it, It's Allah's work!
    "Should anyone play with the Kambili affair,
    I will play with him!"
    The favored wife thus left the Kambili story, no
    lie,
    If you don't fear evil jealousy, you fear nothing.
                                    (Bird 1974: 55–57, 65–66)

From the evidence of the above samples, it should be
clear that charges of "thin narrative texture," if made against
the African oral epic, would be sustainable only if the
standard of narrative texture is baroque excess of detail and
microscopic pointillism in description. Regarding the "chances
of character development" in the oral epic, consider the
passage presented above from *Monzon:* Saran's psychological
state is first described, then dramatized in her dialogue with
her servants, and the consequence of her subsequent conduct
is narrated with succinct detail and force. By offering us

penetrating insights into Saran's character, the passage makes nonsense of the aspersions cast against the oral African epic on the matter of characterization.

From all the foregoing examples, therefore, we can see how unwarranted are those standard charges irresponsibly made against African oral narratives when the charges are tested against good transcriptions and translations of master performances whether of shorter narratives or of longer narratives.

Izevbaye is not alone in disparaging the African oral tradition. Adrian Roscoe makes some other disparaging remarks about African oral narrative which deserve countering here, since they are allied to those made by Izevbaye. Consider the passage that follows, part of which was quoted earlier in connection with Roscoe's gerrymandering of evidence:

> The oral story, then, has been Africa's dominant form. As Borges points out, a piece of the length and complexity of a novel could never be related by word of mouth. In Africa's oral past, and present, texts as long as *Things Fall Apart* or *The Interpreters* are not normally found. Africa has been brought up on much shorter narratives: epics like *Sundiata* being special, occasional, exceptions, belonging more to the category of historical texts, and in any case of fairly short length. The *griot* who can commit *Sundiata* to memory is a rare professional; but even he, with his prodigious memory and his consummate skill with mnemonic devices, would find the complicated turns of plot, the minutiae of physical and scenic description, of even a short novel, an impossible burden. The novel, thus, unlike the story, is not a fact of the African past.
>
> (Roscoe 1971: 75)

In this brief passage Roscoe, characteristically, makes at least six howlers: (1) To say that epics like *Sundiata* are special or occasional, or exceptions in a field of shorter narratives, is to say nothing significant about *Sundiata* since epics the world over are special, occasional, and exceptions in a general background of shorter narratives. (2) When Roscoe says of *Sundiata* that it is of fairly short length, what is his yardstick? If his yardstick is other epics from all over the world, as it properly should be, then he is in error. *Sundiata,* one of the epics of Mali, is 84 pages long in the Longmans prose text of 40 lines per page, but *Beowulf,* the British national epic, is only 75 pages long in the Penguin prose text of 34 lines per page, and *Gilgamesh,* an epic from the ancient Near East, is only 59 pages long in the Penguin prose text of 32 lines per page. *El Cid,* the Spanish national epic, is 127 pages long in the University of California prose text of 33 lines per page; and *Song of Roland,* the French national epic, is 100 pages in the Macmillian verse text of 28 lines per page—and of course it would be considerably shorter in a prose text. Given these comparative facts, it is difficult to sustain Roscoe's charge that *Sundiata* is "of fairly short length." True, Roscoe might claim that there are longer epics, but he should make sure that those epics whose lengths are of a different magnitude are not indeed *epic cycles* whose individual epic components have been written down and threaded together and put between two covers, as is the case with the *Iliad,* the *Odyssey,* and the *Nibelungenlied,* for example.

(3) Roscoe's claim that a griot who can commit *Sundiata* to memory is a rare professional is true but inconsequential; for so is the writer of big novels in Europe, or the oral epic narrator anywhere in the world.

(4) And as for his claim that even such a griot would find the complicated turns of plot, etc., of even a short novel an impossible burden, consider the case of the Nyanga bard Serungu, as reported by Daniel Biebuyck:

> During a year's sojourn at the research center, he
> began at my request to dictate his memoirs to my two

Nyanga assistants, Mr. Kubuya and Mr. Tubi. He developed these memoirs in his own manner, free from direct intervention by us, but included in them at my explicit request all the songs, proverbs, riddles, prayers, formulas, incantations, praises, and tales he knew. The text of his autobiography covers 3,456 closely written pages. To my great surprise, it was in this context that he provided me with the text of epic IV, in addition to several longer tales in which Mwindo or other characters associated with the epics occur. He also supplied a fascinating epic which he said he had heard a certain Wanowa sing in a hunting camp. . . . Included in the autobiography are 386 riddles, 82 "true stories," 41 "thoughts," 22 tales, 371 songs (mostly proverbs or one or two-line songs), and a large number of dreams, reminiscences, prayers, praises, formulas, omens, incantations, taboos, and medical recipes.

(Biebuyck 1978: 12)

Clearly, the existence of Serungu alone would invalidate Roscoe's claim. However, there are many more Serungus in Africa, as shall soon be seen from more evidence supplied below by Daniel Biebuyck.

From the example of Serungu, and other evidence also supplied by Biebuyck, it becomes indubitably clear that it is false to assert, as Roscoe does, that (5) "a piece of the length and complexity of a novel could never be related by word of mouth," or that (6) "in Africa's oral past, and present, texts as long as *Things Fall Apart* or *The Interpreters* are not normally found." Clearly, as the passage quoted below will show, Roscoe did not bother to consult those who had investigated the matter. In his essay, "The Epic as a Genre in Congo Oral Literature," in which he discusses one of the three major regions of Africa where the epic has, to date, been investigated with some thoroughness, Daniel Biebuyck reports:

Epic texts seem to have a wide distribution in the

Congo Republic. . . . In general surveys of African oral literature, little attention has been given to these epics, because many of them are unknown or inaccessible and many are available only in fragments which tend to be classified together with the myths and tales.

The discussion limits itself to what is sometimes more narrowly referred to as the heroic epic. This can be defined as a long narrative that recounts in a coherent manner the deeds of a legendary hero with human traits and with supernatural attributes that are set against a background of extraordinary events, within the framework of a certain time span and a certain stretch of space. . . .

The heroic epic can be contrasted with what is loosely called the historical epic, which deals on a more limited scale with the genealogies, the migrations, and the chiefs of a particular people. Because of its strong cultural linkages, the heroic epic obviously recalls explicitly or implicity certain historical events in the life of a people, but this is subordinated to the extraordinary and fictional element. The historical epic also frequently requires a verbatim recitation, which is limited to special annual or other occasions. The heroic epic leaves much room for improvisation and loose elaboration of the central themes and is not restricted to a particular circumstance. . . .

Epic cycles centering primarily around anthropomorphized animal heroes or more-or-less theriomorphic heroes are widespread in Africa. . . .

As a distinctive category of literary composition characterized by a particular style, form, content, function, and meaning, the Central African epic has barely received any systematic treatment. And yet it is perhaps the most fascinating and profound literary achievement of Africa, because of the wealth of cultural information it provides, the richness of the language in which it is formulated, the complexity and loftiness of its style, its synthesizing character, and the deep thought patterns it reflects.

In the Lega and Nyanga areas, where I undertook my research, the epic is classified as a separate genre in the linguistic taxonomy of the people. The Nyanga call it *Kárisi* to distinguish it from other, well-isolated categories of literature such as the tales with or without a mysterious content *(uano, mushinga),* the "true" stories *(kishambaro),* the narration of extraordinary events that happened to particular individuals *(ngenu-riro),* and other genres. The Lega classify the epic as *lugano* and contrast it, as a distinctive category, to their other genres.

Unlike the other genres, samples of which are widely known to, and narrated by, vast numbers of individuals of different sex, age, and social status, the epics are known and recited only by very few individuals. . . .

The mode of presentation of the epic has special features. Invariably, the narration of oral texts draws a participating crowd in the African communities. Song, recitation, and pure narration frequently alternate as part of a single performance. Musical instruments are often played in conjunction with the narration. The narration leads to much social interaction, and sometimes to dramatic action as well. The mode of presentation of the epic, the total setting in which it takes place, although leaving room for improvisation and individualized ways of doing things, follows a formalized and prescribed method. The epic is sung, episode by episode; then the episode is narrated and dramatically acted out. The entire epic cannot, of course, be performed in a single evening or a single day. A series of consecutive evening performances may be scheduled, but a single performance may also be limited to one evening and restricted to a couple of episodes. . . .

In form, style and content, the Mongo, Lega, and Nyanga epics have many distinguishing features. The language in which the epic is formulated is usually rich and subtly used by the bards, who are true masters of verbal art. The vocabulary is abundant and there are many refined variations in the use of grammar. The texts abound with complicated metaphorical expressions and subtle nuances in the choice of verbal expression and their conjugation. The structure of the sentence is terse, succinct, precise, incisive. The style is lofty in the narrative and the speeches, and poetic in the songs. There is a true cult for sylistic effect. In the Nyanga epic, indirect discourse, unfamiliar reversal of word order in the sentence, epithets, and repetitive formulaic expressions are very numerous. All possible stylistic effects are drawn into the narration, and here the creative genius of the individual artist can manifest itself most strongly. Certain bards whom I have heard performing among the Nyanga had a special gift for the use of sonorous effects, obtained particularly through reduplication of words and a generous application of ideophones. Others were specialized in the extremely refined and nuanced metaphorical usage of verbs.

The mastery of the bard manifests itself most strongly in the completeness, the consistency, and the logical coherence of the epic and of the constituent episodes. There are beginnings and ends to the Lega and Nyanga epics, and between these there are sequences of events that flow from one to the other without interruption or break in the plan, the plot, and the themes. The quality of the bard is largely judged in terms of the control that he has over all of this. Among the Nyanga, I was brought into contact with several individuals who were said to know the Mwindo or Kárḭsḭ epic. When they were invited to perform and demonstrate their art, they were sometimes promptly dismissed because they were unable to keep episodes and sequences of events clearly apart from each other. . . .

The epic is, so to speak, a supergenre that encompasses and harmoniously fuses together practically all genres known in a particular culture. The Mwindo epic is typical in this respect. There are prose and poetry in the epic, the narrative being constantly intersected with songs in poetic form. The prose narrative to some extent, and the songs to a large extent, incorporate proverbs, riddles, praises, succinct aphoristic abstracts of tales, prayers, improvisations, and allusions and references to "true" stories and persons. Among the Lega and Tetela, where the techniques of message drumming are highly developed, drum names and drum formulae are an intrinsic part of the story. This mixture of prose and poetry, of song and narration, of aphorisms and improvisations is also present in the Mongo epics.

The content of the epic constitutes an encyclopedic inventory of the most diverse aspects of a people's culture. There are direct and indirect statements about the history, the social institutions and social relationships, the material culture, and the system of values and ideas. The Lianja epic provides considerable insights into the social, economic, and religious life of the Mongo. It gives information about customs related to birth, marriage, and death; about the various economic activities (agriculture, hunting, trapping, food gathering, fishing), and the arts and crafts; about God, the ancestors, magic, witchcraft, dreams, rituals. It is also a historical document that offers information about migrations, and interrelationships of different groups. The Mwindo epic makes direct statements about such diverse features as the material culture; the economy; the technology of hunting, gathering, and cultivating; the marriage system; the kinship terminology and the code of social relationships; the political structure; the religious conceptions and the cults; and the values and sentiments. It also makes abundant reference to the physical world in which the Nyanga live. The choice of actors in the Mwindo epic provides, by itself, a wide sample of significant social personalities and beings in Nyanga social organization and thought. The hero himself has fully human, Pygmy-like characteristics, but has, in addition, supernatural gifts. He is surrounded by animals, other humans with whom he may stand in a kinship position, divinities, fabulous beings, and abstract characters (such as the idiot and the Smart One). . . .

In addition, the sentence structure, on the one hand, and the entire plan of the epic, on the other, indirectly provide deep insight into a key feature of Nyanga thinking: their preoccupation with space and place. The sentences abound with repetitive locative expressions and place indications. The plan of the epic follows all major cosmological divisions recognized by the Nyanga. The action takes place on earth *(oto),* in the underworld *(kwirunga),* in the atmosphere *(mwanya),* and in the remote sky *(butu).* Earth itself is subdivided between the inhabited world *(mbuka,* i.e., village, hamlet and ancient village site); the forest of immediate utility *(mundura),* with fields, fallow land, and secondary forest; the virgin forest *(busara);* and the water *(rusi).* The epic is, in other words, complete, because it is comprehensive and consistent in its ground plan with the total Nyanga view of the world. The hero becomes, so to speak, a true hero only after he has successfully completed the whole cycle of events and deeds that put him through all the relevant spheres of the world . . .

The Nyanga and Lega epics cannot simply be qualified as mythical, etiological, didactic, or moralizing. All these elements are implicit, and sometimes explicit in the narrative. The epic harmoniously blends these elements with historical fact and actual culture. The Mwindo epic, for example, partially revolves around the constant interaction between the supranatural and the human worlds, between the hero and various divinities, mythical beings, and semi-divine theriomorph personages. The origin of several customary practices, such as the worship of Lightning, is explicitly mentioned, and there is an implicit interpretation of how homogeneous kingdoms came to be fragmented. The didactic nature is implicit throughout, because of the encyclopedic character of the text. The moralizing aspects are explicitly formulated at the end of the epic and here and there in dialogues or speeches: they are implicit in the direct and indirect reference to the value system. The action itself, although mostly at the heroic level returns steadily to the familiar village context, with common people (the counselors, the princes, the commoners, the women, the little children) and Pygmies interacting with the hero. The entire epic is placed against the background of a well-known region in Nyangaland itself.

(Biebuyck 1972: 257–73)

Again a detailed comparison of Roscoe's assertions and Biebuyck's testimony, quoted above, will show how unwarranted are Roscoe's aspersions against the longer oral narrative in Africa.

Now, for the benefit of those too quick to disparage oral narrative, whether of the longer or shorter form, the following observations by Philip Noss on Gbaya narrative art are well worth noting:

One of the primary factors in blurring the aesthetic qualities of the African tale has been the belief that good literature has dimension and depth while the African folktale lacks description and therefore dimension. When the Western reader thinks of literature, he thinks of the short story or the novel in which description is a conscious art with paragraphs and chapters devoted to the embellishment of setting, event, and character. Or he may think of poetry with its metaphors and similes, whose principal purpose is that of description. When one reads tales that are meant to be presented orally, usually in a language other than the original, with little awareness of the cultural setting or the aesthetic principles and assumptions underlying the tale, it is not surprising if he concludes that the tales are merely action-packed episodes involving stock characters whose only dimension may be comic. Yet, to the audience for whom the tale is created, every dimension is explicit. The performance is a complete living event.

The Gbaya people of Cameroun and the Central African Republic were traditionally semi-nomadic hunters and farmers. They developed what they called *to*, an art form that was oral and dramatic. It was performed by an artist through the medium of the spoken word. When the printed word is the medium of expression, it alone must evoke whatever imagery exists; it alone must create dimension. The spoken word in contrast has many dimensions. It is heard and seen and felt; it is experienced as the narrator becomes a one-legged swinging creature, a character with a long nose or with two noses, or an ugly old lady with mattery eyes and black mushrooms all over her back, or when he is simply Wanto receiving a richly deserved beating at the hands of his wife. With varying degrees of animation, body movement, facial expression, tone of voice, and rhythm of speech, the narrator presents the character and his plight.

The narrator's audience must be attracted and held; it is not captive. The easiest way to hold the listener's interest is through action, and the Gbaya language is grammatically well suited to the rapid development of plot. Sequences of three or four verbs are quite common, as in the sentence: "The baboon wandered coming came arrived found them." . . . But narrative action that may lead to speedy resolution of the plot cannot alone sustain the attention of the listener. He wants to know not only what is happening, but what kinds of characters are performing the actions, what kinds of environments and circumstances they find surrounding themselves, as well as details such as the time of day and the darkness of the night. The oral performer must weave these details into his story just as the novelist does, but with considerably less leeway for error. Unlike the reader, who puts the book down for an hour or who skips to the next chapter, the audience either begins disrupting the performance or simply disperses. Thus the oral performer, like the poet, must create new ways of describing his people and their places and actions. His tale must be imaginative, concise, and beautiful.

Inherent in the development of the *to* was the establishment of aesthetic principles. Methods of description were required in order to provide the dimension necessary to a complete performance. Thus the following descriptive techniques occur in the Gbaya tale as it is performed today:

1) Ideophones
2) Names
3) Imagery
4) Narrative Description
5) Allusion. . . .

Given the potential of the ideophone, of names, of imagery, of simple narrative description, and of allusion, the traditional Gbaya tale need not lack for dimension. In the hands of a skilled performer, the tale is not deficient in any way. It is a complete aesthetic work of art. The conflict arises when a translator or writer attempts to put on paper, through the written word, what was created for oral performance. To fault the traditional art form for being simple and shallow is at best unfair.

(Noss 1972: 72–75, 90)

The testimony of such research as Noss has conducted should reduce by a fair amount the quantity of disparaging nonsense routinely repeated about oral narrative. Furthermore, it does raise the particularly useful research question of how to capture in written notation such oral dramatic art forms as the Gbaya *to*. Clearly, beyond matters of narrative texture, there are other ingredients in oral performance which not even a master verbal artist himself can be expected to capture when he writes down his own telling of a story. The research problem would be one of significantly enlarging the technical capabilities of the written medium so that it can convey the *heard, felt* and *seen* aspects of the spoken word in the performance context in which it is delivered. The point of such notation would be to assist the average reader to recreate in his mind's eye the original performance, in much the same way as a drama director from a written page constructs in his mind's eye a fleshed-out performance before he recreates it on stage. We might obtain a better idea of what kinds of coding devices are needed for transcribing oral narrative performances by examining the coding devices used in writing down instructions for the performance of music, dance and drama.

Narrative texts, as they are presently written down, are merely a sequence of words with minimal punctuation. This kind of notation would be analogous to a musical score made up of only the lines and pitch notes, together with clefs and bars, but without the all-important performance instructions about phrasing, loudness, forcefulness, speed, pace, etc.— such items as *fortissimo, pianissimo, staccato, cantabile, glissando,* pedalling instructions, rest notations, etc. The point of the needed technical research would be to supply to the written versions of oral texts the equivalents for such musical performance directions. Considering that an oral narrative performance has not only musical aspects but also dramatic and dance aspects, there would be need also for scoring their written versions in such ways as would embody stage directions and choreographic instructions. In short, what would be required would be something like a fully scored operatic text, with directions for music, songs, chants, recitatives, as well as dramatic and dance movements. This is because in an oral narrative performance, the pure narrative is interspersed with singing, dancing, chanting, recitals, and dramatic action. These kinds of notations would be needed to supply the reader with things that were the meat and sinews of the performance, such as gestures, body movements, facial expressions, tonal inflections, speech rhythms, mood and atmosphere.

Since even the best available written texts of oral narratives—and they are clearly in the minority—are nevertheless limited in their success at capturing the performance
dimension, scholars have a challenge before them to invent
techniques, notations, formulas and codes for reproducing in
writing such performance aspects of oral narrative as they
have so far not been able to capture in print. The same
challenge extends to both critics and writers: just as Joyce
and Proust and other modern European novelists, when they
had new materials to capture in writing, embarked upon
technical innovations, our scholars, critics and writers have
a responsibility to make innovations for reproducing oral
narratives in full in writing. They should face up to this task
instead of trying to avoid it through the escapist claim that
the oral tradition is inferior to the written tradition and
therefore has little or nothing to offer. The fashionable
idolatry of the written medium, insofar as it leads to auto-
matic and habitual disparagement of the oral medium, is
unwarranted. Even a prima facie look at the evidence shows
that it is unwarranted.

For those scholars who are habitual and prejudiced detractors of the oral medium, Noss's recapitulation of the qualities
of oral performances among the Gbaya is a much needed
reminder that the final authority for generalizations regarding
African oral narrative is the performance itself. His caution
about faulting the oral original for whatever the transcription
process might have left out is very well taken. One may not
allege deficiencies in the oral original simply from deficiencies
observed in a written down version. Moreover, generalized
claims of shortcomings in oral narrative tradition ought not
to be made on the basis of written texts which are liable to
contain important omissions. Eldred Durosimi Jones has
pointed out that

> As critics we must constantly remind ourselves that
> the central document is the work itself. It must even-

tually be judged by what it contains or what can
legitimately be implied from it.

(Jones 1975: editorial)

For literature the central document is the written text itself. For orature the central document, the work itself, is the live performance. Claims that a work of orature does not have one thing or another and is therefore inferior to a comparable work of literature are not to be taken seriously unless it is made clear that the work itself, i.e., the performance, has been consulted, or that an adequate copy of the performance, or an adequate written transcript, has been examined. In the present state of things, an audio-visual record of the performance, if competently done, is the best copy of the performance. If such is not available, a written transcript of a performance by a master of the verbal art, especially a transcript done by such a master himself, e.g., Diop, Postma, should be consulted. Where none of the above is available, scholars would do well to rely upon reports provided by careful scholars, especially by those scholars with a good ear for verbal artistry, such as Noss and Biebuyck, who have consulted an actual performance or an audio-visual record thereof. If this is not done, generalizations alleging this or that deficiency in the oral medium, however confidently delivered, should not be taken seriously.

Having dealt rather exhaustively with the first two in our list of issues raised by Izevbaye's passage, we shall now address the third. Izevbaye correctly attributes to Willie Abraham the views that "undeveloped characters are typical of African fiction," and that this phenomenon should be attributed to "the traditional African conception of the individual and society." Here is how Abraham himself stated it:

One finds that characterisation, the limning of the individual in the round, was notably absent in the traditional Akan literature. This has an explanation in the very conception of society and of the individual. Since society was thought of as comprising individuals with antecedent duties and responsibilities, the three-dimensional individual, completely subsistent, and a distinct atom, was non-existent. Literature did not therefore portray him. . . . Character types were therefore more interesting to Akan literature than characters in the round. It is probably this different tradition of type-characterisation, typical of African literature, which has made three-dimensional characterisation by African novelists in English and French so far a failure. Their characters have tended to be flat and canvassy.

(Abraham 1962: 96–97)

Izevbaye and Abraham both agree on this much: that the African conception of the individual and society has produced what Abraham calls type-characters, which are said to be typical of traditional African oral literature or orature. Izevbaye goes the further step of regarding such type-characters as a deficiency in the orature. Abraham's terms "flat," "round," "three-dimensional" and "type-characterisation" (terms borrowed from E. M. Forster), are not without problems of their own, as we shall show later on in this essay; however, for convenience, we shall employ them for now.

Now, whatever the case may be about "the communal character of traditional societies," or about the traditional African "conception of society and of the individual," this cannot be said to have at all limited characterization in African orature to type-characters, because, in fact, it has not. As we have shown, in both shorter and longer oral tales from Africa, we do indeed have character development that is as detailed, as "un-typed," and as "rounded" as any in European novels or in epics from anywhere. Simply put, Abraham's and Izevbaye's notion of what kind of charaterization there is in African orature is wrong. And most certainly African society, or the nature of African society, cannot be responsible for something that just isn't so. Abraham's explanation explains nothing because there is nothing here for it to explain. What he and Izevbaye claim is typical of our orature is in fact only typical of the poor transcripts they have read, not of African orature itself. To try to use the "communal nature of traditional societies" as a scapegoat for some non-existent deficiency in the African oral tale, as Izevbaye does, is to try to use it to disguise his own misperceptions about the African oral tale. Such scapegoating is a tendentious exercise, and indeed a libellous defamation of traditional African society. And as for Abraham's specu-lation that characters in the African novel are "flat and canvassy" because of the influence of type-characterization in African orature, and thus ultimately because of the tra-ditional African conception of society and the individual, it cannot be taken seriously; for even if it were true that characters in African novels are "flat and canvassy," you could not hold the oral tradition responsible for that without misrepresenting and maligning that tradition.

Having demonstrated at length the absence of these alleged deficiencies in the oral tradition, and having thereby shown that, in the respects considered, the best from the African oral tradition is as good as the best from the European written tradition, we must therefore maintain that: (1) Whatever real failings our writers suffer from cannot be laid at the door of the oral tradition, especially when it is doubtful that they have learned well from it. All such failings must be attributed to the writer himself, either for not having learned his craft well, or for not having chosen well what to learn his craft from, or both. (2) Such false allegations cannot be used either by eurocentric taskmasters or by embarrassed Africans to exhort our writers to model them-selves exclusively on the Western tradition.

A word is in order here on these professional detractors of Africa and on their eurocentric procedure. In evaluating African literature and matters related to it, they start out by taking outstanding written material from Europe as their standards; they gather whatever African material they find convenient, usually of middling quality or worse, and compare them adversely with the best from Europe, and thereby unctuously confirm themselves in their initial prejudice that Europe is "good" and Africa "bad." When it comes to the African oral tradition, their anti-African prejudice is reinforced by their anti-oral prejudice. They therefore gather the most grossly inadequate versions of African oral material they can find, and proceed, once again, to unctuously confirm themselves in their double-barrelled prejudice against things both African and oral. To proceed in such a manner is of course bad scholarship, however ego-salving it might be to these scholars. It is certainly none of our business to cure them of this bad habit they have of blaming the African oral and written traditions for their own shortcomings in scholarship and commonsense. We only wish to point out to our fellow-Africans that if such detractors were not certified university professors, one would call them ignoramuses, just as one might call a man in the street a fool if he blamed a right leg for not being a left leg.

AN AFROCENTRIC DEFENSE OF THE AFRICAN NOVEL

The Premises and Prejudices of Eurocentric Criticism

Now, before dealing with the specific charges listed at the beginning of this essay, it is necessary to determine from where within the Western tradition these charges emanate. Most of the genuinely technical charges would appear to attempt to impose canons of the 19th century European "well-made novel" upon the 20th century African novel, entirely disregarding both the tradition of African orature and the revolution in the techniques of the European novel initiated by Proust, Joyce and Kafka, and extended by Faulkner, Hemingway, Beckett and many others.

When in their complaint against succinct sketches these eurocentric critics demand of the African novel detailed physical description, elaborate portrait painting, detailed psychological investigation with elaborately subtle probing of motivations, and a cartographer's spatio-temporal map, they would seem to be calling for a Balzacian luxuriance of minutiae. These watchdogs of eurocentric propriety would appear in their pronouncements either totally oblivious to the passing within their own Western tradition of the "well-made" or "pure" novel since the era of Joyce and Proust, or they would seem to be deliberately engaged in scotching literary and cultural experimentation in Africa.

Proust, Joyce, Kafka and their heirs are an incitement to technical experimentation. They challenged the traditional Western modes of presenting time, character, setting and other aspects of reality. They promoted word coinages, unorthodox uses of language, asymmetric or random renderings of sequences of events—developments that would appear anarchistic and dangerous to any mind imbued with reverence for the 19th-century European status quo. In addition, they extended the range of materials that could be presented in the novel, and how. For instance, the anticlericalism and sexual explicitness that pervade Joyce's novels, the explicit homosexuality in Proust's work, and the presentation of joyful adultery by Lawrence, naturally offended the residual Victorianism, puritanism, and prudery of the keepers of their respective national orders.

Developments since Joyce, Proust and Kafka, as for instance in the French *nouveau roman,* overwhelmingly demonstrate that the novel is an open form, and that there is no ideal form to which all novels must conform. In particular, we should not be misled by the connotations of the terms "well-made" or "pure" into idealizing or strenuously imitating the forms of the 19th-century European bourgeois novel. The forms of the novel are capable of change in every direction. In the making of the novel, it is "morning yet on creation day," to borrow a phrase from Chinua Achebe.

Most of the objections to thematic and ideological matters in the African novel sound like admonitions from imperialist motherhens to their wayward or outright rebellious captive chickens. They cluck: "Be Universal! Be Universal!" And what they don't consider universal they denounce as anthropological, atavistic, autobiographical, sociological, journalistic, topical ephemera. When they first encountered African novels, eurocentric critics praised their detailed descriptions of African setting and customs as "quaint," "exotic," "fantastic" and "bewitching"; but now that their nouveaumania has tired of such material, they denounce it as anthropological data and "local color." Those works which they denounce as autobiographical, sociological, journalistic and topical, are usually those works whose subject matter, if handled from an African perspective, cannot but indict the colonial order. For instance, an African brought up under colonialism, when employing autobiographical material in his fiction, would be hard put to avoid an at least implicit criticism of colonialism.

When these critics denounce what they consider didacticism, propaganda, or inconsistency of moral attitude, they usually do so only when these things criticise or militate against European bourgeois values. In their concern with promoting the Western brand of individualism, they denounce as "situational" those presentations in which some individual does not dominate or wilfully tower over his social environment. And of course they do not want to hear or read "protest literature" since the protest is, and has to be, overwhelmingly against what the bourgeois order, which is managed from and in the primary interest of the West, is doing to the African.

Furthermore, when some critics complain against "too many *Things Fall Apart*," or when some others call for "an urgent release from the fascination of the past," reminding everyone that the past "is not a fleshpot for escapist indulgence," they could be said, at least in part, to be urging a moratorium on literary examination of the colonial experience. If their complaint is meant to also imply that African writers should focus exclusively on the modern African state and turn a blind eye to its colonial antecedents, it should be rejected as anti-historical and misleading. We see no reason why all kinds and periods of African experience should not be open to the writer to explore.

To the allied charge that there is a preponderance of autobiographical novels, we ask: why not? Autobiography is a legitimate literary quarry; autobiographical novels are a species of the the historical novel. Perhaps what irks the critics who levy this charge is that the Euro-African conflict is the theme of a large part of these autobiographical novels. We should point out that for those who grew up under colonialism, this conflict is the central event of their environment.

Considering Africa's recent history, it would indeed be surprising if autobiographical novels, and, through them, the Euro-African conflict, did not feature heavily in African literature. Is this charge against an abundance of autobiographical novels not another effort to block examination of colonialism and its impact on African society and individuals? Indeed, other themes should be explored, but that should not require a reduction in the number of works dealing with autobiography or culture conflict. Given our history, we can't have too many autobiographical novels, or too many *Things Fall Apart*.

Fidel Castro once described the attitudes and interests from which such criticisms emanate:

> Novels which attempt to reflect the reality of the world of imperialism's rapacious deeds; the poems aspiring to protest against its enslavement, its interference in life, in thought, in the very bodies of nations and peoples; and the militant arts which in their expression try to capture the forms and content of imperialism's aggression and the constant pressure on every progressive living and breathing thing and on all

that is revolutionary, which teaches, which—full of light and conscience, of clarity and beauty—tries to guide men and peoples to better destinies, to the highest summits of life and justice—all these meet imperialism's severest censure.

(Castro 1962: epigraph)

It is therefore not surprising that the eurocentric critics of the African novel, concerned as they are with keeping upon us the hold of the mythologies of imperialism, choose to ignore new developments within their own traditions, and exhort our novelists to bury themselves in an archaic and vestigial branch of the Western tradition. While our writers do not need, in a sort of reflex reaction to these antediluvian critics, to embark on the wild fads of the contemporary European literary scene, the need for experimentation in creating from different traditions a novel adequate for probing African realities, ought to be acknowledged.

In the light of Fidel Castro's remarks we shall now examine three of these eurocentric pro-imperialist critics of African literature and how they go about their task of imperialist censure.

In his book, *Mother is Gold,* Adrian Roscoe's disparagements, and the tone in which he delivers them, are quite remarkable. He conveys an impression of being an articulate member of that breed of expatriate critics whose job is to mind the cultural fences and keep the colonial bailiwick intact. The strategy of his performance appears to be this: to persuade the reader that the African is naturally incapable of producing or enjoying long complex fiction, that short narrative is his natural metier, and that he should stick with what he performs best. "Leave the novel alone; stick to the short story," would seem to be his cathechism:

> The African child, for instance, is faced in school with a written literary form imposed on him by an alien system of education. He may acquire a taste for the novel; but his home life, his society's history—in a

word, his culture—predispose him naturally to the story. It also means that for the moment, the African reader is a short distance performer. And curiously enough, so, too, are many of the writers.

(Roscoe 1971: 75–76)

This passage is like a condensed version of a famous scene in Malcolm X's *Autobiography:*

> Somehow, I happened to be alone in the classroom with Mr. Ostrowski, my English teacher. He was a tall, rather reddish white man and he had a thick mustache. I had gotten some of my best marks under him, and he had always made me feel that he liked me. He was, as I have mentioned, a natural-born "advisor," about what you ought to read, to do, or think—about any and everything. . . . I was one of his top students—one of the school's top students— but all he could see for me was the kind of future "in your place" that almost all white people see for black people.
>
> He told me, "Malcolm, you ought to be thinking about a career. Have you been giving it thought?"
>
> The truth is, I hadn't. I never have figured out why I told him, "Well, yes, sir, I've been thinking I'd like to be a lawyer." Lansing certainly had no Negro lawyers—or doctors either—in those days, to hold up an image I might have aspired to. All I really knew for certain was that a lawyer didn't wash dishes, as I was doing.
>
> Mr. Ostrowski looked surprised, I remember, and leaned back in his chair and clasped his hands behind his head. He kind of half-smiled and said, "Malcolm, one of life's first needs is for us to be realistic. Don't misunderstand me, now. We all here like you, you know that. But you've got to be realistic about being a nigger. A lawyer—that's no realistic goal for a nigger. You need to think about something you *can* be. You're good with your hands—making things. Everybody admires your carpentry shop work. Why don't you

plan on carpentry? People like you as a person—you'd get all kinds of work.''

The more I thought afterwards about what he said, the more uneasy it made me. It just kept treading around in my mind.

What made it really begin to disturb me was Mr. Ostrowski's advice to others in my class—all of them white. Most of them had told him they were planning to become farmers. . . . But those who wanted to strike out on their own, to try something new, he had encouraged. Some, mostly girls, wanted to be teachers. A few wanted other professions, such as one boy who wanted to become a county agent; another, a veterinarian; and one girl wanted to be a nurse. They all reported that Mr. Ostrowski had encouraged whatever they had wanted. Yet nearly none of them had earned marks equal to mine.

It was a surprising thing that I had never thought of it that way before, but I realized that whatever I wasn't, I *was* smarter than nearly all of those white kids. But apparently I was still not intelligent enough, in their eyes, to become whatever *I* wanted to be.

It was then that I began to change—inside.

I drew away from white people. I came to class, and I answered when called upon. It became a physical strain simply to sit in Mr. Ostrowski's class.

Where ''nigger'' had slipped off my back before, wherever I heard it now, I stopped and looked at whoever said it. And they looked surprised that I did.

(Malcolm X 1965: 35–37)

Roscoe's criticism purveys clearly a cultural variant of the genetic pseudo-arguments for the alleged natural inferiority of non-whites which are being advertised by Jensen, Hernstein, Eysenck, Schockley and others. As proof of what he considers the African writer's natural predisposition toward short stories rather than novels, Roscoe points out that

> many African writers (including poets, novelists, and
> dramatists) have naturally worked in this form and
> answered the pull of their home tradition. . . . The
> objection might be raised that the short story is being
> used as journey work, as a stepping-stone to more
> extended performances. But this does not explain why
> established novelists still persist in writing short stories.
> It does not explain why even aspiring dramatists like
> Christina Ama Ata Aidoo have turned their hand to
> this form.   (Roscoe 1971: 76)

Roscoe's theory explains nothing because there is nothing
to be explained; but it gives an insight into his prejudices.
He rather conveniently forgets that many writers all over
the world—poets, dramatists *and* established novelists—also
wrote short stories, for example, Faulkner, Hemingway,
Fitzgerald, Henry James, D. H. Lawrence, Chekhov, Gorky,
Joyce, Mark Twain, Thomas Mann, Maupassant, Kafka,
Oscar Wilde, Tolstoy. If accomplished poets, dramatists and
novelists all over the world have likewise "turned their
hand" to the short story, why does Roscoe feel a need to
invent a special explanation for African novelists who likewise write short stories? It must take a special kind of
insanity to concoct extraordinary explanations for regional
instances of a widespread, indeed universal human phenomenon.

Roscoe continues his litany of put-downs:

> The pull of tradition can even be felt when writers
> are not ostensibly offering the short story at all. Take
> the works of Tutuola or Fagunwa. What are they, if
> not a string of short narratives skillfully bonded into
> one longer tale? (p. 77)

He conveniently forgets that so is any picaresque novel.
After all, what is *Don Quixote* or *Ulysses* but "a string of
short narratives skillfully bonded into one longer tale?"
Clearly, if this is something that Africans are to be faulted
for, then many major Western novels must be faulted, too.

Presumably, now that Roscoe, the Britisher, has named two champions and pitted them against each other, Sierra Leoneans and Nigerians, with their African partisans in tow, will rush out to fight each other—while the British laugh!

Roscoe's amazing catalogue of silly dicta and pompous stupidities—and all in one paragraph!—are obviously aimed at a captive classroom audience, one probably without access to comparative information. Is such abuse what our students have to endure? After reading such a litany of thoughtless put-downs it is hard to resist the temptation to point out that such so-called perceptive critics as Roscoe are probably the best of the intellectual dead wood floated out from Europe to Africa to clutter up our cultureways with their bloated ignorance. Their mission appears to be to disorient our young minds with dicta that are racist, imperialist and half-baked. How does supporting such jaundiced and careless thinking with our public revenue, private fees, and textbook purchases differ from paying tribute to imperial masters?

Let us emphasize that we are not defending any genuine faults and shortcomings of those works, whatever they may be, but merely pointing out that Roscoe's is the wrong kind of attack from the wrong quarters, reeking with malice aforethought. It is stupid and racist criticism. Africa and her writers want none of it. While Roscoe's observation that there are still only a few good novelists from Africa may well be supported, but on grounds far different from his. His statement that "there are still only a few novelists who seem destined for international stature," is nothing more than an attempt to dangle the carrot of Western recognition before aspiring African novelists whom he wants to toe the imperialist literary line. When he further observes: "Africa, indeed, could yet be one area of the world where the quiet remark of Luis Borges, that 'the novel is a form that may pass, doubtless will pass,' is given powerful substance," we would like to point out that the French *nouveau roman* is more likely where the death of the novel will begin. Some of its practitioners are offering short, empty grunts as novels.

While Adrian Roscoe's criticism may be seen as a *bête blanche* of British colonialist criticism, specimen of the separate and unequal school of literature, that of Charles Larson, of America's phony universalist school, is not much of an improvement. To begin with, the title of his book, *The Emergence of African Fiction,* is mystifying. One wonders what African fiction is supposed to be emerging from, and what into. In his closing chapters he makes it all too clear that what he is celebrating is the supposed emergence of African fiction from some "primitive" past or condition into the mainstream of Western literary tradition! "How surprising, we might conclude that with Wole Soyinka and Ayi Kwei Armah, the African novel as a literary genre now moves into the main stream of Western tradition, yet how even more surprising, we might think, that this did not happen long before now." (p. 277) Nigerian critic Omalora Ogundipe Leslie aptly summarizes the presuppositions on which Larson's criticism is based: Larson's celebration, she writes, exposes

> a belief in a literature in vacuo; the myth of a necessary evolutionary progress from a different traditional literature to the mainstream of Western tradition; the movement from a mindless African past to a "civilised" thinking present. And at the heart of the crystal is the shining faith that we are all Americans under the skin; that given time, Western education and the inevitable erasure of cultural aberrations, we shall all walk into our Anglo-American inheritance: of individualism, monogamy and the atomic family; free enterprise and free competition; the collapse of emotional order and a superficial challenge of all forms of authority; masculinity, neurosis and the loss of most human moorings—all of which of course, are not culturally determined.
>
> (Leslie 1973: 89)

A variant of the universalist argument is offered by Eustace Palmer, a eurocentric African critic, as follows:

> Even if the form of African novels were different [from European ones], this would not mean that a different set of criteria should be evolved for their criticism. . . . Since we are still concerned with the same genre, the same criteria should still apply. To allow different critical criteria is to provide loopholes for mediocrities.
>
> (Palmer 1972: x)

None of Palmer's three propositions is true, and each is demonstrably false: (1) the proposition about providing loopholes for mediocrities merely serves to intimidate disagreement with the other two propositions; (2) different criteria do often have to be applied to different branches of the same genre; and (3) because literary forms are socio-historical cultural products, they, as well as the terms for evaluating performances guided by them, do tend to vary from society to society, and even from period to period within a given society. Therefore we see no logical grounds, no non-political grounds, for not evolving for the African novel a different sort of criticism than the prevailing eurocentric one. African realities are sufficiently different, and our concern to liberate our culture from European imperialism sufficiently antithetical to Europe's imperialist purposes, to demand of us new forms, new genres, and critical criteria radically different from the European. The one thing we do not need is to emerge into the Western tradition. What we do need instead is to emerge out of its mind fetters.

These pronouncements by Roscoe, Larson and Palmer are instructive examples of the kinds of prejudices and false premises which are routinely brought to the criticism of the African novel by eurocentric critics. We shall proceed now to demonstrate how these prejudices show up disguised as technical, esthetic or philosophical criticism of the African novel.

The So-Called Problem of Space and Time

Larson's treatment of the "problem" of space and time
in the African novel is a classic of sorts. His commitment
to a phony universalism, which is nothing other than a
commitment to a Western imperialist world view, comes
through clearly when he commends Lenrie Peters' novel,
The Second Round, for its "universality, its very limited
concern with Africa itself":

> That it is set in Africa appears to be accidental, for
> except for a few comments at the beginning, Peters'
> story might just as easily take place in the southern
> part of the United States or, say, in the southern
> regions of France or Italy. If a few names of characters
> and places were changed one would indeed feel that
> this was an American novel or a French or Italian
> novel. In short, Peters' story is universal.
>
> (Larson 1972: 230)

In other words, if the mission of the African novel is to
attain universality, it can be quite easily accomplished, at
least with regard to the problem of setting, by having the
African novel set entirely outside Africa! In short, the proper
setting for the African novel is the West. African novelists
ostensibly create problems for "universalist" critics by setting
their novels in Africa!

Having offered his final solution to that "problem,"
Larson approaches the matter of time and space by trans-
muting his misperceptions and illogicalities into muddleheaded
metaphysical speculations. He claims that "time in an African
sense has little to do with actual blocks of time as measured
in a Western sense, but rather with human values and human
achievements." (p. 106) And for evidence he tells us that
Ouologuem's novel of 300 pages covers approximately 750
years (pp. 20, 106). How this is supposed to pose any
problems, metaphysical or otherwise, is hard to see. How it

constitutes evidence for the alleged difference between the African and Western measurement of time is even harder to see. After all, in one edition of 422 pages, Milton's *Paradise Lost* spans from before the Creation to the Expulsion of Adam and Eve from Eden. How many centuries or eternities is that? Joyce's *Ulysses* covers roughly 18 hours in 783 pages. What, by Larson's logic, should all that tell us about the Western sense of time? Much like Roscoe, Larson concocts extraordinary explanations for what is a perfectly ordinary literary phenomenon.

But Larson's metaphysical preoccupations lead him to further confusions and to elaborate absurdities. For instance, he claims to see a metaphysical problem of time in Tutuola's *The Palm-Wine Drinkard* because the hero's journey to Deads' Town took ten years and his return journey only one year. In Larson's words: "Here alone there appears to be an inconsistency; if the trip to the Deads' Town takes ten years, why is barely more than a year involved for the return?" (pp. 102-3) Following his metaphysical nose, Larson confidently invents the following explanation: "The answer, however, has nothing to do with space or the actual distance between the Drinkard's own village and the Deads' Town. Rather, time is related to the incidents involved in the Drinkard's going and coming from the Deads' Town and in the relative value of these incidents." (p. 103)

The metaphysical confusion appears complete. Even if the narrator had not pointedly said that for the return journey his dead palm wine tapser "showed us another road and it was really a road not a bush as before" (Tutuola 1953: 101), still it must take a compulsive ingeniousness for anyone to avoid a commonsensical explanation and instead laboriously insist upon constructing ontological problems and fanciful solutions. For one thing, rather than unnecessarily invoking a "time in an African sense" that allegedly is metaphysically different from "time as measured in a Western sense," it seems far more sensible to remember that the Drinkard on his way out wandered about asking directions, being delayed by numerous trails and ordeals and sidetracking tasks whereas on his return journey, even if he had not found a short cut and had merely retraced his original route with a minimum of delays, he could conceivably have gotten home ten times faster. Instead of taking a commonsensical approach and examining the evidence in the text, Larson prefers to invent fanciful metaphysical explanations.

Larson continues by trying to explain the obvious by the obscure. He tries to explain Tutuola's presentation of time by concocting the categories of "evil time" and "good time." What do these mean and what is the warrant for positing them? Larson does not explain. Further on he tells us: "Clearly, the Skull catches his victims because he operates in a time different from theirs." (p. 103) What does this mean? Larson doesn't know what he is talking about. He demonstrated his confusion most clearly when he started the discussion of Tutuola's sense of time by flatly contradicting himself. First he says:

> In *The Palm-Wine Drinkard,* the reader is always conscious of time, because Tutuola constantly makes references to hours, days, weeks and months, even years. (p. 102)

Then in the very next sentence he says:

> One is reminded that many years ago, Spengler maintained that interest in time is peculiar to Western civilization. If lack of interest in time may often be more typical of non-Western cultures, Tutuola is in many ways a perfect example.

Larson, it would appear, has already forgotten what he said in the preceding sentence! It seems strange to accuse a man of being "a perfect example" of "lack of interest in time" immediately after you have said that he "constantly makes references to hours, days, weeks and months, even years."

On the matter of space, Larson also tells us that

> space and its treatment in *The Palm-Wine Drinkard* is also something frequently quite removed from the Western concept as shown in much Western fiction. (p. 106)

In support of his contention he says that Tutuola's hero and other characters are capable of covering vast distances

> in very limited periods of time in spite of the fact that in many cases there are no roads or pathways from one place to another. (p. 106)

What Larson has chosen to forget is that a tale of this sort is not in the realistic mode; and that in this regard Tutuola's treatment is no different from stories in non-realistic modes in any land, and that therefore no special explanation is called for. In any case, Tutuola's hero tells us quite early in his story that he is a magician, "Father of gods who could do everything in this world." (Tutuola 1953: 10) This should have served as sufficient that this story is in a non-realistic mode.

Larson compounds his gaffe when he compares Kafka's and Tutuola's treatments of time and space as "surrealistic"—and then fails to draw the proper inference and abandons his theory that Tutuola's handling of time and space is peculiarly African. Has he, perhaps, in his somnambulist fashion also forgotten that Kafka was not an African?

Emmanuel Obiechina devotes a chapter in his book *Culture, Tradition and Society in the West African Novel* to an investigation of cultural forms for delimiting space and reckoning time as they appear in West African novels. We believe this is the right approach to the matter. Western or urban man does not have an ontologically different time, or space, or sense of time, or sense of space from African or non-urban man; they simply reckon them with different measures, much as the same distance might be measured in either meters or feet or roods. We should always bear in mind that the Gregorian calendar is not the only one available for reckoning the astronomical cycle of the solar system which we call the year. There are other calendars—lunar, Julian, Chinese, etc. Also, the 24-hour clock is not the only possible chronometer for the earth's daily cycle. Convention could have divided the duration of the day into 5, 79, or 113 units instead of 24.

Aside from this, especially when astronomical precision is not required, people in all ages and places have adopted less rigorous measurements. For instance, it is for the most part sufficient to indicate period of year by season, e.g., winter, fall or autumn, spring, and summer in temperate lands; rainy and dry season in tropical lands; monsoons and harmattans where these apply. When they thought it necessary to be more precise, people have referred to, say, harvest time, planting time, the time when migratory birds pass through the locality, etc. In denoting times and periods of the day, people in all parts of the world have always used such markers as cock-crow, sunset, sunrise, when the shadow reaches a certain length, or the sun is in a certain region of the sky. The general utilization of the 24-hour clock and the Gregorian calendar has not entirely displaced these usages anywhere. Time continues to be denoted by whatever convenient units are locally available. This, as is implicit in Obiechina's investigation, is a matter of cultural form, not of special senses or kinds of time.

The same may be said for space: the markers available range from street names to natural or man-made landmarks such as hills, mountains, valleys, gorges, streams and rivers; temples, shrines, skyscrapers, squares, markets, etc. Maps, whether of the locality or of the globe as a whole, are used according to need; they have not displaced other modes of showing directions or spatial relationships. As in the case of time, space relationships are indicated by what is available, and by what suits specific needs. When these appear in novels they should be no cause for surprise; and when, in particular, they appear in African novels, they constitute no warrant for obtuse speculations regarding African metaphysics and epistemology.

Although Obiechina's approach is generally sound, some trace elements from the muddled thinking in contemporary literary criticism still do creep into his presentation. For instance, he opens his discussion of space and time by saying:

> The novel is unlike oral literature in its insistence on
> the "precise spatial and temporal location of individual
> experience." (p. 122)

At least two errors are contained in this comment. First, the appropriate opposition is not between oral and written works, but between realistic and non-realistic modes of presentation. Though the required degree of precision will vary from work to work, the demand for "precise spatial and temporal location" applies to realistic presentation as much in oral as in written narrative. Secondly, as far as the novel is concerned, this demand would apply only to the realistic novel, or to the realistic portions of a novel in mixed modes. For instance, dreams, hallucinations and visionary experiences, when presented in a novel, would only be distorted by the kinds of precision appropriate for the presentation of normal waking experiences. And even then, the requirement of "precise spatial and temporal location" does not commit a novel to exclusive use of the clock or the Gregorian calendar in measuring or indicating time; nor to miles, meters and the cardinal points for measuring distance. To think that it does is pure prejudice—even if a fashionable one.

The proper question of "precise spatial and temporal location" in realistic fiction (and there are gradations of realism) is not: where is Ouologuem's Nakem? Or Robinson Crusoe's island? Or Achebe's Umuofia? Or Robert Louis Stevenson's Treasure Island? Or Swift's Lagado or Brobdingnag?—meaning, presumably, where on a real-world map might these places be found? After all, it is fiction, not history. Would telling these stories without mention of a place name at all invalidate these stories in any way? Ditto for time.

On the other hand, a legitimate question of space and time in fictional works in the realistic mode is one of internal consistency and coherence. The north part of a country should not, a few pages later, suddenly become its east, nor should a distance of a hundred miles suddenly become a thousand; and if in telling his story the narrator gives enough information, it should be possible to construct a coherent map of the location—as is indeed possible from the *Iliad, Odyssey* and *Sundiata,* for instance. If the narrator does not find such exact information necessary to his purpose, "once upon a time" (or "once upon a place") should be sufficient, and should not be assumed to place the action automatically "in a never-never land where fantastic things happen." (Obiechina, p. 122)

This matter of precise spatial location has been regularly misused by "universalist" critics, especially when they accuse African novels of "local color." They choose to forget that in describing an African setting, you can't meet their call for precise spatio-temporal location at the same time as their absurd demand for a "universal" setting (meaning, outside Africa). If you are precise they accuse you of "local color." They probably want you to be quite precise about a British, French or American setting, and as vague as you can about an African setting—in which case you are all right for them, you are an accomplished sleight-of-hand "universalist" who can write with "precision" and no "local color" all at the same time. Clearly, the game of literary criticism is being played, at least on African literature, in bad faith. It might be helpful to remind these eurocentric votaries of universality what T. S. Eliot said on the matter:

> Universality can never come except through writing about what one knows thoroughly. . . . And, though it is only too easy for a writer to be local without being universal, I doubt whether a poet or novelist can be universal without being local too.
>
> (Eliot 1965: 55, 56)

An observer might wonder what colonialist critics of African literature are up to when they spin off pseudo-problems such as we have been examining above. It seems to us that these critics come to African literature carrying problems which have arisen in the centuries of criticism of Western literature. Having been trained to deal with such problems, they frantically search for their equivalents in African literature, and if they don't find them they create them. And they are quite willing to go ingenious lengths in creating them. One notorious procedure of theirs is to start from some particular problem they see in a particular text, then quickly generalize it for all of African literature, and irresponsibly theorize as to its origins in African society as a whole. Even with compelling evidence, these would be two extremely large steps to take.

What is remarkable is that responsible critics of Western literature do not at all proceed in this fashion. For instance, there is a problem in the handling of time in Shakespeare's *Othello:* by one set of time indicators, Othello and his bride have lived together in Cyprus for only a few days, no more than a week at the most. In that case, Desdemona could not possibly have committed the acts of sexual infidelity she is accused of, alleged acts for which a credulous Othello executes her—if for no other reason than that there just hasn't been time enough. But the "short time" seems necessary to reinforce the impression that Othello has not had time to know his bride well enough to know these accusations to be false; worse, that he acts precipitately and does not give himself time to think. However, by another set of time indicators, the couple have lived together in Cyprus much longer, months at least, and it is by this set of time indicators that Iago's accusatory portrait of Desdemona as a cunning and habitual adulteress could be made plausible even to a man as credulous as Othello. In other words, there are two parallel and contradictory time indicators or clocks running in the play, and scholars have labored for centuries to reconcile or explain them.

Similarly, there is a problem of time, timing and psychology in Shakespeare's *Hamlet*. Why did Hamlet not execute his uncle until near the end of the play? Did he distrust the ghost even after his play within the play had so clearly revealed his uncle's guilt? Western scholars have spent considerable time trying to unravel this question. They have come up with various answers, some commonsensical, some alarmingly ingenious; but nobody in his right mind has attempted to go on from there to generalize about medieval Danish psychology, Danish (or, in *Othello*, Italian) sense of time, or English psychology or sense of time. What they have done instead has been to view these questions as technical problems. Shakespeare may have made a mistake, or he may have kept Hamlet vacillating and ruminating either in keeping with Hamlet's character, or because he had to keep the play going for five acts, and if Hamlet killed the villain too soon, Shakespeare would be hard put to fill in the rest of the time.

Now, it might be said of the latter explanation that Shakespeare could have solved that technical problem another way; after all, he had Julius Caesar assassinated in the first scene of Act III when the play was less than half over, yet he more than managed to fill in the rest of the time. Either he couldn't handle *Hamlet* in the same manner, or he simply chose not to. The important point is that it is a technical problem within the work, and it constitutes no warrant for fantastic pronouncements on Elizabethan cosmology or Danish psychology.

The African equivalents of such problems have, similarly, no implications for African cosmology or psychology. If a problem or issue arises within a work, it should be dealt with within the work. Critics should not glibly generalize and say that the handling of time in a given novel proves *anything* at all about African society. In order to prove anything about African society, you need to have considerably more evidence to go on than the work of one writer or one work of one writer, or one sentence in one work of one writer. Unfortunately, this is the situation we have in the case of Larson's discussion of *The Palm-Wine Drinkard*. The protagonist tells us in one sentence that it took him one year to get back from Deads' Town; in another sentence he tells us that the journey to and from Deads' Town required a total of eleven years. It is largely on this slim evidence, those two sentences, that at least one ingenious critic has constructed labyrinths of metaphysical speculations regarding an African sense of time. The first question should have been: is this handling of time by Tutuola, if it is irregular (which it is not), characteristic of other African writers? Do we find it in works by other African writers? If we do, then we might go on to consider whether this is a peculiar characteristic of each of these writers, or whether it is a manifestation of something endemic in the society as a whole. Rather than do this, such critics jump from a problem they find, or choose to find, in some particular author, to generalizations about African sense of time, cosmology, metaphysics, etc.

Just like the above mystifications of spatio-temporal matters, a penchant for mystification of sociological matters is also most noticeable in conventional pronouncements on time and the clock. These mystifications involve allied, radical mistakes. Whereas the metaphysical mystifications examined above involve the hypostatization of spatio-temporal matters, the sociological mystifications which we now examine involve the reification of sociological relations. For instance, Obiechina states:

> Time in the traditional consciousness is less significant than social institutions—ethics, religion and aesthetics. Since the traditional setting is largely an agrarian society and small in scale, time and space have less significance than in urban or industrial setting. So West African novelists show an awareness of this relative irrelevance. Some of the novelists even draw attention to the peculiarity. According to Nkem Nwankwo, "Punctuality is not one of the virtues of the Aniocha man. He takes time over his snuff and his palm wine and if you attempted to hurry him from either he would excuse himself by reminding you of the proverb: where the runner reaches there the walker will reach eventually. . . ."
>
> In the urban environment time acquires significance. Bureaucratic systems of administration in industry, commerce and the civil service, the need to have numbers of people drawn together from different parts of a large metropolis, require adherence to time schedules. People's lives are being increasingly controlled by the clock. The tempo of life in towns is strict because there are so many things making demands on the time of the townsmen; to attend to them all he has to be very mobile, physically and mentally. Life has become a nightmare rush to keep up with things—with one's profession, with social engagements, with trade union and political meetings, with funerals, marriages and outings, with football matches, with the theatre and the cinema, and even with one's sex and drink. Time is master and the townsman its slave.
>
> (Obiechina 1975: 135, 136)

Now, these are important but relatively straightforward sociological matters. Whether in industrial or non-industrial settings, the kind, degree and extent of control is determined by how work and other activities are organized, by whom

109

and for whom. In industrial settings, control is not by the clock but by the social order, the power structure, and the boss who determines whether you get paid or not, which in turn determines whether you eat or not. The boss insists you come to work at a particular time and place or else be dismissed. The worker's life is controlled not by the clock but by his bosses and those whose economic power they represent. In contrast, the man in a non-industrial setting, like the Aniocha man, could afford to be leisurely and unhurried because he is his own boss, the individual free-holder of his own land or one working his share of communal land, and he therefore has the power to regulate his comings and goings as he pleases. This privilege still exists in the industrial community where the individual trader, bank president or Permanent Secretary(?), being his own boss, can afford to independently determine his own comings and goings.

Furthermore, although the worker, wherever he may be, is constrained to come to work at a particular time, he nevertheless may be in full control of other portions of his day. While he might be as hurried and punctual at work as he is required to be, he might be cavalier in those of his after-work social appointments where there are no similar constraints. But even in the non-work segment of life, other equally powerful constraints might come into play. For instance, if you are going to a funeral in which you are exptected to be a chief mourner, whether in town or village, in an industrial or non-industrial setting, you would do well to be there on time, *no matter how time is actually indicated,* or face social censure or even sanctions. Again, if a boy has to arrive to sweep the village square with his mates at the first cock-crow, and he comes late, he will face censure and his mother might even have to pay a fine on his behalf. But in matters where there are no constraints, whether it is a village festival or an urban drinking party, you could, like the Aniocha man, take your own sweet time getting there.

The real opposition in this matter of time, punctuality, hurry and leisure is not urban vs. rural, or industrial vs. non-industrial, as much as it is whether or not there are economic, moral, political or other social sanctions for punctuality or precise timing in the particular activity. And certainly the "villain" is not time, or the clock, but rather the norms and sanctions of the social order, and those in whose interests these are established and regulated. The issue, therefore, should be seen as one regarding the social consequences of different modes and organization of production, not as a matter of clocks or no clocks.

As against the expatriate critics, who import such wrongheaded problems into the criticism of African literature, it would appear that some of our African critics, having inherited a set of issues, don't analyse them, but repeat all manner of inherited pronouncements upon them. But really, that something has been long bandied about in the critical literature does not at all mean that it is a genuine or noteworthy problem. It may be entirely wrongheaded and should be abandoned. The narcotic attention of previous or other scholars does not legitimize it.

Plot, Structure, and Dialogue

Larson charges a good many African novels with having a loose narrative structure, instead of the structure of a "well-made story." According to him, Tutuola's novels, and such other novels as Elechi Amadi's *The Concubine*, Ngugi's *Weep Not Child*, and Achebe's *Things Fall Apart* and *Arrow of God*, consist of "a series of short tales strung together" or "a collection of short stories tied together" or "many unrelated essays and stories." (pp. 18–19) In Euro-American criticism such expressions are used to describe a novel that is picaresque or quasi-picaresque. So Larson's claim amounts to saying that many African novels are picaresque or quasi-picaresque. But then, so what? That the picaresque is not

111

the currently dominant kind of novel in Europe is no reason why it shouldn't be in Africa—different cultures, different dominant forms, if they so choose.

John Povey makes the same charge but lays the alleged fault at the door of an alleged preponderance of autobiographical material in African novels:

> Too often other West African novelists, experimenting with their first novels, disregard structure; so that the pattern ceases to be a series of organized aesthetic choices and becomes merely the shapeless sequence of one thing after another. So close are many African novelists to the events they record that there is none of that artistic distance which is the basis for the writer's art. Plots mirror the autobiographical information proffered in the fly-leaf of the book's dustjacket and this causes the balance of events to be seen only through the single self-satisfied vision of the protagonist, and the end, unless it has the shock of unexpected melodrama, can be a mere finish, for the novel has failed to develop any impetus more structural than that of the author's own life.
>
> (Povey 1972: 97)

Since the same matter can be plotted and told differently, we see no necessary connection between autobiographical material as such and any particular plot structure. The legitimacy of autobiographical novels should not therefore be impugned because of any substantiable faults of structure.

As for Larson's dismissive claim that many African novels have "the situational construction wherein not one person but an entire group (a village, a tribe, a clan) becomes ultimately affected (usually for the worse) by the major event of the narration" (p. 19), we must ask: who says a novel must focus on an individual rather than on a group or community? Is this sheer bourgeois individualist prejudice? Is it even part of the Western definition of the novel that it must deal with "one person"? If so, in what sense could it possibly be said that only one person is ultimately affected by the major events of the narration in *War and Peace, The Brothers Karamazov, The Forsyte Saga, Man's Fate, Pride and Prejudice, A Tale of Two Cities, Les Miserables, The Red and the Black,* or *Madame Bovary?* Indeed, if there is any novel whose major events ultimately affect only one person, we would appreciate hearing about it from Larson. Not even in *Robinson Crusoe* did that happen. If a genuinely "non-situational" novel is such a rarity in the world, why should African novels be singled out for censure for being "situational?"

Larson further reports that, in the judgment of some critics, there is a "dialogue deficiency" in some African novels, and that in some others the dialogue is "laden with Churchillian vocabulary, sometimes quite out of character with everyday settings either in England or Africa." (p. 18) The notion of a "dialogue deficiency" seems rather odd. Is there some minimum quantity of dialogue required by some dialogue health regulation board, below which a work suffers from dialogue malnutrition? And if some dialogue is Churchillian or stilted or out of character, let us note that it probably results, at least in part, from the fact that English is a second language for these writers, one whose literary uses they have learned mostly from books and from old-fashioned teachers who not only frown on the use of pidgin, patois creole, colloquialisms and other species of "bad English" in "serious" writing, but who also hold up and almost exclusively teach prose stylists of the pre-Joycean, pre-experimentalist eras. Ironically, if African writers should continue to heed the lessons and examples of such teachers and critics, they would produce more, not less, of such stilted Churchillian, Victorian and Shakespearean dialogue.

Characterization and Description

Among the specific charges made against the African novel in the area of characterization and description are the

113

following: that characters are undeveloped; that character portraits are not full or detailed enough; that personality traits are not probed in depth; that complete characterizations are hard to come by; that dialogue is not much used to develop characters; that the motivations of characters are not really probed; and the pictorial descriptions are sketchy.

On the matter of undeveloped characters, let us now consider those among the questions raised by Izevbaye's formulation which we had deferred: (1) However popular the view, in what sense, if any, of the term "undeveloped" could it be true that "undeveloped characters are typical of African fiction?" (2) Are undeveloped characters, however defined, a shortcoming in written fiction, and if so, why? (3) Is it true that characters in the drama are not as fully "rounded" as characters in narrative fiction?

The notion of developed and undeveloped character is in need of analysis, for there is a confusion of usages to be untangled. Various renditions of this same charge in the critical literature speak of characters that are "types" rather than "individuals," of characters "lacking in depth," of characters "not imagined with any fullness," and of characters whose individual psychologies are not sufficiently probed.

There are at least three common usages of the term "undeveloped": an "undeveloped" character is sometimes said to be "static" rather than "dynamic"; it is said to be "flat" rather than "round," a "type" rather than an "individual," "one-dimensional" or "two-dimensional" rather than "three-dimensional;" or again, it is said to be one whose presentation is ineptly executed. A static character is said to be one which changes little in the progress of the narrative, one which, though revealed by action, does not show changes in response to action; whereas a dynamic character, in contrast, is said to be changed or modified by the action through which it passes. A one-dimensional, two-dimensional, typed, or flat character is said to be one with a single dominant trait, whereas a three-dimensional, individualized or round character is said to be endowed with a convincing congeries of personality traits.

The distinction between flat and round is not very sharp, but rather elastic. For, as E. M. Forster, the English novelist who brought these terms into general usage, states:

> In their purest form [flat characters] are constructed round a single idea or quality: when there is more than one factor in them, we get the beginning of the curve towards the round.
> (Forster 1927: 103–4)

Presumably a miser, if presented with only one dominant trait, is flat; but if the miser also loves his wife, he begins to balloon out into the round.

These metaphors, insofar as they suggest that a character is either "round" or "flat," are misleading, for it is not the character that is "round" or "flat" but rather the author's presentation and our consequent preception of them. For whether a character is presented with one or more dominant traits is less a characteristic immanent in them than a description of how we view them. In other words a "flat" character may possess other dominant traits than that which is shown. Forster himself seems to have realized the elasticity of his distinction, for he says that a character might start out flat and end up round (pp. 113–116). Moreover, here is the test he offers for recognizing a rounded character:

> The test of a round character is whether it is capable of surprising in a convincing way. If it never surprises, it is flat. If it does not convince, it is a flat, pretending to be round. It [the round character] has the incalculability of life about it, life within the pages of a book. (p.118)

This test makes very clear that it is our perception of the character rather than the character itself which determines whether it is to be considered flat or round. For instance, almost any character would be surprising to the naive, but

115

not to the widely experienced observer. Also, what surprises a given observer may not surprise another; and what surprises a given observer on first presentation need not surprise him on a second presentation: the observer now knows what to expect, and his capacity for being surprised has diminished or vanished altogether. In this usage, then, the very same presentation of the same character could be correctly said to be flat or round, depending on the perceivers, or upon how many times a given perceiver has perceived it.

The question of whether a character is perceived as static or dynamic turns on what kind and degree of change it undergoes and with what consequences for itself. Some literary extremists sometimes demand that a character be considered undeveloped unless it starts out one way and ends up the exact opposite; unless, for instance, it starts out a "good man" and ends up a "villain." Such a demand for melodramatic transformation can, of course, be disregarded. In its more realistic version, this view calls for the transmutation of a character, something rather more like a chemical change or a growing up process, where character traits firm up and trace elements become distinct veins; or to use the parlance, the potentialities of the character are realized.

It is interesting to note that the two interpretations of "undeveloped character" so far discussed are not mutually exclusive, for we can have a static, one-dimensional, flat character as well as a static, multi-dimensional, rounded character; and we can have a rounded, dynamic character as well as a flat, dynamic character, i.e., a dynamic, one-dimensional, flat character as well as a dynamic, multi-dimensional, rounded character. Since these various combinations are possible, it is important for critics to specify exactly what they mean when they say that a character is simple or complex. For instance, a character may be described as complex because it is seen "in the round," with many dominant character traits, and yet be regarded as simple because it is static, where the traits presented do not change during the course of the narrative. For example, a character can be miserly in one situation, loving towards his daughter in another, patriotic in another, and ruthless towards his enemies in another, and could still be considered static, wooden and therefore undeveloped, especially if each given character trait is regularly manifested in similar circumstances. Consequently, agreeing on the details of a case, critics might yet disagree on whether the character is to be judged simple and therefore undeveloped.

A mode of discourse marred by such basic problems should, if not abandoned entirely by critics, be approached and employed with the greatest of judicious care. And insofar as the terms continue to be used it should be borne in mind that neither flat, typed, one-dimensional characters nor round, individualized, multi-dimensional ones are to be generally considered preferable. In some circumstances one kind is preferable to the other. In real life some characters *appear* flat, others rounded, and the universe of a novel, as a simulacrum of reality, should be expected to contain both. The real issue is not which kind should be considered a fault in itself, but rather which kind of presentation, in a given story, is effective in the terms of the story. For example, in a parabolic story, where only one character trait is being explored, to present more than one would be superfluous and sometimes even confusing or distracting. To claim that a character in such a story is undeveloped and hence faultable would be absurd. Critics would do well, therefore, to bear in mind that, before they ascribe fault for any given presentation of a character, they need to demonstrate that a different treatment was called for by the internal exigencies of the story. That a character in a story is a "type" or "undeveloped" is not necessarily a fault. Even Forster himself recognized this when he concluded as follows:

> One great advantage of flat characters is that they are easily recognized whenever they come in. . . . In

> Russian novels, where they so seldom occur, they
> would be a decided help. . . . A second advantage is
> that they are easily remembered afterwards. . . . Part
> of the genius of Dickens is that he does use types
> and caricatures, people whom we recognize the instant
> they re-enter, and yet achieves effects that are not
> mechanical and a vision of humanity that is not
> shallow. . . . His immense success with types suggests
> that there may be more in flatness than the severer
> critics admit. (pp. 105, 109)

Clearly, Forster is speaking as a pragmatic craftsman, and not as a dogmatic critic operating by rote formula.

In discussing those charges of undeveloped characters which are attributable to dissatisfaction with the author's techniques of presentation or description, we would do well to remind ourselves that a cardinal aim of characterization is to so credibly present the imaginary persons of fiction that, within the limits of that fiction, they appear real for the reader. The key term here is the credibility of their presence. This is something that would depend on culturally variable norms, and on culturally variable narrative techniques.

Techniques of characterization in Western narrative include explicit description and direct exposition, whether by means of an initial block of detailed portraiture, or by piecemeal presentation throughout the work; presentation of the character in action, with little explicit commentary by the author; reports of what the character says and does, of what others say of him, and what the author, in his own voice, says of him; and presentation of the character through the workings of his mind, whether directly as in stream of consciousness, or through reports by the author, done without authorial comment. These techniques, as we demonstrated earlier, are also employed in African oral narratives. In addition, the oral narrative tradition favors characterization through allusions with which the audience is familiar; through the character's salient traits as evoked by praise names or by metaphoric identifications of the character with animals or objects known to be associated in the minds of the audience with certain traits or qualities, e.g., the leopard for bravery, the elephant for strength, the gazelle for graceful movement, and the mountain for insurmountable hugeness. Thus, in each tradition, a narrator has a range of techniques available to him, but he need not employ each and every one of them in each and every story.

Therefore, even within a given literary tradition, critics would do well to make sure that when they say that a character is undeveloped, and mean that they consider its presentation technically faulty, they do not really mean that some of their favorite techniques have not been used. They should also bear in mind that standards of adequacy or excellence in the use of any particular technique vary from culture to culture.

We would now like to examine some of the explanations and speculations offered by some who, from the perspective of the "well-made" European novel, assert that characters in African novels are "undeveloped." In his attempt to lay the blame for this alleged fault on influences from African oral narrative, Izevbaye asserts:

> . . . the oral tale made up for its thin narrative texture with a dramatic vitality, and it is now usually accepted that dramatic characters are not as fully "rounded" as fictional ones.
>
> (Izevbaye 1975: 5)

Let us now examine the question we raised in connection with this assertion: is it true that characters in the drama are not as "rounded" as characters in narrative fiction? We do not think that the dramatic genre limits the possibility of character development. In fact, many of Shakespeare's characters are as "rounded" and "fully developed" as any in the European well-made novel. It is therefore invalid to say that the dramatic mode, in and of itself, makes for undeveloped characters. In any case, as is well known, many characters in many novels are flat instead of rounded, and sometimes judiciously so.

We have already discussed some of the problems with the fashionable use of such terms as "flat' and "round," "developed" and "undeveloped," "type" and "individual," "one-dimensional," "two-dimensional" and "three-dimensional," etc.; nevertheless, where it is shown that an African writer has presented a "flat" or "undeveloped" character where a "round" or "developed" one was required by his story, the blame cannot correctly be laid at the doors of African orature by way of its dramatic nature or "dramatic vitality," but must be laid on the particular writer's handling of that particular character.

Abiodun Adetugbo offers another extenuation for this alleged fault in African fiction:

> In general, Nigerian novels are concerned with outer reality: that is, with conflicts that are socially significant. Hence characterization is often of types rather than individuals and the types are meant to have large ranges of public experience summed up in them. Soyinka tries in *The Interpreters* to portray some characters with an inner reality of their own and psychological interest; to do this he uses interior monologues that present the movements of the consciousness of their characters directly through either their feelings or their moods. But there is only a little of this. The style of the Nigerian novels is often studied and artificial. Only occasionally do we have a feeling of spontaneity in the dialogues.
>
> (Adetugbo 1972: 180)

And Bruce King, editor of the book in which Adetugbo's essay appears, reiterates and elaborates upon Adetugbo's points with a few extra speculations of his own:

> Nigerian writers, for example, seem more interested in communal rather than personal problems. Conse-

quently, characterization in their novels and plays is often lacking in depth. Does this result from a new approach towards literature in which individual psychology is less important than public themes? Or is it simply the result of being unable to imagine characters with any fullness? Do the unwieldy plots of Tutuola, Soyinka and Ekwensi show an inability to handle form or are they closer to some as yet ununderstood Nigerian aesthetic norm?

(King 1972: 8)

There are serious errors of logic and locution in these proffered explanations. First, there is no logical connection between interest in "communal rather than personal problems" and lack of depth in characterization, nor between "conflicts that are socially significant" and protrayal of characters as "types rather than individuals." This way of thinking bristles with false dichotomies. An interest in communal problems need not exclude interest in personal problems, nor does the presentation of some characters as types or with lack of depth preclude the treatment of others as "individuals." Most novels deal with both kinds of problems and contain both kinds of character treatment. When the balance of concern lies with communal problems rather than with personal ones, there still can be depth of characterization. For example, in Malraux's *Man's Fate,* whose central theme is revolutionary insurrection, Kyo, May and Ch'en and other leading characters are probed in depth; even the sexual needs and hang-ups of Kyo and May are explored in detail. In Ousmane Sembene's *God's Bits of Wood,* where the central issue is a general strike, such characters as Maimouna the blind woman, Sounkare the watchman, Penda the leader of the women, and Bakayoko the leader of the men, do have their personal problems and characters explored.

Similarly, where the balance of concern lies with personal problems, some important characters are presented as "types" or with relative lack of "depth." For instance, in Dickens'

121

Great Expectations, a *bildungsroman* where, naturally, the focus is on the growing up of a young man who is presented in depth, such important characters as Miss Havisham, Joe Gargery, Mrs. Gargery, and Mr. Jaggers are presented as stock types with relative dearth of depth. And in Cheikh Hamidou Kane's *Ambiguous Adventure,* another *bildungsroman,* whereas Samba Diallo is characterized in depth, such other important characters as the Fool, the Knight, the Chief, and the Most Royal Lady are not. Clearly, the insinuation of a logical connection between the nature of the problems discussed and the degree of characterization employed is erroneous.

Moreover, a further confusion underlies the notion that a "type" character cannot be probed in depth. They often are. For instance, Balzac's Père Goriot and Dickens' Scrooge are stock characters, misers in this case, but each is explored in great depth. And it is, in fact, this depth of psychological exploration that makes them effective and memorable representatives of the type. This is nothing unusual; rather, it is in the nature of such things, for as F. Scott Fitzgerald aptly observed in "The Rich Boy": "Begin with an individual, and before you know it you find that you have created a type."

Critics caught in this mess of invalid dichotomies ought perhaps to note that whether a character should be probed "in depth" or not, and to what degree or in what direction, depends far more on other sorts of detailed considerations than on whether the work is primarily about "outer reality," "inner reality," "communal problems," or "personal problems." Idolators of the European bourgeois psychological novel who try to legislate its characteristics into a norm for *all novels* have a few questions to answer: who says that the proper concern of the novelist is the probing of "inner reality," and on what grounds is this said? Who says that the probing of "outer reality" is not as much a province of the novelist as any other reality? Or that the probing of one reality automatically precludes or subordinates the probing of any other? Besides, why is it sometimes implied that a discussion or presentation of "inner reality" may not be "socially significant"?

And what exactly is meant by the fashionable demand for "full" or "complete characterization"? There is an important error of locution here. It is in the nature of a characterization, description or word portrait that it can never be full or complete. All that might properly be said is that one description is sketchier than another, since they are by their nature language approximations of whatever is being described. Therefore any demand for "full" or "complete" characterization, description or portrait is inherently misguided. Perhaps what these charges mean is that descriptions, characterizations and portraits are sketchier or less detailed than those in standard European novels—whatever these might be. In that case these charges are no more than an underhanded way of imposing eurocentric norms on African sensibilities. We would like to state categorically that African novels need not meet eurocentric standards of any sort, for standards are culture-bound, and the imposition of eurocentric standards on Africa is nothing but cultural imperialism.

In particular, African novels do not need to meet standards based on the European "well-made" or "pure" novel. It perhaps needs to be stressed that the adequacy of a sketch depends upon its purpose, its context, and also upon what its beholders accept as normal or proper. If a certain amount or level of detail in a sketch is found by the writer's primary audience to be adequate for the purposes of the story, and suitable for its context, then the writer has succeeded. Therefore, if African readers don't feel that the descriptions, portraits and characterizations supplied by their writers are sketchier than they would like, the objections of Westerners, with their alien sensibilities, won't matter. Westerners, being at best a secondary audience for African literature, will have to learn to overcome their distaste. With time and effort and a sloughing off of their racist superiority complexes and imperialist arrogance, they might acquire a taste for whatever degree of detailed sketching African writers and their African audiences establish as the African norm. But if they never do, that too will not matter.

These same positions hold for the probing of motivation; for the amount of dialogue used to develop characters; and for the intricacy of plots. In these matters, too, the norms that apply are culture-bound. Differences between European and African norms should neither cause surprise, nor bring admonitions from cultural agents of Western imperialism. Those African critics who parrot eurocentric demands should stop doing so, unless they can produce non-eurocentric grounds for demanding the same norms. We should always insist that the West is not our standard. If our autonomous standards are equivalent to theirs, well and good; if they are different that is not a fault. "Different cultures, different norms" should be the reasonable expectation, if we believe in cultural freedom.

It might be instructive to consider a few examples of where our sense of adequacy differs radically from that of eurocentric critics. First, the matter of the treatment of white characters in African novels. In his evalutaion of Ngugi's novels, W. J. Howard complains about Ngugi's treatment of Howlands in *Weep Not Child* and of the colonials, especially Margery, in *A Grain of Wheat*. About Howlands, he seems disturbed at finding the deterioration of a white man presented in an African novel:

> The character who had formerly been presented quite simply as loving the land and worried about the strike has become a child-beater and castrator, haunted by Njoroge's eyes, a drunk, consumed with hatred for Ngotho because Ngotho loves and protects his sons, dim-witted (only slowly does he realize Boro's involvement), a satyr with black women (although he doesn't know why he misses his wife), cringingly clinging to

life. Ngugi should have employed the art of understatement here instead of over-writing.

(Howard 1973: 111)

Notice how Howard, by claiming that the characterization
is overwritten, and by recommending understatement, wants
to transfer his own moral and psychological problems with
the contents of the passage to Ngugi, and to Ngugi's alleged
use of "inappropriate technique." But inappropriate for what?
Certainly, not for exposing the moral degeneracy of white
colonialists! Howard's discomfort with the passage is indeed
an indicator of how very well Ngugi's chosen technique
succeeded.

Furthermore, Howard maintains:

> Even if certain men are capable of the cruelty described,
> pincers and all, that "the red beard and grey eyes
> laughed derisively" (p. 128) when Howlands walked
> out after torturing Njoroge seems bordering on grade
> B Hollywood theatrics, and is unworthy of Ngugi. It
> is the gesture of a villain of melodrama and should
> have been edited.

(Howard 1973: 111)

In the matter of Margery, he appears to think that the
sexual escapades of white women should not be explored in an
African novel.

> The two episodes that have no function in the novel
> are precisely the two that include Margery, Thompson's
> wife, and Dr. Lynd; both deal with the sexual adven-
> tures of the two women. Neither has an aesthetic
> purpose in the novel, and neither is necessary for the
> developmment of the central theme, or of any particular
> episode in the book for that matter. One is then
> prompted to ask why they are included.

(Howard 1973: 118)

We would instead like to ask: why should these passages
about Howlands and Margery be edited out or excluded?

Could it be because they bring the white man and woman off their imperialist pedestals, strip them of their airs of virtuous superiority, and expose their human frailty? Does Howard want to continue to perpetuate the colonial myth that whites are gods or godlike, incapable of cruelty, sadism, sexual incontinence, infidelity or moral degeneration? If anything, the whole history of imperialism proves just the opposite. When he claims that such protrayal "is unworthy of Ngugi" we ask: why? Is it, perhaps, because, according to one strand of imperialist mythology, Africans are expected to be "noble savages"—all-forgiving, patient, all-enduring, and loving of our enemies? The insolence of these Europeans seems to know no limit! They not only steal our Land and Liberty, but they also expect us to love them!

Writing about Achebe's *Arrow of God,* K. W. J. Post also complains:

> In his treatment of the white characters in this book the author is perhaps a little unfair. They are not a very attractive group. The senior administrator, Winterbottom, is concerned with his duty; Africa, as he believes, "never spared those who did what they liked instead of what they had to do." His main function in the novel is to establish in our minds the attitudes of the British toward those they sought to rule, the "natives," who "like children . . . are great liars," who have "elemental cruelty" in their "psychological makeup." Clarke, Winterbottom's deputy, is concerned with his career, afraid to speak out lest he offend his seniors, even by refusing to drink more than he wishes. There are no humane personal relations between white people in this book; Winterbottom's relationship with the lady doctor he eventually marries is scantily mentioned, and then as a sort of joke. Throughout, the white characters are vehicles for the ideas and attitudes of the colonial system. They are caricatures rather than real human beings, and it is in this that the possible unfairness of treatment lies, for

it contrasts markedly with the rich and complex delin-
eation of the Africans in the book.

(Post 1969: x)

And writing about Ousmane Sembene's *God's Bits of
Wood,* Eustace Palmer observes:

> The weakest point of Ousmane's art in this novel is
> probably his protrayal of the white characters. One
> has the feeling that they lack the depth of the blacks.
> Nevertheless, Ousmane still achieves variety in their
> protrayal. . . . The uncomfortable feeling persists, how-
> ever, that Ousmane makes his white characters just a
> bit too stupid and beastly; they are, in fact, rather
> one-dimensional.

(Palmer 1973: 11)

Do Palmer and Post mean to suggest that whites should
never be caricatured in African novels? Are Africans not
routinely caricatured in novels by European writers? Have
the Europeans been faulted for doing so? Have they stopped
doing so? Or is it perfectly alright to satirize or present
Africans unsympathetically or maliciously but wrong to do
so to Europeans? Certainly, whites in colonial settings are
not a very attractive lot—certainly not to those whose land
and liberty they have stolen. Moreover, white colonial offi-
cials were interchangeable cogs or functionaries in the service
of the empire. They were not allowed to intrude their
personal values into their relationships with Africans—if these
values differed from or would interfere with official ideology.
Upon arrival in the colonies, they were instructed and
repeatedly reminded not to let down the white race by
treating Africans on terms of human equality. And, in fact,
any who deviated from required behavior were treated as
mavericks and pariahs. If they persisted in fraternizing with
Africans they were recalled to Europe.

Given this nature of their relationship to Africans, it
would be surprising if they did not appear to Africans as
wooden, distant and hostile figures without warmth or psy-

chological depth. Why then should they be entitled to be portrayed differently in stories written from the African perspective? To those Europeans who complain about the treatment of white characters in African novels, we can only say: don't blame the mirror for what you see in it. In particular, to those Europeans who object to being satirized or caricatured in African novels, we say: what can one do with gods, invented or self-appointed, except worship or satirize them? One can't treat them on terms of human familiarity, for that is precluded by their own claims.

In the matter of characterization by physical description, our sense of adequacy differs radically from that of euro-centric criticism as represented by Larson. Larson says:

> Interestingly enough, initially we do not have the kind of description of Okonkwo that we might expect, that is, a description of his physical stature, which is so fitted, we may assume, for wrestling. Achebe has found other ways of coveying this, however. In the second paragraph he states, "Amalinze was a wily craftsman but Okonkwo was as slippery as a fish in water. . . ." And in the third paragraph: "He [Okonkwo] was tall and huge, and his bushy eyebrows and wide nose gave him a very severe look."
>
> These few sentences of pictorial description are about as much as Achebe ever uses to describe Okonkwo, at least physically. . . . There is not one place in the novel where authorial commentary extends beyond a few descriptive facts—nothing comparable, for example, to Joyce Cary's initial description (on the first page) of Mr. Johnson in his novel of that title.
>
> (Larson 1972: 32)

Let us compare the passages Larson is talking about, first, the Joyce Cary:

> Johnson is not only a stranger by accent, but by color. He is as black as a stove, almost a pure Negro, with

short nose and full, soft lips. He is young, perhaps seventeen, and seems half-grown. His neck, legs and arms are much too long and thin for his small body, as narrow as a skinned rabbit's. He is loose-jointed like a boy, and sits with his knees up to his nose, grinning at Bamu over the stretched white cotton of his trousers. He smiles with the delighted expression of a child looking at a birthday table and says, "Oh, you are too pretty—a beautiful girl."

(Quoted in Larson 1972: 32)

Then, the Achebe:

Okonkwo was well known throughout the nine villages and even beyond. His fame rested on solid personal achievements. As a young man of eighteen he had brought honor to his village by throwing Amalinze the Cat. Amalinze was the great wrestler who for seven years was unbeaten, from Umuofia to Mbaino. He was called the Cat because his back would never touch the earth. It was this man that Okonkwo threw in a fight which the old men agreed was one of the fiercest since the founder of their town engaged a spirit of the wild for seven days and seven nights.

The drums beat and the flutes sang and the spectators held their breath. Amalinze was a wily craftsman, but Okonkwo was as slippery as a fish in water. Every nerve and every muscle stood out on their arms, on their backs and their thighs, and one almost heard them stretching to breaking point. In the end Okonkwo threw the Cat.

That was many years ago, twenty years or more, and during this time Okonkwo's fame had grown like a bush-fire in the harmattan. He was tall and huge, and his bushy eyebrows and wide nose gave him a very severe look. He breathed heavily, and it was said that when he slept, his wives and children in their houses could hear him breathe. When he walked, his heels hardly touched the ground and he seemed to

walk on springs, as if he was going to pounce on
somebody. And he did pounce on people quite often.
He had a slight stammer and whenever he was angry
and could not get his words out quickly enough, he
would use his fists. He had no patience with unsuccessful men. He had had no patience with his father.

(Achebe 1969: 7–8)

Larson considers Achebe's description of Okonkwo inadequate in comparison with Joyce Cary's opening description
of Mister Johnson. We do not find it at all inadequate for
either Achebe's purpose or for our taste. We dislike the
baroque excess of Cary's portrait. Such pointillism does not
conform with our sense of propriety. We do not find it
edifying, for instance, to be shown every pore of a Brobdingnag
giant where a mere glance from afar would do. Where is
Larson coming from? After he has been given a brief and
succinct sketch of Okonkwo, does his dissatisfaction stem
from a fear that he might not recognize him on a street or
village path from fifty feet away?

Now, Cary, with an imperialist's jaundiced eye, wants to
give us an initial mugshot whereby any colonial policeman
might recognize Johnson. So he uses his method to paint a
still-life portrait of Johnson. But Achebe's purposes are
different: he offers us a historical description of a man of
action through a physical description of some of his more
spectacular deeds, his skills, his reputation, his attitudes, as
well as those characteristic aspects of his physical presence
which stamp him who he is. Achebe's technique serves his
purpose so well and so economically; how a still-life portrait
of the man would have conveyed him better is not easy to
see. Larson is asking for a snapshot when a movie sequence
with flashbacks is what is required, and he is fatuous enough
to fault the artist for not satisfying his own misguided
expectations.

On the question of characterization through dialogue,
Larson tells us:

Indeed, in many African novels, dialogue is quite sparse, and in others it appears to have nothing beyond a fuctional purpose. . . . In Achebe's novel . . . there is no characterization of Okonkwo established by dialogue in the first chapter—Okonkwo says nothing until the last page of Chapter Two. Throughout the novel, it will also be seen that Achebe rarely uses dialogue to develop any of his characters.

(Larson 1972: 18, 33)

These remarks prompt a few retorts. First, would Larson have us believe that in Western fiction dialogue serves as mere padding or baroque decoration? Otherwise, what would be wrong with dialogue having nothing beyond a functional purpose? Secondly, since when did it become a requirement to establish characterization by dialogue in the first chapter of a novel? And if it is, on what grounds? In the matter of Okonkwo's charaterization in particular, Achebe tells us in the novel that Okonkwo was "not a man of many words" (Achebe 1969: 103). Why then should one expect more dialogue from Okonkwo than is given? If Achebe was writing about a chatterbox, this charge might conceivably make sense.

Consider all the gaffes, mispresentations, false accusations, wielding of double standards, phony universalisms, etc., which have characterized all of Charles Larson's pronouncements which we have examined. If by this time the reader feels thoroughly fed up and exasperated with Larson's criticism let him know that he is not alone. Similar exasperation with Larson's brand of criticism has driven Ayi Kwei Armah to make a modest proposal which we hereby wholeheartedly second. Armah says:

Larson, the critic of African literature, is a Westerner. From the evidence of his work, he is plainly committed to the values and prejudices of his own society, just as much as any other Western expert hustling Africa, be he a businessman, an economic advisor or a mercenary wardog.

Personally, I do not feel like appealing to him or protesting against him and his work. I have taken his measure from his work, and seen his qualities: his integrity is low; his intelligence is average; what he has in high degree is ambition. I suspect, in fact, that Larson would like to rise high above the generality of Western critics of African Literature, to become not just one Western critic among many, but *the* Western critic of African Literature, his name a household word, at least in academic households.

Animated by a desire to do something to help Larson achieve this noble ambition, I hereby make a modest suggestion in the hope that scholars, critics, experts and even mere creative writers in the field of African Literature might some day adopt it and thus quicken their ongoing intellectual discourse. It would only be a fitting tribute to this bold, resourceful and enterprising Western critic of African Literature if his name became synonymous with the style of scholarly criticism of which he is such an inimitably brilliant exponent, that style which consists of the judicious distortion of African truths to fit Western prejudices, the art of using fiction as criticism of fiction. I suggest we call it "larsony."

(Armah 1977: 55)

The examples we have considered so far should make it quite clear that Larson is far from alone. Many Western critics are guilty of *larsony*. Some, like Adrian Roscoe, are guilty of *larsony* in the first degree.

The accusations of minimal description, thin plots and inadequate characterization made against the African novel, appear in part to be outcries from these eurocentric critics' frustrated demand for bulk. An addiction to the "well-made" novel might be responsible for their addiction to bulk. Given the same story, a non-"well-made" treatment is liable to be shorter than a "well-made" treatment. For instance, if Balzac threw out his initial descriptive segments—place setting,

introductory character portraiture, lengthy exposition, etc.—
some of his novels would be shorter by more than a third.
Besides, who has time or incentive to read or write bulky
novels today? Bulk might have made sense for the bored,
unimaginative genteel aristocrat in 18th or 19th century
Europe, who had servants to do everything for him, and
solid stretches of lazy afternoons to fill up, and who could
not imagine a character or setting unless a detailed baroque
portrait was first provided. Today, even for those of the
same leisured class, the novel has to compete with radio,
TV, cinema and investigatory journalism for their attention.
How much more for the rest of us who, in addition, have
to work all day, and often far into the night. More important,
if a given story can be well told in 100 pages, why drag it
out to 500 for fear of being called a short-distance performer
by some British savage?

On these matters, it should be noted once again that
since the era of Joyce, Proust, Kafka, Faulkner and Dos
Passos, standards of the "well-made" novel have been largely
abandoned in the West. When judged against those standards,
many contemporary novels in the West are short, their plots
are thin, their descriptions rather undetailed and sketchy. If
they felt so strongly in favor of "well-made" novels, it
would make far more sense for these Western critics to
apply their energies to curbing or reversing these trends
away from the "well-made" novel within their own culture.
In dissociating ourselves from eurocentric norms and in trying
to establish our own, one place to begin would be to find
out what levels to detail in characterization, description or
portraiture were or are considered adequate in African orature
and why. And we ought to show good cause before we
abandon such norms.

Whereas these European critics, who clutch at anything
to support their prejudices and indulge their racist and anti-
Africa malice, should be dismissed entirely and out of hand,
it is necessary to say a word to those Africans whose sloppy

scholarship and careless speculations give aid and comfort to imperialist criticism. They should stop doing sloppy work. In particular, we find unacceptable the disparaging cliches being regularly bandied about in the wake of Willie Abraham's pronouncements on charaterization in African oral tradition and in African novels (Abraham 1962: 92, 96-97). The matter, in our opinion, should be re-examined and Abraham's errors should be retired, not shovelled from mind to mind.

Didacticism and Moral Attitude

Some critics charge African novels with being didactic. This charge usually amounts to a claim that the moral or social purposes of the novelist are overtly rather than intrinsically expressed. Critics of this sort see themselves as part of a European tradition which has outgrown its "primitive" taste for moral tales, especially those of the sort that carry an adage or moral tag at the end. They therefore view such African novels and stories with distaste or embarrassment. Charles Larson, still bent on larsony, states:

> Another major difference commonly noted in the fiction of African writers is the frequent occurrence of the didactic ending. The following novelists especially belong in this category, though in a certain sense, there are few African novelists among the first generation whose works are not somehow related to this moral overtone: Cyprian Ekwensi, Chinua Achebe, William Conton, Ferdinand Oyono, Camara Laye, Amos Tutuola, and James Ngugi. The Western reader is especially conscious of the high frequency of didactic endings because our own literary tastes have changed so considerably since the nineteenth century.
>
> (Larson 1972: 19)

If by these statements Larson is expressing a distaste for overt didacticism and explicit moral tags of that sort commonly found at the end of fables, we do not find them in the works of most African novelists. If Larson considers the above authors didactic, perhaps he means that he disagrees with the moral attitudes intrinsic in their stories; and that, insofar as he thinks these attitudes are implicitly being urged, he considers the works didactic. In that case, let us point out that these African novelists are no more explicitly or intrinsically didactic than Jane Austen, George Eliot, Dickens, Hardy, Henry James, Conrad, D. H. Lawrence, Flaubert, Stendhal, Balzac, Cervantes, Thomas Mann, Tolstoy, or Dostoevsky. Those who think they have outgrown the taste for didacticism would have to view the works of these Western writers with the same distaste or embarrassment as they claim they feel for African novels.

But really, has the European tradition (writers and readers alike) lost its taste for didacticism, especially of the intrinsic sort? That the didactic intent of an author is subtly communicated through the structure and organization of the novel and the treatment of characters and situations in it, does not mean that didacticism has been abandoned. The most that perhaps could be granted is that the current tastes of European literature require that direct authorial announcement of the moral point of a story or tale be suppressed.

But even if the European tradition has lost its taste for didacticism of any sort, does that mean that the African tradition must do the same? What is perhaps behind this alleged distaste for didacticism is that these critics perceive such didacticism as coming from traditional African values whose communalist ethos they find antithetical to a bourgeois ethos which cultivates possessive individualism. One wonders if they would take exception to didacticism in African novels were such didacticism not of the sort that would militate against their imperialist interests. Of course, as Borges has pointed out, "Those who say that art should not propagate doctrines usually refer to doctrines that are opposed to their own" (Borges 1968: 87).

135

Other critics blame some African novelists for not taking a moral stand on their characters, and argue as if failure by an author to do so is cause for judging a work a failure. What this usually means is that the authors do not take the particular moral stand which the critics would prefer.

Eustace Palmer in his *An Introduction to the African Novel* attempts to evaluate Ekwensi's *Jagua Nana* in order to explain why Ekwensi is not one of the authors he presents. His procedure merits examination. But before we go on we wish to make it clear that we are not evaluating *Jagua Nana,* but instead are analysing and evaluating Palmer's criticism of it. Palmer says:

> And although his characters usually end badly, it is doubtful whether this is due to any conscious moral concern. Ekwensi hardly ever manifests a consistent moral attitude, his main preoccupation being the sensationalism created by vice. All these weaknessess are clearly present in his most successfull novel *Jagua Nana.* Like Defoe's *Moll Flanders,* which it resembles in several respects, *Jagua Nana* gives a very realistic picture of the seamy side of Lagos life. . . . One would not indict Ekwensi for taking us into the world of prostitutes, pimps, dishonest politicians, organized crime and thuggery, but one can indict him if he fails to take some moral standpoint. In *Jagua Nana* Ekwensi could either have tried to make excuses for his characters and show plausibly that they are victims of their society, or he could have used various techniques, such as irony, to indicate that he disapproves of them. But like Defoe, Ekwensi fails to do either. . . .
>
> Whatever internal unity the book possesses is imparted by the figure of Jagua herself. *What is Ekwensi's attitude towards Jagua? This is central to one's evaluation.* There is no doubt that Jagua is an immoral woman. Unlike Moll Flanders, she does not turn to prostitution because there is no other means of survival in a money-conscious man's world. She

refuses several offers of marriage from the local boys with whom she has had sexual experience, on the grounds that they are not sufficiently expert. Jagua is a nymphomaniac with a crazy passion for sex and the bright lights of Lagos. Moll Flanders at least was only kept by one man at a time; Jagua on the other hand is not content with one man. It is doubtful whether she is capable of being in love with anyone. Her "affection" for Freddie, the only man she seems to have been really fond of, is most probably motivated by a need for future security, and at the end she joins forces with Uncle Taiwo to destroy him. Jagua can also be ill-tempered, vengeful, and unscrupulous. All these faults might have been pardoned if she ever showed signs of remorse. But Jagua only repents when she realizes she is finished in Lagos. One would expect a serious novelist to show some signs of disapproval of Jagua's conduct, but instead Ekwensi seems to try to persuade the reader to share his captivation with her: there is very little criticism, either of her or of the threat which the dangerous Lagos underworld presents to civilized standards. The quality of Ekwensi's moral vision is weak. The characterization is just as weak. The only fully realized character is Jagua herself, the others being hazy figures whom the reader soon forgets. The style is obviously that of the sex-and-crime school.

Jagua Nana represents Ekwensi at his best, and yet by any standards it is a failure.

(Palmer 1972: xii-xiii. Italics added)

In Palmer-type criticism, as exemplified by the above, it appears that an author's attitude towards his characters is of utmost importance in evaluating a work; for he asks: "What is Ekwensi's attitude towards Jagua?" And asserts: "This is central to one's evaluation." For Palmer, Jagua is an immoral woman; she especially irks him by showing no remorse for her ways. Ekwensi doesn't criticise, ridicule or make excuses for her, but instead appears quite captivated with her. From Palmer's standpoint, a book in which an author appears to be captivated with an immoral character cannot be a good book. That is to say, if an author has failed a critic's morality test, his book cannot be judged successful. This is a rather odd critical procedure, as we shall soon demonstrate.

But first, if an author's moral attitude is indeed central for the critic, what is Shakespeare's attitude towards Cleopatra, or Richard III, or Iago, or Macbeth? What is Achebe's attitude towards Okonkwo, Ezeulu, or Chief Nanga? How does one know? Would Palmer claim to know? In particular, how does Palmer determine Ekwensi's attitude towards Jagua? Palmer's logic seems to be that if an author does not clearly express or indicate disapproval of a character, he must be presumed to approve; for since Ekwensi expresses or indicates no disapproval of Jagua's conduct, Palmer concludes that Ekwensi must necessarily approve of her. In other words, his logic does not allow for authorial neutrality.

In this matter of guessing an author's attitude towards a character, it is useful to remember that in four centuries of Shakepearean scholarship no one has yet succeeded in pinning down Shakespeare's attitude towards the characters named above. Those who thought they had succeeded merely advertised their foolishness. In fact, no critic worth his salt has considered the effort worth his while.

What would Palmer's attitude be towards Cleopatra who, though a queen, might accurately be described, like Jagua, as a whore and "a nymphomaniac with a crazy passion for sex"? Or towards Richard III, that ugly hunchback and sweet-tongued murderer whose person was an esthetic offence to regal splendour, and whose villainous deeds were a moral danger to "civilized standards"? Or to Iago, that infamous troublemaker and bearer of false witness whose calculated villainy led to the slaughter of innocents? Or to Macbeth, that ambitious regicide, usurper and provoker of civil strife? What would be Palmer's attitude towards this parade of villains, whores, murderers—clear dangers, one and all, one would think, to "civilized standards"? What moral values would Palmer impute to Shakespeare for presenting them as he did—that is, without making excuses for them, without showing them as victims of their societies, and without indicating that he disapproved of them? If Palmer disapproved of these characters, and thought that Shakespeare does not criticize them and is captivated with them, would he therefore declare Shakespeare's moral vision weak? And would that be grounds for downgrading these works and excluding them from attention? If one knew an author's view of his characters, would it change one's view of the work? We think not; but it might change one's view of the author as a human being. To take an example from outside of fictional literature, Jean-Jacques Rousseau wrote *Emile,* a treatise on how to educate children, but had his own children farmed out to orphanages. Over the centuries, his behavior has been denounced while his book has continued to be important in that field.

Were Palmer's procedure followed, it would lead to misplaced censorship; for a book would then be censored not because of what was in it but because the critic did not like what he thought it told him about its author's morality. A very different matter indeed, and a rather amazing sort of ideological criticism. Coming from Palmer, it is all the more remarkable, because Palmer is loud among those who condemn what they consider intrusions of ideological considerations into literary criticism. In the controversies surrounding his *Introduction to the African Novel,* the very book in which he performs this exercise on Ekwensi, Palmer says:

> I will never accept that the critic should allow his commitment to influence his criticism. . . . He must approach the work in question with an open mind, honestly prepared to evaluate and illuminate what he finds there. It is dangerous for any critic to try to

> read his ideological prejudices and preoccupations into
> a work.
>
> (Palmer 1975: 126)

Perhaps Palmer really meant that he would never accept that any other critic should do the things he here objects to.

In our view, ideological considerations always do enter into literary criticism, and this is as it should be. For a work has to be evaluated not on issues of "pure craft" alone, but also on the values it urges upon its readers, implicitly as well as explicitly. Moreover, even issues of "pure craft" embody social values. The proper and inevitable question therefore ought to be, not whether there is ideology or not, but rather which ideology—European, African, Christian, Islamic, Buddhist, capitalist, socialist, communist, communalist, individualist, or what have you. We should therefore at all times be suspicious of claims of ideological virginity. We should indeed probe all the harder for hidden ideological agendas whenever a critic makes a pretense at offering "objective," "value-free" criticism.

But even though ideological considerations do always enter into literary judgments, there are inappropriate as well as appropriate ways in which they can enter. It seems cockeyed that they should be brought in in the Palmer fashion, not through an assessment of the values expressed in the work, but through attitudes attributed to an author towards his characters.

In criticizing a book, what values should an African critic have? Certainly not imperialist, eurocentric ones, for they are incorrigibly anti-African. Also it will not do to judge a work by the quality of its craftsmanship alone, nor by its moral and ideological commitments alone. Both are needed. Nor will it do to allow moral judgments to masquerade as artistic ones. A book which slanders Africa and Africans, however exquisitely crafted, should not expect to be judged good by any self-respecting African. In like manner, a book that flatters Africans, if badly crafted, should not expect to be considered of literary merit. We should bear in mind that, given the fundamental antagonism between Europe and Africa, an antagonism rooted in racist and imperialist relations of some five hundred years duration, Europeans are quite likely to consider good those works which successfully slander Africans. The better executed they are, especially if they conceal their slanderous nature, the better they are likely to be judged by Europeans. Clearly, a book judged good by Europeans need not be a good book from the African point of view. And we, as Africans, should be preeminently concerned with the African point of view.

According to Palmer, a vision which does not defend "civilized standards" is morally weak—which is to say that a vision which does not defend Western bourgeois culture and its values is morally weak. Which again is to say that a vision which does not defend the culture which brought us Africans the pains and indignities of colonialism and imperialism is morally weak. For it is quite clear from Palmer's pronouncements that for him "morality" means conventional bourgeois Christian morality, and "civilization" the culture of Europe.

Given that Palmer is committed to defending these "civilized standards," we who are judging from an African point of view would not be surprised at what books he chooses to exclude from his *Introduction to the African Novel*. A minor controversy has arisen around his exclusion of certain books which many other African critics consider among the very best so far produced. These include Ousmane Sembene's *God's Bits of Wood*, Mongo Beti's *King Lazarus* and *The Poor Christ of Bomba*, Ferdinand Oyono's *Boy* and *The Old Man and the Medal*. These happen to be books in which European colonialists and their African collaborators are uncompromisingly criticized or satirized, and in which, as in the case of *God's Bits of Wood*, Africans seize and exercise initiative, strike against their colonial masters, and *win*. It would appear that, insofar as the Euro-African confrontation is concerned, Palmer rigorously and vociferously excludes works dealing with those areas of African experience in which European power is successfully challenged or in which European pretensions are stripped bare. Against this kind of ideologically motivated censorship by Palmer, we must insist that works dealing with any part of our experience should not be excluded by hidden ideological decrees from any recommended canons of good works.

Palmer's exclusion of Tutuola, especially without explanation, also raises some important questions. Might it be because Tutuola writes about ghosts and transformations of humans into animals—things that have been viewed by some as manifestations of "primitive" mentality, and therefore as dangers to "rational," scientific bourgeois, "civilized standards"? One wonders what Palmer would make of European gothic novels. Would he welcome them in spite of the fact that they have ghosts as characters? If so, might it be because they are white ghosts in English country houses, European chateaux, castles with moonlit turrets, rather than black ghosts in tropical African bushes at "2 a.m. in the midnight"—African ghosts that could bring esthetic terror to the white bourgeois mind?

As for transformations of men into animals, Kafka, whose works Palmer appears to approve of, uses them. In Kafka's *The Metamorphosis* the protagonist turns into a beetle, retains his human consciousness, crawls all over the place, continues to share the dwelling with his family, and, like any good German, remains as preoccupied with anal cleanliness as ever. A mind that is comfortable with Kafka but not with Tutuola needs to reexamine its racist commitments.

Palmer's performance is quite instructive about his biases. Perhaps for him it would be all right for a great writer like Shakespeare not to express disapproval for his immoral or villainous characters but all wrong for lesser writers. Similarly, it would, for him, probably be all right for queens to be whores, kings to be murderers, and high-placed citizens to be villains of all sorts, but not at all right for ordinary folks. Such a bias against the non-privileged, together with his puritan tirade against Jagua's sexuality, raises questions about the kind of moral vision by which Palmer wishes works to be judged.

Let it be noted that Palmer judges the morality of Jagua, *Jagua Nana* and Ekwensi exclusively by sexual conduct. His obsession with a puritan revulsion for sex, his commitment to a defense of Western bourgeois culture, and his internalization of white esthetic terrors expose his advocacy for moral vision and his insistence on a "consistent moral attitude" for what they are. Does Palmer's morality and ideology amount to more than the following creed?

> Thou shalt not mock the white man.
> Thou shalt not frighten the imperialist.
> Thou shalt despise the poor.
> Thou shalt not criticise the rich.
> Thou shalt not rob a bank.
> Thou shalt not make fun of anybody in tails or top hat.
> Thou shalt not bestow thine sexual favors on more than one if thou art female.
> And on pain of hell and damnation,
> Thou shalt not bring "civilized standards" into disrepute.

A catalogue of such commandments is probably the sum total of Eustace Palmer's "morality." Any deviation from this would probably be denounced by him as a lack of "consistent moral attitude." And by the way, Palmer should object to this procedure of speculating on his values from evidence so fragmentary; or should object to a judging of him by the result of such speculation—results which he might want to claim as not representing his actual values— we would like to point out that what we have attempted is merely a close parody of his procedure of Ekwensi. But let us return to more substantial matters.

Now, seriously, if one maintains a "consistent moral attitude," then of what kind should it be? Palmer appears to forget two things: first, that there is more to morality than sexual conduct; secondly, that there is not one "morality" but many—the morality of the rich, the morality of the poor, the morality of the Christian, the morality of the Moslem, the morality of one village, and the morality of the next village, homegrown African moralities, and the moralities brought in and imposed by European and Arab invaders, and so on and so forth. If the items in our parody happen to be correct, Palmer's requirement that an author display a "consistent moral attitude" would therefore mean no more than that he should consistently defend privilege, no matter the cost in misery to the many. Such an ideological bias, when smuggled into literary criticism, would lead an African critic to consistently exclude from his canon of important African novels those works which, with exquisite craft, mock the imperial masters or show them defeated in struggle.

Palmer's whole performance is in keeping with his view of decolonization which, as Adeola James has pointed out, is utterly ridiculous (James 1975: 149). Palmer writes:

> The decolonization of African literature is already in progress. Novelists are becoming less preoccupied with cultural and sociological matters, and more concerned about exposing the corruption and incompetence which are so widespread in African political and governmental circles. Ayi Kwei Armah's first novel—*The Beautiful Ones Are Not Yet Born*—is one of the most successful results of this exercise.
>
> (Palmer 1972: 129)

By what strange definition of "cultural and sociological matters" does Palmer exclude them from, and contrast them with, "corruption and incompetence . . . in African political and governmental circles"? More importantly, to view the exposure of African corruption as "decolonization" is to miss entirely the meaning of cultural and literary decolonization. If by decolonization of African literature Palmer means that interest is shifting from the Euro-African clash to problems that are intra-African in their manifestation, he ought to be reminded that the decolonization of African literature, as we have painstakingly tried to show in this essay, involves far more than a change in the subjects and themes treated in African literature. It is a matter of rooting out from African literature colonial attitudes, norms, world views, values, and techniques. It is also a matter of replacing them with others that are conducive to African dignity and autonomy in the world.

Summation

In summation, let us point out that we have considered the particulars, circumstances, backgrounds, aims and ambitions of eurocentric criticism of African *literature,* and have shown that eurocentric critics make illegitimate demands and cast disorienting and unwarranted censure upon the African novel. On our way to doing so, we have also considered the particulars, circumstances, backgrounds and ambitions of eurocentric criticism of African *orature,* and have shown that eurocentric critics defame our oral traditions. Our close examination shows every one of their charges to be unfounded. Contrary to their malicious aspersions, our orature is rich in themes, attitudes, and technical devices from which we cannot afford to not profit.

So much for eurocentric criticism of African prose narrative literature and orature.

Now, having chased away the marauding hawks from alien skies, it is time for a family conference with our novelists. Though we have found those eurocentric charges against the African novel to be unwarranted, we nevertheless feel, from an afrocentric liberationist perspective, that our

Transition: An Asymmetry in the Criticism of African Poetry and of the African Novel
▼▼▼▼▼

There is a general tendency among eurocentric critics of giving high praise and encouragement to African poets, while firing shrill-voiced, pompous strictures against the novelists. Once again, Adrian Roscoe is a representative voice in this matter. On the one hand, he contemptuously implies that African novelists should yield to what he considers the pull of their indigenous tradition of "short-distance" performance, give up on the novel, and confine themselves entirely to the short story (Roscoe 1971: 75–79).

On the other hand, in the same book, and in the name of "artistic freedom," he encourages African poets to see themselves as "modern scholar(s) inheriting a world culture," as "inheritors of a universal tradition of art and letters and not just as the recipients of an indigenous legacy." (p. 67) Similarly, in appraising their works, Roscoe applies his standards inconsistently. He describes Soyinka's "Idanre" as a work that satisfies the "lofty requirement" of the epic (p. 70); five pages later in the same book, Roscoe most grudgingly admits *Sundiata* to the rank of epic—grudgingly on account of what he considers its "fairly short length" (p. 75). Presumably, "Idanre," in all its 25 pages of verse and 3 pages of notes, compares favorably with Homer's *Iliad* or *Odyssey,* but *Sundiata,* with its 84 pages of prose text, which if displayed in verse form would easily run to 200 pages, does not. Doesn't this seem a little odd, especially coming from a critic who makes so much of length? Is

Roscoe perhaps using the term "epic" in two different senses? If so, one would at least expect him to say so.

Gerald Moore displays a similar inconsistency of critical attitude toward African novels and African poetry. On the one hand he urges surface clarity in prose, and on the other encourages obscurity in poetry. While commenting on Camara Laye's prose, he says:

> The art of symbolic fiction depends upon the interest and variety maintained on the immediate level of perception. The mind should not be continually aware of "pregnant significances" as it reads, but should be fully entertained and absorbed by the story itself. The search for parallel or inner meanings should come later. This means that the surface narrative and dialogue must be largely naturalistic and even sprightly in tone, though the events and conversations described may be bizarre enough. A heavy portentous style, drugged with its own significance, and continually drawing attention to its own profundity, must be abjured above all.
>
> (Moore 1962: 37–38)

But while defending Christopher Okigbo's poetry, and, like Roscoe, in the name of artistic freedom, Moore declares: "An African poet has got just as much right to be obscure as anybody else" (Moore 1965: 83).

This critical schizophrenia is sufficiently remarkable to merit some probing. Why do these critics dislike what the novelists are doing, but like what they, the poets, are doing? What do they [like] about what the poets are doing? Why? What standards are they holding up to the African writers? What specific poetic or prose traditions are they striving to induct our writers into by way of these standards?

We have already shown that these critics are holding before our novelists the standards of the pre-Joycean Anglo novel, that is, the standards of what F. R. Leavis codified as the so-called Great Tradition. In other words, they are attempting to induct our novelists into the Anglo pre-modernist prose tradition which pointedly excludes Joyce and his experimentalist influences.

In poetry the situation is reversed: these critics, again following Leavis, have abandoned their pre-modernist tradition and embraced the modernist revolution of Eliot and Pound, and we find them enthusiastically rallying African poets to the standard of anglomodernist poetry. We find Gerald Moore, for instance, defending obscurity and upholding privatism in African poets, using T. S. Eliot to sanction the view and the practice of *poetry as puzzle*. Again speaking of Christopher Okigbo, Moore says:

> I would agree that his poetry is extremely private—
> he uses a great deal of private imagery. But at the
> same time so does a poem like *The Waste Land*. It
> is only because we have been reading *The Waste Land*
> for forty years and have since been treated to some
> notes on it by Eliot that we now say *The Waste Land*
> is not obscure. If a poet is good enough, I think he
> can get away with writing rather private poetry, and
> the reader will in time—if he decides that the poetry
> is good, if he wants to study it, likes it and wants to
> read it again—find ways and means of elucidating
> some of the imagery.
>
> (Moore 1965: 102)

Such, of course, are the hallmarks of the recondite kinds of poetry which anglomodernism says it likes.

This preference for pre-modernist prose and for modernist poetry is rather surprising. One would have thought that these critics would recommend either anglomodernism in both prose and poetry, or Anglo pre-modernism in both. Why this schizophrenic asymmetry? Is this indeed a remnant of the influence of F. R. Leavis on English literary taste? Whatever the case, their praise for our poets and dispraise for our novelists show that the poets are doing as they are told from England, and that our novelists are not. Their reasons for hectoring our novelists gives their whole imperialist game away.

As we have demonstrated at length, it is not so much that our novelists are not operating within the pre-modernist "Great Tradition" that is favored in England, but rather that an African nationalist consciousness permeates the materials they treat in that approved mode. From the anglocentric viewpoint, that our novelists are not modernists is quite fine; what isn't fine is that they refuse to play by the rules of an alleged universalism which is merely a cloak for the hegemonic thrust of Anglo-Saxon cultural nationalism. What confirms all of this is the way in which our poets are strenuously praised, not merely for the modernism of their techniques but for the alleged universalism of either their attitudes or the presuppositions which underlie their modernist practice. For instance, Gerald Moore praises Okigbo for supposedly having made the "painful choice, to abandon all the possibilities of his own vernacular when he decides to write in English" (Moore 1965: 103). Adrian Roscoe underlines the matter by his insidious praise of a critical lecture by Michael Echeruo in the following terms:

> [Echeruo] established himself as one of the best literary critics in modern Africa. It was a skilful performance, tackling a difficult topic with incisiveness and tough intellectual independence. An exercise in the kind of scholarship that is kicking away the row of little boxes that have long stood before the house of criticism, it brought to a discussion of African verse insights gained from Eliot and Pound, from Tennyson, Arnold, and Vergil.
>
> (Roscoe 1971: 64)

Is one supposed to believe that an African shows "tough intellectual independence" by being beholden to Eliot, Pound, Tennyson, Arnold, Vergil and other mentors of the European tradition? Our great grandfathers, who had to face the brunt

150

of the European invasion of Africa would have thought otherwise!

The modernist retreat of our poets into privatist universalism makes it quite easy for them to shed whatever African nationalist consciousness they have before they cross the threshold into the sanctum of "poetry in the clouds." And this suits the English literary establishment just fine, since they would much prefer it if an African nationalist consciousness, inevitably anti-British, was not promoted or cultivated, through literature, in the young African elite.

Why have the critics been successful in encouraging our poets to abandon the African poetic tradition and insert themselves into the European modernist tradition of poetry? Clearly there has been pressure from the school milieu; but why has this pressure not been resisted? A case can be made that two of the most powerful inhibitors of such resistance have been: (1) the formal obstacles to the perception of an indigenous and independent African poetic tradition, and (2) the absence in anglophone Africa of a powerful cultural nationalism with its cohesive and comprehensive cultural consciousness.

Within the European culture of African schools, the notion reigned that poetry was something written, which had meter, rhyme and stanzaic form. Such a notion contributes to a disregard and abandonment of the African poetic tradition by promoting the view that Africa had no poetry. Since there were no immediately visible African equivalents of such European poetry as is written in such forms as the sonnet, rhyme royal, sestina, ballade, villanelle or rondeau, Africa had no poetry—so went the illogic.

Now, if one proceeds to look at African orature with such criteria in mind, it would be quite plausible to conclude that there was indeed no poetry in Africa. First of all, most African poetry is not written. Secondly, if transcribed and written down, African poetry would not display the formal features of European poetry (meter, rhyme, stanza, etc.).

151

Given the differences between stressed and tonal languages, there is no intrinsic reason to expect metrical regularity in tonal utterances. There are other devices of rhythmic regularity and repetition available to poetry besides Greek-derived meters, stresses and syllabic quantities. Similarly, regular stanzas are only one way of dividing a poem into segments. There is no intrinsic reason why it should be preferred to divisions dictated by narrative, logical, or musical paragraphing. And end-rhyme, though emphasized in the European tradition, is only one of several available sonal devices that may play a part in poetry. Though African poetry has not emphasized end-rhymes to the eccentric degree which European poetry has, it makes abundant use of internal rhymes, assonance, dissonance, alliteration, homophones and other devices for sonal and word play.

But one trained to see poetry only in meters and end-rhymes is likely to overlook all these riches and feel satisfied in concluding that Africa has no poetry. Indeed, many ethnologists didn't recognize African poetry when they heard it. If they thought it was poetry, they would have transcribed it in versified form in accordance with their notion that versification was a definitive feature of a poem. Since much of their collections of African poetry was not written down in versified form, subsequent readers who share the same assumptions and who identify poetry through versified form, would not easily recognize that such passages were indeed poetry.

Thus, indoctrination into a narrow and parochial European view of poetic form enables one to declare, in the absence of written form, meter, stazaic divisions or end-rhymes, that works employing many other peotic devices not considered definitive in the European tradition are not poetry. The idolatry of such European norms and forms might easily prevent even bright African would-be poets from seeing the abundance of African poetry and learning from its resources. What one sees depends on what one has learned to see.

The European and African traditions differ in how they train us to see works of orature and literature. The notion of oral poetry is, even today, held in question and considered illegitimate or of doubtful validity in eurocentric criticism. Furthermore, in the European tradition, there is a strict segregation of versified literary forms from the non-versified. In particular, in the traditional European view, poetry has been a versified form. In contrast, within the African oral tradition, the distinction between "poetry" and other kinds of utterance has been fluid, and rigid use of versification to segregate a sub-section of utterance as poetry and treat it as intrinsically distinct from the rest has been neither necessary nor fashionable. Thus, passages that could be versified if written down are found interspersed with universifiable passages in stories, drama, epic, oratory, etc. Now, it is easier to go looking for poetry if you've been trained to see it as something special and apart, something cast in distinctive form by versification, than if the distinctions had been kept fluid. In the latter case, felicitous, moving and memorable utterances of all kinds would be considered remarkable, but there would be no compulsion to segregate them together in versified form.

Incidentally, a de-emphasis of versification and an emphasis on memorable felicity of utterance would clean up the European classification schema quite considerably. Treatises have been written trying to separate mere verse from poetry, prose poems from prose, etc. The insuperable difficulty in such efforts lies, in our view, in the attempt to find purely *formal* criteria for a distinction that is more one of *effect*. It is a virtue of the African approach to the classification of orature forms that it avoids a rigid grouping of specific forms into "poetry" and "prose." In other words, though African critical usage recognizes specific forms, along with their various sub-types, such as *izibongo, maboko, ebyevugo, ebirahiro, ijala, oriki, iwi, rara, odu ifa, afa, ofo, heho, hwenoho, aigo, halo, ngoma, tumbuizo,* and *zitengulo,* it wisely avoids the Western compulsion to ask of any literary specimen: Are you poetry or are you prose?—as if that merely formal classification was of earth-shaking importance. Consider the following passage:

> The griots, fine talkers that they were, used to boast of Niani and Mali saying: "If you want salt, go to Niani, for Niani is the camping place of the Sahel caravans. If you want gold, go to Niani, for Bouré, Bambougou and Wagadou work for Niani. If you want fine cloth, go to Niani, for the Mecca road passes by Niani. If you want fish, go to Niani, for it is there that the fishermen of Maouti and Djenné come to sell their catches. If you want meat, go to Niani, the country of the great hunters, and the land of the ox and the sheep. If you want to see an army, go to Niani, for it is there that the united forces of Mali are to be found. If you want to see a great king, go to Niani, for it is there that the son of Sogolon lives, the man with two names."
>
> (Niane 1965: 82)

Can you imagine some dunderhead ethnologist or critic, after hearing this utterance, asking it: "Are you poetry or are you prose? . . . But you are not rhymed verse!"

In brief, literary passages and artifacts are divided up differently by European and African traditions. persons brought up in the one are likely to classify items differently from persons brought up in the other. And even persons brought up in both, unless they learn to accept differences in cultural forms and categories between different traditions, are liable not to see as equivalents things which must, in spite of appearances, be seen as equivalents. To deny legitimacy to oral poetry, is to insist that what is not written cannot be poetry and to forget that a man is still a man whether his skin is white or black. To insist that unless a passage is versified it is not poetry, would be analogous to saying that an umbrella is not an umbrella if it is rolled up, not spread out. And to insist that a literary passage is not poetry unless it is versified by means of meters, stanzas and end-rhymes, is analogous to saying that a man is not dressed unless he wears European clothes.

Even though the European notion of poetry has with, say, free verse, moved away from some of its old-fashioned and straight-laced rigidities, those old notions were still entrenched when many of Africa's anglophone poets were in school and were learning about poetry. Besides, we still have to be on the lookout for new and stranger versions of the same old errors, especially since they have not been entirely eliminated in Africa.

The disorienting authority of this eurocentric view of what constituted poetry might have been challenged had there been an effort to look for African equivalents of European poetry. But given their derogatory attitudes about African capabilities, the imperialists felt no need to do so. Those Africans who had accepted or internalized the malign European view of the African, felt no need to look for such functional equivalents either. Among those Africans who resisted the European view, the absence of a powerful and comprehensive cultural nationalism blocked or discouraged attention to African poetic traditions.

Thus, given the situation of malign neglect, the stylistic features from African poetic traditions could not be brought in as factors in the writings of anglophone euromodernists. In contrast, in francophone Africa where there was the active cultural nationalism of negritude, deliberate and dedicated attention was paid to the resources of traditional African poetry, and these resources were integrated with the prevalent French poetic practice of the time to create the style of negritude poetry.

One result of these two circumstances, namely, the formal obstacles to eurocentric perception of an indigenous African poetic tradition, and the absence of a powerful and comprehensive cultural nationalism which would have helped to overcome those obstacles, is the unmitigated eurocentric reference of modernist poetic craft and criticism in anglophone Africa. Traditional African poetry and its criticism has been little studied; knowledge of it is haphazard, leaving fertile ground for botched mimesis and for the smug attribution of those botches to alleged influences from the African oral tradition. Thus, critics would try to defend the incompetencies which stem directly from the imported European tradition by claiming that they are, instead, manifestations of African oral tradition. Stanley Macebuh, for instance, attributes Soyinka's linguistic obscurity to an alleged fidelity on Soyinka's part to Yoruba "mythopoetics" and "masonic diction" (Macebuh 1975–76: 79–84). Soyinka's obscurantism, however, would seem more readily explainable in terms of his fidelity to the Hopkinsian butchery of English syntax and semantics, and to his deliberate choice of Shakespearean and other archaisms as models for his poetic diction.

Another consequence of these circumstances is the atmosphere of cooperative tutelage which exists between the critics and the poets. Insofar as the poets perceive themselves and are perceived as apprentices working exclusively within the European modernist tradition, the critics' job would be seen as that of encouraging them to perform within the canons of that tradition and that tradition alone, and to abandon the devices and approaches of African poetry for those of European modernism. In addition to the examples of such encouragement which we already cited from Roscoe and Moore, there is Echeruo's notorious encouragement to his fellow African poets to avoid explicitness and cultivate deliberate obscurity (Echeruo 1966: 150). And the poets who are sufficiently indoctrinated and without recourse to other authority seem to have felt comfortable in heeding such disorienting advice.

Since no African tradition was perceived as a counter-authority to that of European modernism, this atmosphere of cooperative tutelage in deracination went beyond matters of poetic form and reached into questions of theme, subject matter, treatment and ideology. The poets seem to shun searching treatment of overtly political and social matters and display a marked preference for private topics. But even when they stray from private matters, their critical guardians and mentors are not unduly alarmed since their political views and insights are safely wrapped in obscurantist diction.

Thus, the injunction to obscurity has served well to insulate from their public much of whatever political insights they have had to convey through their poetry. Thus, all is fine and dandy, and the critics have no ideological cause to hector them for alleged esthetic sins. The actual performance of the poets poses no challenge to the eurocentric values of the critics, and therefore the tone of their criticism has not been one of acerbic hectorings but rather one of cooperative tutelage and encouragement along the paths of euromodernism.

This situation in poetry is in marked contrast to the acerbic hectorings which the critics aim at African novelists. We have shown that the critics are beholden to the pre-modernist European tradition of the "well-made" novel; and many critical studies have demonstrated that most African novelists have been working within that same tradition, e.g., studies linking Achebe with Conrad, Ngugi with Dostoevsky, etc. Given the view that both the critics and the novelists are working within the same pre-modernist prose tradition, one would naturally expect a similar air of cooperative tutelage between them as we have observed between the modernist poets and their modernist critics. But, surprisingly, this is not the case. Why?

Although they are working within the same tradition, the critics and the novelists have serious formal, thematic and ideological disagreements. Their disagreement on formal matters is largely attributable to the fact that whereas the critics are beholden exclusively to the canons of the "well-made" pre-modernist European novel, the novelists' practice is guided by a mixture of at least three different narrative traditions, namely: (1) African oral traditions; (2) the euro-modernist prose tradition; and (3) the pre-modernist European narrative tradition. Of course, there are clear cases of novelists attempting to execute a passage under the canons of the pre-modernist tradition who are rightly chided by the critics for incompetence; but it is not such cases that make for the persistent hectoring of "the African novel." It is rather because the critics are reluctant to concede the authority of the other two rival traditions that they prefer to see and hector as artistic incompetence much of what can be seen as justifiable practice within the other two traditions.

This lack of complete authority by the critics over the novelists extends from formal into thematic and ideological matters, in marked contrast to their complete authority over the poets. Their thematic and ideological disagreements with the novelists are sometimes presented as if they were dis-agreements over matters of form. In this way, the ideological and political character of those disagreements is masked and their origins in the clash between imperialism and anti-imperialism, a clash which is an implicit and powerful aspect of any colonial situation, is obscured. By attempting to suppress forms and techniques that help to display for understanding the nature and workings of imperialism the critics actively seek to protect imperialism. In this clash, anti-imperialist novels have withstood pro-imperialist criticism and reduced it to acerbic rantings. Their ability to do so is quite important and deserves to be explained, especially in light of the general absence of a powerful cultural nationalism among the novelists, and in light of the capitulation of the poets to imperialist blandishments and authority.

In our view, the most powerful factor working for the novelists in their defiance of imperialist criticism has been the perceived and contrasting authority of African narrative traditions on matters of theme, treatment, and ideology as well as of form. In contrast to the situation in poetry, there has never been any doubt in anyone's mind that Africa has an indigenous prose tradition independent of the European, even though under imperialism it was held in contempt for being oral and "folk." The existence of this palpable and recognized indigenous tradition as a resource and model to work from, made it impossible for the novelists to be conned into an idolatry of any eurocentric tradition. If you saw the novel as a long story which happens to have been written down, you were less likely to be persuaded that it was so unique and apart that the only way to attempt it was to ignore the entire African narrative tradition and settle exclusively to a slobbering imitation of European models.

Thus, though eurocentric critics insist on making pompous and bloated claims about the uniqueness of the novel, its formal characteristics have posed no obstacles to a recognition of it by our novelists as having equivalents in the indigenous and palpable tradition of African narrative. So that while the novelists, just as the poets, undertook their tasks in a milieu which lacked a coherent movement for nationalist cultural consciousness, they could manage without and still produced works which were influenced by, and obtained legitimizing authority from, an indigenous narrative tradition clearly perceived. And on almost every point of contention with eurocentric criticism, African novelists could find support for their practice in the African narrative tradition—for instance, the communalist ethos; the unexaggerated prominence of the individual within his society; the open and healthy treatment of sex in contrast to the Western obsession with either prudery or prurience; the utilization of proverbs; succinctness of description as against pointillist excess or rhapsodic luxuriance; the use of stock characters and situations in parabolic presentations; magic, ghosts, and the supernatural; characterization through allusions, praise names and metaphors.

Thus, whereas euromodernist teachers and critics have monopolized authority over the definition of the form, themes, treatments and ideology allowed in African poetry, they are unable to monopolize control over the definition of such matters in African prose because there has been a rival authority to theirs immanent in a perceived African narrative tradition. Similarly, whereas there is a widespread prejudice that politics is not a proper theme for poetry, efforts to enforce this sort of political prudery upon the prose have never worked, for an anti-imperialist presentation of realities could readily find sanction in the anti-authoritarian stories and social and political satires that exist in the African narrative tradition.

Incidentally, this banishment of overtly political and sociological matters from the thematic province of European poetry is itself a recent (late 19th century) development advantageous to a European bourgeoisie which had finally won power and which needed to shield itself from criticism. Even in the West itself, poetry has felt quite free, down through the ages, to handle scientific treatises, political and sociological satires and discourses, as well as the more narrowly subjective private effusions of sentiment which have come to be grouped together as "lyric poetry" and which have further attempted to monopolize the name of "poetry." By trying to encourage the notion that only lyric poetry is poetry, and by promoting privatist obscurantism, imperialist critics are effectively censoring treatment of socio-political matters and attempting to limit the impact of whatever treatment of such matters still manage to slip into the poetry, since only a few hard-working initiates would be able to decipher whatever political messages are coded into obscurantist poems. Thus, the promotion of obscurantism is an indirect way of enforcing the fashionable injunction to keep politics and poetry apart, since the example of the entire tradition of poetry argues unanswerably against such an apartheid.

Since prose happens to be a far more popular genre than poetry, and since African prose writers have not avoided political and sociological matters, the potential impact of their dealing with such themes, given the anti-imperialism dictated by their circumstances, has naturally been a matter of great concern for the imperialist controllers of African thought—hence the persistence and acerbity of their hectorings. Their cultural containment job is practically nonexistent when it comes to the poets and their poetry, but is in danger of being unaccomplishable with regard to Africa's prose writers; hence the point we began with, namely, the general tone among eurocentric critics of giving high praise and encouragement to Africa's euromodernist poets while firing shrill-voiced, pompous strictures against African novelists.

CHAPTER 3

African Poetry and
Its Critics (1950-1975)
▼▼▼▼▼

MAJOR TENDENCIES IN AFRICAN POETRY

During the period under consideration, there were three major tendencies discernible in African poetry in English, namely: (1) the euromodernists, who have assiduously aped the practices of 20th-century European modernist poetry. These include Wole Soyinka, J. P. Clark, and the early Christopher Okigbo; (2) the traditionalists, who have sought to model their English-language poetry on elements from traditional African poetry. These include Mazisi Kunene, Kofi Awoonor, Okot p'Bitek, and the later Okigbo; (3) a miscellany of individual voices of the middle ground who, unlike the euromodernists or the traditionalists, share no strongly distinguishing characteristics. These include Gabriel Okara, Lenrie Peters, and Dennis Brutus.

However, of these three groups or tendencies, the critics of African poetry have paid the most attention to the euromodernists and indeed have boosted them far beyond their merits. This might well be expected, considering that most of the criticism of African poetry is modernist and eurocentric. True, the traditionalists generally came to notice later than the euromodernists; true, their appearance was duly noted—but there has been no enthusiastic boosting or cultivating of their tendency by the African critical establishment. Thus, the net result is that euromodernist criticism has promoted euromodernist poetry in Africa and has sought to make it dominate the African poetry scene.

The present dominance and entrenchment of the euromodernist tendency is a fact reflected in (1) their prominence in major and influential anthologies such as Gerald Moore and Ulli Beier's *Modern Poetry from Africa* (1963, revised 1968) and Wole Soyinka's *Poems of Black Africa* (1975), which both serve as representative portraits of poetic activity during the period under discussion; (2) the quantity and quality of critical attention they have received; and (3) their entrenchment in the curricula of schools and universities in anglophone Africa. Our discussion of African poetry and its critics (1950–1975) shall therefore concentrate upon the euromodernist tendency—its characteristics, origins, cultivation, wrongheadedness and neocolonialist sensibility. Discussion of the other two rather neglected tendencies we shall defer to the proper context where their strengths and merits shall be highlighted for what they can contribute towards the development of an afromodernist poetry.

The euromodernist tendency was promoted into prominence in Nigeria during its years of emergence there, 1957–67, and its best known practitioners in all Africa were Nigerians associated with the University of Ibadan and the University of Nigeria, Nsukka. These poets studied or taught at either institution and formed a clearly distinguishable literary coterie. They knew one another, cross-influenced one another, and were products of literary values and attitudes traceable to euromodernist teaching in those two institutions. They were given powerful and early prominence, occupied center stage, and were the darlings of the critics. Today, they still occupy a dominant position and exercise considerable influence in anglophone African poetry from within the Nigerian literary establishment. Thus, the *Ibadan-Nsukka school of Nigerian poetry* serves as an excellent representative of the euromodernist tendency in anglophone African poetry. We shall therefore examine their products and the kinds of criticism that have nourished them.

EUROMODERNISM: THE CASE OF THE IBADAN-NSUKKA SCHOOL OF NIGERIAN POETRY

There is a failure of craft in the works of the euromodernist Ibadan-Nsukka school of Nigerian poetry. Despite the high praise heaped upon it from all sides, most of its practitioners display glaring faults, e.g., old-fashioned, craggy, unmusical language; obscure and inaccessible diction; a plethora of imported imagery; a divorce from African oral poetic traditions, tempered only by lifeless attempts at revivalism.

Language and Surface Meaning

Their language is archaic: they seem to pattern their language after 19th-century or even 16th-century British writers. For example, J. P. Clark's "Ivbie" is replete with such clichés and Shakespeareanisms as "thereby hangs a tale," "bade us hold our tongue/Bade us note," "sleep no more." In "Heavensgate" Christoper Okigbo writes: "Singeth jadum the ministrel/. . . Singeth jadum from Rockland . . . ." The poem is dotted with latinisms: *Lustra; Lacrimae Christi; Lumen mundi.* Michael Echeruo's *Mortality* bristles with *corpus christi* formulas: *ne nos inducas; ure igne; nobis quoque peccatoribus; qui tollis peccata mundi; miserere; non sum dignus*—"according to the order of Melchisedech." Wole Soyinka's syntax and verbal structure is Shakespearean: he speaks of "unsexed," "such webs as these we build our dreams upon," and "Propitiation sped/Grimly on, before." (*Idanre,* pp. 7, 10)

Partly as a result of this addiction to archaisms, the

poetry of the Ibadan-Nsukka poets tends to be craggy, lumpy, full of obstructions, unnecessarily and artificially difficult. Simple ideas are often deliberately clothed in esoteric idiom. For instance, what exactly does Echeruo's "Sophia" mean? What is he trying to communicate?

> Left hand is God's hand
> Devil's hand across Chaos
> When Eve began
> Was hers in Eden farm
> Through cat's tiger's fur
> Through Adam's core.
>
> 'Increase and till the earth.'
> Plough on virgin-land is temptation
>
> There was a fountain
> Of rain and grain
> Force fountain down gorge
> Into valley of shoots
> (*Is not spilling*)
> But will not bloom on Martha
> Or *Vita Nuova*
>
> Eat apples by the left hand
> Much sweeter.
> Right hand is Right's hand
> Bitter.
>
> Sweet gorgeless Sophia.

A poem cannot just *be,* it must also *mean*—regardless what anyone says to the contrary. Is "Sophia" a simple erotic experience? Or some archetypal ritual? And it is not enough to say that we miss the whole point. That we miss the whole point is the point! The poem doesn't make sense, not even if we know that Sophia means Wisdom. If he is talking about a simple erotic experience with some woman by the name of Sophia (or Martha) on whom the copulation will not bring conception and new life ("will not bloom on Martha/Or *Vita Nuova*"), why the unnecessary associative indirection? If this is not what he is talking about, then what on earth is he talking about? Poetry is not a puzzle.

Christopher Okigbo, one of the more accomplished practitioners of all the vices of the school, writes:

> The only way to go
> through the marble archway
> to the catatonic pingpong
> of the evanescent halo. . . .
>
> ("Distances")

Again we ask: what does this mean? Is this a joke? Or is he seriously trying to communicate something, and if so, what? But whatever it is, at least it reads well, it is smooth, it has music, its images are striking, it is pleasurable. Nonsense perhaps, but pleasurable nonsense. But we cannot say the same for Soyinka's "Dawn," for instance:

> Breaking earth upon
> A spring-haired elbow, lone
> A palm beyond head-grains, spikes
> A guard of prim fronds, piercing
> High hairs of the wind
>
> As one who bore the pollen highest
>
> Blood-drops in the air, above
> The even belt of tassels, above
> Coarse leaf teasing on the waist, steals
> The lone intruder, tearing wide
>
> The chaste hide of the sky
>
> O celebration of the rites of dawn
> Night-spread in tatters and a god
> Received, aflame with kernels.

167

Not only does it not make immediate sense (you have to puzzle it out), but it is not even easy or pleasurable to read. On the contrary, it is heavy, tongue-twisting, difficult to articulate, and it cannot keep the listener's attention. *And poetry is an auditory medium.* We have emphasized the need for readily available surface meaning in poetry because without it, it is futile to attempt to discover and appreciate whatever deeper levels of meaning a poem might contain.

Imported Imagery and Attitudes

These poets compound the problem of meaning by insisting on importing imagery from alien environments and sometimes shamefacedly apologizing for doing so. Clark speaks of Io (Greek mythology) in "Cry of Birth," and of Joan of Arc (medieval France) in "Olumo." Can't he find an outcast or a woman of stubborn heart in indigenous African mythology or history? We have already spoken of the latinisms rife in Okigbo and Echeruo. Companion to that is the vast array of Catholic impediments which clutter their poetry. Just about every other line we stumble against a chalice, crucifix, marble sarcophagus, halo, incense, rose, passion flower. In their presentation of the accompanying rites, if their intention is to mock, it rarely comes through; and when it does, it sounds like the pusillanimous mockery of an initiate on the verge of disenchantment:

> Anna of the panel oblongs,
>   protect me
> from them, fucking angels;
>   protect me
> my sandhouse and bones.
>   (Okigbo, "Heavensgate")

> Storms rage; fires consume
> and after (so they say),
> all shall be restored in the Lord,

all shall be forgiven by the Lord—
or so has he promised O'Brien.

(Echeruo, "Ure Igne")

Too often their manner of presentation tends to give legitimacy to these alien religious rites. Contrast, for instance, Okot p'Bitek's outright and obvious mockery of the Christian church:

He says
When we suffer misfortune
We should say:

Look Mariya
Mother of the Hunchback. . . .

We should pray to Joseph
And Petero, and Luka
And the other ancestors of white men!
He says
It is stupid superstition
To pray to our ancestors
To avert the small-pox,
But we should pray
To the messengers of the Hunchback
To intercede for us.

(*Song of Lawino,* p. 155)

With Okigbo and Echeruo the presentation is straight-faced, whereas Okot, for example, transliterates "Melchise-dech" and "Gregory" into "Meldikijedeki" and "Gilirigo-loyo." Surely all three poets must have grown up under Catholic tutelage, for they speak as insiders. How is it that one is able to debunk the foreign religion so unequivocally, whereas the other two pamper it?

Into their obscurantist cesspool the Ibadan-Nsukka poets drag everything: foreign images, foreign attitudes and forms, and assorted mannerisms. Okigbo's pictograms in his original version of "Distances" (*Transition* 16, September–October, 1964) are senseless and superfluous; they hark back to the wild and purposeless experimentation of some decadent Western poets. Okigbo's "great boys of child" ("Heavensgate") is awkward and adolescent. In "Malediction" Soyinka curses a woman who rejoiced at the massacre of her fellow countrymen. But he curses her in language that is a blend of Shakespeare and the Victorian English poets. He does not curse the way his forefathers cursed, nor the way his contemporaries curse—for it is important to remember that African orature is at once traditional and contemporary. It is happening out there in the village, on the streets, and even in the halls and corridors of the university campuses. All that the poet has to do is open his ears, and listen to his contemporaries who have not lost touch with tradition, and write the way they speak.

The following are some curses in traditional style:

> May you go mad at the height of your prosperity.
> May you run naked through a crowded market.
> When you die may your body be thrown into the evil
> forest.

Soyinka's curses in "Malediction," had they been rendered in simple English, might have come across with something of the straightforward vigor of the traditional:

SOYINKA ORIGINAL

> Giggles fill the water-hole
> Offsprings by you abandoned,
> And afterbirth, at crossroads
>
> So when the world grieves, rejoice
> Call to them in laughter . . .

Even thus
for your children
and your children's
children

that their throats laugh Amen
on your bier, and carousing hooves
raise dust to desecrated dust—Amen

SIMPLE ENGLISH

May you give birth to monstrosities at crossroads
And when the world comes to commiserate with you
May you burst out laughing with joy

May your children and children's children rejoice when
    you die
May they desecrate your funeral with their drunken
    and boisterous behavior

It may be asked: what's wrong with cursing the way
Englishmen of the 16th or 19th century (supposedly) cursed?
The answer is simple: (1) It is voluntary cultural servitude—
and worse, servitude to somebody else's dead past. It is a
denial of the validity of our own culture. The poet is saying
in effect that our cultural style is not good enough to curse
in. (2) It blocks the channel of cultural transmission. Two
hundred years from now, when perhaps everyone has gone
to school and our orature may have changed drastically,
people will go to books to find out how we cursed, and
they will say: "this is how they cursed, enh? like 16th or
19th century Englishmen?" What sacrilege!
    The same may be said for Soyinka's dirges "For Fajuyi"
and "Massacre, October '66." At the conclusion of his
"Massacre" Soyinka apologizes:

I borrow seasons of an alien land
In brotherhood of ill pride of race around me

> Strewn in sunlit shards. I borrow alien lands
> To stay the season of a mind.

Why does Soyinka find it necessary to "borrow seasons of an alien land" to mourn our dead? In his play *The Road* he models several dirges on traditional forms. If he could do so then, why not now, on this most important national occasion? In any case, why import and then apologize?

We have nothing against foreign imagery ("seasons of an alien land") as such. All we are saying is that when the context and setting is African and tropical, it is asinine to drag in spring, snow and other arctic paraphernalia. When the context or locale is unspecified, as in Okogbule Wonodi's "Love Song," anything goes. Cultural servitude aside, the issue here is one of internal consistency and fidelity to fact. The issue is one of craft.

Unsuccessful Mimesis: The Hopkins Disease

The Ibadan-Nsukka poets are for the most part *ineffectual imitators*. When they imitate the European tradition, they too often botch it; and when they consciously attempt to write in the African manner, they also botch it. Let us take a look at the kind of botch they make when they imitate the euromodernist tradition, and, while doing so, also consider the kind of literary appreciation which tries to convince the reader that such botches are indeed gems of profound art.

The idols in the poetic pantheon of Nigeria's euromodernists are the Leavisite modernist trinity—Ezra Pound, T. S. Eliot and Gerard Manley Hopkins. Since their university days, Nigeria's euromodernist poets and critics have been apprenticed to the works of these idols and trained to consider them the epitome of modernist poetic culture in the English language. Now, for those who are familiar with the poetry and critical pronouncements of this trinity, and who are impressed with the solidity of their achievements, the performance of their Nigerian disciples is rather curious and disappointing. The only things these disciples appear to have learned from their models are their well-known faults. Prominent among the characteristics of Nigerian euromodernist poetry are Hopkinsian syntactic jugglery, Poundian allusiveness and sprinkling of foreign phrases, and Eliotesque suppression of narrative and other logical linkages of the sort that creates obscurity in "The Waste Land." In their prosody, they seem to be addicted to Hopkinsian sprung rhythm, and to the only slightly loosened up metrical rigidity of Eliot's *vers libre*. Pound's expansive open forms have had very little impact upon their prosody.

It would appear that while avidly acquiring these faults of the anglomodernist masters, these poets have uniformly shunned their strengths. For instance, in the best of Hopkins there is an energy and felicity that survives the syntactic jugglery and word play. There is an elegance of Pound's wit and a carrying power to his eloquence. Eliot is famous for his vivid, concrete images and *mots justes*. Both Pound and Eliot extensively use varieties of colloquial diction in their poetry. Little of such strengths are to be found in Nigeria's euromodernist poetry; but if one combines the individual faults of Pound, Eliot and Hopkins one obtains the hallmark of Nigeria's euromodernist poetry.

Surprisingly, the dominant influence among them is Hopkins. The individual and group indebtedness of these Nigerian poets to Hopkins is stark and heavy. In the early Okigbo and in Clark, Echeruo, Soyinka and Wonodi, as well as in the younger members of their coterie, there is an abundance of such Hopkinsian infelicities as atrocious punctuation, word order deliberately scrambled to produce ambiguities, syntactic jugglery with suppression of auxiliary verbs and articles, the specious and contorted cadences of sprung rhythm, the heavy use of alliterations and assonances within a line, and the clichéd use of double and triple-barrelled neologisms. The employment of these devices amounts to a widespread mannerism, a species of modernist practice which we have called the *Hopkins disease.*

The heavy indebtedness to Hopkins is easily verified by reading through the extant works of these Nigerian poets (there isn't that much of it—it can all be read in less than one day). Their practice can be compared with the following excerpts from Hopkins:

> Not, I'll not, carrion comfort, Despair, not feast on
> thee;
> Not untwist—slack they may be—these last strands of
> man
> In me or, most weary, cry *I can no more.* I can;
> Can something, hope, wish day come, not choose not
> to be.
>
> ("Carrion Comfort")

> I caught this morning morning's minion, king-
> dom of daylight's dauphin, dapple-dawn-drawn
> Falcon, in his riding
> Of the rolling level underneath him steady air,
> and striding
> High there, how he rung upon the rein of a wimpling
> wing
> In his ecstasy!
>
> ("The Windhover")

> Look at the stars! look, look up at the skies!
> O look at all the fire-folk sitting in the air!
> The bright borough, the circle citadels there!
> Down in dim woods the diamond delves! the elves'-
> eyes!
>
> ("The Starlight Night")

There is something rather odd about Hopkins sprouting on Nigerian soil, considering that the native owners of Hopkins have wisely chosen not to imitate him much, treating him as an inspired dead-end in the development of British poetry. Dylan Thomas, the most accomplished of Hopkins' few imitators, was judiciously selective in his imitation. He managed to make a virtue of the Hopkinsian lust for assonance and alliteration and other word play, and minimized syntactic jugglery and atrocious punctuation. But Soyinka, Clark and Company have chosen to resuscitate in Nigeria, and without amelioration, the worst aspects of this vestigial branch of the anglomodernist tradition. O Hopkins! What strange roots your mangled ghost has sprouted in these distant African provinces of the bloody British empire!

Now, why has this happened? Is it merely that fools rush in where angels fear to tread? Or is this the doing of some Hopkins-struck teacher at Ibadan in the 1950s? Or is it that given the two seminal sins of anglomodernist poetry, namely, Poundian allusiveness and Hopkinsian syntactic jugglery, the Nigerian neophytes chose the one that was within their intellectual means? After all, people of little or narrow learning have little to allude to. Whatever the case, it appears that the recipe for writing and reading "serious" and "significant" poetry, Nigerian style, i.e., Hopkinsian poetry, can be reduced to the following formulas:

THE HOPKINS DISEASE

I. How to Write "Serious" and "Significant" Poetry in Seven Easy Steps

1. Take any everyday sentence, as prosaic as possible.
2. Chop it up into metric lines.
3. Take each line and juggle the word order, breaking as many punctuation and syntactic rules as possible.

4. Suppress all auxiliary verbs and as many other logical or narrative linkages as you can, always with an eye to creating at least seven types of ambiguity per line. By now you should be able to write such lines as:

> Mystery, which barring
> the errors of the rendering
> witnesseth
> red-hot blade on right breast
> the scar of the crucifix.
> (Okigbo, "Heavensgate," *Labyrinths*, p. 7)

> In the desert wildness, when, lone cactus,
> Cannibal in his love—even amidst the
> Crag and gorge, the leap and night tremors
> Even as the potsherd stayed and the sandstorm
> Fell—intimations came.
> (Soyinka, "Prisoner," *Idanre*, p. 44)

5. Inject as many neologisms as you can, preferably in double- or triple-barrelled phrases, using as many alliterations and assonances as you can, e.g.: fresh-firecoal; chestnut-falls; wring-world; fire-folk; dapple-dawn-drawn; couple-colour (Hopkins); grain-spray; feather-flakes; flesh-birds; milk-thread; moon-breasts; fire-surrounds; glow-swarms (Soyinka); brow-beat bribe-beat; roll-glow; lead-tether'd; self-split selves; adrizzle-damp, draw; calm from flush of cam; kestrel-together-leaf flaps; tick-twit; dabble, dip paddle blades; fear frou-froued in fronds (Clark); he-goat-on-heat; *malisons malisons mair than ten* (Okigbo).

6. For prosody, shake up the rigid metric lines and free them up a little, tickling some phrases into "sprung rhythm," and as often as you can ending each line at the first word after a punctuation mark, preferably a comma, as in the following:

April is the cruellest month, breeding
Lilacs out of the dead land, mixing
Memory and desire, stirring
Dull roots with spring rain.
Winter kept us warm, covering
Earth in forgetful snow, feeding
A little life with dried tubers.

> (Eliot, "The Waste Land")

Now, garnerers we
Awaiting rust on tassels, draw
Long shadows from the dusk, wreathe
Dry thatch in a wood-smoke. Laden stalks
Ride the germ's decay—we wait
The promise of the rust.

> (Soyinka, "Season," *Idanre*, p. 45)

Mist-hung curtains, adrizzle-damp, draw, fall
Apart, spring a forward catch in the sky
That swift over us spreads, all
Of a lift, this fresh burst of blue, freckled dye
In running decks
Of quicksilver flakes and flecks.

> (Clark, "Ibadan Dawn (after *Pied Beauty*),"
> *A Reed in the Tide*, p. 13)

7. If you have sufficient erudition, sprinkle in as many foreign phrases and allusions as you can—allusions to obscure persons, places and events from some foreign folklore, mythology or history, such as those of ancient Sumer, Stonehenge, or Tegel, or from some document which you found on shipdeck at Hong Kong or El'brus (it doesn't matter if the place is landlocked); or allusions to something which you dredged up from your dreams or memories— always taking care (some would call it "security measures") not to tell where or what these are, for that would give your game away and deprive the reader of the privilege of hunting down these phrases and allusions himself. By now

you should be able to stud your lines with allusions like the following: Kepkanly; Haragin; *etru bo pi alo a she* (Okigbo, in the original version of "Heavensgate"); Flanagan; Irkalla; Enkidu; Guernica; Eunice at the passageway; a branch of fennel on an empty sarcophagus; where the beast is finishing her rest (Okigbo, in the original version of "Limits"—please, please don't look in his collected poems, *Labyrinths,* where most of these allusions are explained in footnotes, thereby giving the game away!). If you happen to have the rare gift and mastery of Pound, you might be able to string your foreign phrases and allusions compactly together into a passage like this:

> He was playing there at the palla.
> Parisina—two doves for an altar—at the window,
> *"E'l Marchese*
> *Stava per divenir pazzo*
> after it all." And that was when Troy was down
> And they came here and cut holes in rock,
> Down Rome way, and put up the timbers;
> And came here, condit Atesten . . .
>   "Peace! keep the peace, Borso."
> And he said: Some bitch has sold us
>   (that was Ganelon)
> "They wont get another such ivory."
>
>   (Pound, Canto XX)

Now, poet, you have written a "serious" and "significant" poem worthy of close scrutiny, textual explication and critical interpretation; whatever specimen of *the Hopkins Disease* you now have in hand is an authentic product of "autochthonous" African esthetics—so some distinguished critics would have you believe! . . . Now, poet, if you faithfully apply this recipe for poetic ineloquence, you can transmute even psychotic babble into a work of genius. If you need further coaching in this literary game, please read

about an American version of it in Langston Hughes' "How
To Be a Bad Writer (In Ten Easy Steps)."

II. How to Read "Serious" and "Significant" Poetry

Now, reader, all you have to do is "to restore the words
to their normal order or supply the missing links to come
to a position to appreciate the poems" (Nwoga 1974: 36).
Here is an exercise to teach you how:

IN PATHS OF RAIN

In paths of rain, in rock grooves, may
These rare instants of wild fox-fires
Write on moments, lives.

The moment's lightning felt
On wire-tips, as fire-surrounds
To heartbeat of a trembling hare

The last despairing pause, birth-teasing
Yields dues on precipice, to love,
Reassurance, and strangled seeds

Unleashed, exult. From wells
Deep in the brute's denials comes
A captive tenderness

Sky lights from your night redress
My darkness, sable oil still-traps
A straining thunderhead

In unguent silt to rest
Roots of rage held to a lucent stance
Glow-swarms lightening

High thorn-bushes. Clean vistas—
Flecked mica after rain, plankton in antimony
Off rain-washed shores.

Till the chronicle of severance,
Gold spelling, lantern sanctuaries around
Birth-point, and chapter . . .

Ground skins of the unshelled
                              hand over hand of fire
A kernel's freak communion
                    windpools in the ash of palm.

(Soyinka, *Idanre,* pp. 39–40)

Dear reader, are you having trouble coming to a position to appreciate the poem? Well, Professor Eldred Jones has been kind enough to supply the following help; in order to do so he finds it necessary to put the poem in the context of the preceding poem in that section of *Idanre:*

> The seed which comes to fruition in "To One, In Labour" is sown during one highly charged explosive moment in a compulsive instinctive act, when the deep drives take control, and conscious attempts to strangle the seed give way. The seeds assert themselves with an independent will of their own at this charged moment: "and strangled seeds/Unleashed, exult . . ." These are the seeds of life which in the opening lines of the poem "In Paths of Rain" write lives on moments:
>
>> In paths of rain, in rock grooves, may
>> These rare instants of wild-fox-fires [*sic*]
>> Write on moments, lives.
>
> (Here as elsewhere syntactical analysis helps to reveal the meaning of complex passages: "These rare . . . fox-fires" is the subject of "write" and "lives" is the object. "On moments" is adverbial. In stanza 2 [*sic*] "strangled seeds" is subject to "exult." In stanza 5 "still-traps" is a verb to which "stable oil" is subject,

and "a straining thunderhead" is object.) Even this early stanza suggests the momentary nature of the essential process which is vividly symbolized in succeeding stanzas. But the momentary act is produced in a social context and thus breeds a train of consequences of an entirely different nature from the act itself. The act is instinctive; marriage is social. The act may be begun and ended in total mutuality; the vistas are clean:

> Clean vistas—
> Flecked mica after rain, plankton in antimony
> Off rain-washed shores.

But the end of the poem suggests that the mutuality of the instinctive act may produce quite other results in the larger context of the society. The suggestions of this section are very compactly presented—the earlier part of the poem is more expansive; the structure itself is suggestive. Everything is bright, the poem suggests,

> Till the chronicle of severance [*sic*]
> Gold spelling, lantern sanctuaries around
> Birth-point, and chapter . . .

> Ground skins of the unshelled
>   hand over hand of fire
> As [*sic*] kernel's freak communion
>   windpools in the ash of palm.

The "severance" in contrast to the mutuality implied in the earlier stanzas takes place in an atmosphere suggestive of church and ritual: "lantern sanctuaries" and "chapter." In this context "gold spelling" would suggest a book with gold lettering—for example, the prayer book. "Birth-point" suggests an advanced stage of pregnancy. Altogether, the suggestion is of a marriage required by society because of a pregnancy. The two "unshelled" (ungloved) hands are here in a "freak

> communion" in contrast to the more natural commu-
> nion portrayed earlier. The glitter of "mica after rain,"
> the fruitful suggestion of "plankton in antimony" have
> become a more barren "windpools in the ash of palm
> . . . ." This union in fact has, ironically, become "the
> chronicle of severance." The poem separates the
> instinctive physical act from the social rigidities which
> often complicate it. It is an important variation to the
> theme of this section.   (Jones 1973: 131–32)

Thus, according to Jones, Soyinka's "In Paths of Rain" is about "a marriage required by society because of a pregnancy." If that is indeed what this poem is about, namely, Soyinka's explorations of the process and consequences of irresponsible fucking, why does he wrap it all up in obscurantist turgidities? Isn't such a treatment a literary version of the intellectual dishonesties of Anglo-puritan prudery? Why should anyone in his right mind undertake or be compelled to sort through such elaborate mountains of pompous chaff in order to discover some incoherent little thought allegedly buried in it? Waste work! waste work! abominable waste work! And after you have endured it all, you are supposed, as Professor Jones does, to gush over the vivid symbolization that is alleged to be in the poem!

Of course, dear reader, in disentangling Soyinka's syntax you need not agree at all with Professor Jones; after all, what are ambiguities and suppressed linkages for if not to generate a multiplicity of "profound" interpretations? Now, if after patiently toiling to puzzle out your own version of the "significance" in this "serious" poem, you are dissatisfied with it, you must count yourself among "the deaf, the dull, the lazy"—so says the hard-working and brilliant author of the unsigned obituary, "Death of Christopher Okigbo," in *Transition,* No. 33, October/November 1967, p. 18. If all this nonsense makes you angry, then that is sufficient proof that you are not one of the few in Africa who are "whole enough or bright enough" to judge poetry—so says this same anonymous obituarist. And if you balk at participating in this elaborate and obvious con game of puzzling out gratuitous conundrums, and you raise a "hue and cry" against such waste work, then you should know that you are suffering from "insensibility and slavish inability to adjust to novel creations that immensely enrich a universal store of vision"—so says Nigerian critic, Theo Vincent (Vincent 1975: 59).

Ah, yes! Such is the profound esthetic wisdom of the Ibadan-Nsukka school of the Hopkins Disease, and their intellectual spawn and kindred. But really, is this the sort of intellectual waste work we must foist upon our children? What sort of socially useful intellectual work can possibly come from minds intensely and elaborately drilled in such pompous trivia?

As for these poets themselves, one consequence of their addiction to Hopkinsian mannerisms is that when they attempt to write in traditional African modes, their Hopkinsian techniques get in their way, and they botch their traditionalist efforts. For instance, on the rare occasions when they attempt love songs or harvest songs or songs of sorrow or songs of abuse that embody the traditional African milieu, they too often sound limp; it doesn't come off. They fail to convey the tenderness or exaltation or bite or whatever it is they are trying to convey. An alien technique, based on an alien sensibility that is rather too formalist—ambiguity for ambiguity's sake, alliteration for alliteration's sake, sprung rhythm for sprung rhythm's sake, etc.—obstructs them as they try to present or explore thoughts, actions, emotions, or moods that are rooted in the traditional African setting. They often end up merely *referring* to these emotions or celebrating them in the abstract. Take Romanus Egudu's "The First Yam of the Year":

> I have dug it fresh,
> this boneless flesh

of air, earth, warmth
and water, this
life out of the heart
of death;
its cap of fibre
will mail the elder's
head against grey rain,
and its body proof his
to spite time's arrows.

For he is the rope
tied at the foot
of our past hooking
its fingers round our waist,
and reaching for the sable
gourd on the forked stump
where the unfeathered chick
chirps a sacrificial song.

He will eat this long-root
of earth, and after spread
my skin under the Red-Sun
to collect his rays
for washing my blood,
and plant the ageless
sun-tree into my heart.

Now contrast it with this traditional harvest song, "New Yam," translated from the Yoruba:

Cassava and maize are only the poor relations of yam.
Yam is a warrior who brings strife wherever he goes:
The children quarrel for the biggest portion
The landlord complains it was not pounded
    smooth like yesterday.
To plant yam is costly—but it amply repays
    its own debt.
You put the yam to bed in the ground

it will bring you money
that will plant you on top of a beautiful woman.

(Beier 1970: 89)

Egudu maintains a personal esthetic distance, dissecting the yam under a monocle, whereas the traditional poem focuses on the social significance of the yam and presents a lively and dramatic picture of its impact on all those who come in contact with it. The traditional poem is *engagée,* it is lively, and it works. The other is privatist, sterile, and sounds like a labored and lifeless attempt at nostalgic revivalism. By the time you dig through the contorted syntax, blurred images and structural inconsistencies of the poem, you are no longer interested in finding out what the new yam is all about and why it needs to be celebrated. On the other hand, the classic simplicity and terseness of the traditional poem comes through even in translation. And from the traditional poem, because it presents the yam in the dialectical nexus of a yam-farming society, even a foreigner will begin to appreciate why we celebrate the new yam.

Again, witness how Wonodi attempts to capture the flavor of traditional life in "Moonlight Play":

Touching those that us do not
In moonlight night—suffix to daylife
Partnered to food and laugh
    and cry:
Centre circle the players
    and the moonhouse—safe citadel!
The stars' calm and wind blows,
The searcher bellows
And in surge the children,
    the happy ones—soul and body;

    Banana stands mask
Marshes' fair futility;
Furtive fare would feign
Magic turns of turgidity;

Then up sentinel down the search—
Bustle, scuffle and ruffles!
And out the hidden dash
Down to centre-safe;
Chatter, teeth, breath and laughter!
He shudders, mutters and murmurs;
Ogboo-o-uu-o-u-
Bellows of once failed.

We start afresh
Until the touched turns searcher.

Contrast this with Matei Markwei's "Life in Our Village":

In our little village,
When elders are around,
Boys must not look at girls
And girls must not look at boys
Because the elders say
That is not good.

Even when night comes
Boys must play separately,
Girls must play separately.
But humanity is weak
So boys and girls meet.

The boys play hide and seek
And the girls play hide and seek.
The boys know where the girls hide
And the girls know where the boys hide—
So in their hide and seek,
Boys seek girls,
Girls seek boys,
And each to each sing
Songs of love.

Markwei's poem is simple and vivid, without surface complexity or clutter. His language does not get in his way. It conveys the action and experience of moonlight play in an African village, as seen from the point of view of a pubescent youngster. Wonodi's "Moonlight Play," in contrast, is dark and dense: the actions are mangled by words which seem preoccupied with making alliterations and other verbal mannerisms presenting what is happening. Such dismal results by faulty and inappropriate techniques point up the grave problem of a severance from an oral African tradition which is rooted in communal communication.

Euromodernist Nigerian Poetry and the Oral Tradition

The severance of modern Nigerian poetry from what should be its oral African roots manifests itself most glaringly in matters of religion. Several poets have attempted to revive or imitate traditional religious poetry but have failed damnably. What, for instance, should one make of Soyinka's highly touted "Idanre"? His prose preface promises the communication of an intense religious and mystical experience. But the poem itself, 28 pages long, provides the reader no feel for the experience. The imagery is imprecise and opaque and lacking in evocative power. All we can decipher is the names of the various deities: Ogun, Sango, Ajantala, Esu, Orunmila, Orishanla. But in this narrative poem it is never clear who does what to whom and with what consequences. It is often difficult to tell who the many pronouns— *he, she, we, us*—refer to. We are shut off from the experience on both the intellectual and emotional levels. The language is a formidable barrier; and even after you have hacked your way through it, you still cannot understand what, if anything, is supposed to be going on.

"Idanre" is a failure. At best it is a private cipher meaningful to no one but the poet himself—perhaps. It may be that mystical experience is, in the final analysis, verbally incommunicable. If so, why try? If Soyinka's educated countrymen, who have access to the mythology and local custom that inform the poem, cannot figure out what he is saying, even after several careful readings, then who on earth can? This kind of exercise in senseless narcissism, this publicly enacted retreat into a private language must stop. When in public, speak a public language!

Traditional African poetry speaks a public language. Some of our obscurantist poets may retort by pointing to the existence of cult poetry and religious incantations which, in traditional society, were intelligible, not to the general public, but only to initiates of secret societies and the priesthoods. True. There was such poetry. But the initiates were the public for such poetry. Such poetry had a limited audience but was certainly not privatist, was certainly not coded in language intelligible to their composers alone. Besides, such poetry was only a small part of the traditional repertory. If our privatists of today claim that they are descendants of that small tradition, we must ask them: of what cult are you the priesthood? Of what secret rites are your poems the incantations? And if, indeed, your poems are cultic utterances aimed at initiates, why publish and distribute them to the general public? Why not circulate them among initiates only?

As we said before, traditional African poetry speaks a public language. The following invocation and praise of Alajire, a god of suffering, comes from Soyinka's own Yoruba tradition:

> Alajire, we ask you to be patient,
> you are very quick-tempered,
> and we worship you for it.
> We ask you to be moderate,
> you are wildly extravagant
> and we pray to you for it.
> We ask you not to be jealous,

you are madly jealous,
and we love you for it.
Alajire, you have a strange kind of pity:
will you swallow my head,
while you are licking away the tears from my face?
Alajire, you frighten me,
when you fall gently, like a tired leaf.
Do not covet the beauty
on the faces of dead children.
Alajire, I am lost in the forest,
but every wrong way I take,
can become the right way towards your wisdom.

(Beier 1970: 30)

In nineteen lucid lines this poem communicates the nexus of feelings that bind the worshipper to the god. A sense of the worshipper's terror at the god's unpredictable nature comes through clearly. The worshipper has to flatter the god's vices, love his jealousy, and distrust his pity. Even the god's gentleness carries an umbra of fear. But the worshipper is never unaware of the possibility of attaining wisdom. Thus, at the end of the poem the reader understands something of the nature of this god and has shared in the experience of worshipping him.

Among the Igbo poets the situation is much the same. Their attempts to revive traditional religious poetry have been equally unsuccessful. For example, Okigbo opens "Heavensgate" with an invocation to Mother Idoto, an African water goddess. But most of the poem is preoccupied with Catholic liturgy and jargon—in fact, the whole framework of the poem is Christian and Catholic, with snippets of traditional African ritual thrown in. Some may want to view this as a case of syncretism, as a fusion of Christianity and African religions. But one can charge Okigbo with insincerity in his approach to African religion. For instance, the opening invocation, supposedly traditional African, is in fact Christian in language and spirit. With a few minor

189

adjustments in vocabulary, one can convert this invocation into a Christian prayer:

OKIGBO ORIGINAL	ADJUSTED (Christian)
Before you, Mother Idoto naked I stand; before your watery presence a prodigal	Before you, Father Almighty, contrite I stand, before your divine presence, a pilgrim
leaning on an oilbean lost in your legend	waiting at your altar; lost in awe . . . .

But one cannot by similar substitutions convert an authentic traditional invocation into a Christian prayer:

ORIGINAL (African) Prayer to Ekwensu	ADJUSTED (Christian) Prayer to the Devil
Ekwensu we place our hands on you . . . <div align="center">(Beier 1967:16)</div>	Devil we place our hands on you. . .

Can a Christian say prayers to the devil, that exiled incarnation of evil, and risk damnation from his jealous God? But in an African pantheon, good gods are thanked, difficult ones are appeased, bad ones are bribed, and so on. Again, witness the following:

ORIGINAL (African) Prayer to the Dead Father	ADJUSTED (Christian) Prayer to Saint Peter
My father I am giving these yams to you when you are reborn may you be a farmer of many yams.	O Saint Peter, Fisher of Men, Keeper of the Gates of heaven I bring these biscuits to you when you are reborn may you be a baker of delicious biscuits.

(Beier 1967: 17)

The trouble with this adjustment is of course that the belief in reincarnation which undergirds "Prayer to the Dead Father" is outside of Christian doctrine. If Okigbo had, at that stage of his career, had the humility of a votary and wanted to learn how properly to invoke a divine or ancestral spirit, he could have listened to the village elders or priests whose invocations would have run something like the "Prayer to the Dead Father," translated from the Igbo original:

> My father
> I am giving these yams to you
> when you are reborn
> may you be a farmer of many yams.
> My father
> I am killing this goat for you
> When you are reborn
> may it be as my own son.
> My father
> I have brought this dog to you
> When you are reborn
> slay not your children
> and may they not slay you.
> May you kill none by accident
> but may you kill your enemies with intent.
> My father
> I am sacrificing this cock to you
> when you are reborn
> may your *ikenga* stand straight.
> As you are now in the spirit world
> avert all evil from us.
> Let your son who is succeeding you
> look after his family
> as you did before him.
>
> (Beier 1967: 17)

But having first invoked an indigenous goddess in supposed reverence, even if in the language and spirit of a foreign religion, Okigbo then proceeds to refer to her rep-

resentatives as "idols," using deprecatory Christian terminology. To reverence the gods and then deprecate their
representatives at the altar!—you can't do that!

Worse still, Okigbo desecrates the sacred palm groves
with his "cannons," and claims his Messiah ("Lumen
mundi . . .") will come there "after the argument in heaven"
to receive from penitents "vegetable offerings/ with five/
fingers of chalk." What incongruous nonsense! What sacrilege
for the penitents to enact indigenous rituals to propitiate an
alien god!

All in all, "Heavensgate" is a dressed-up Christian ritual—and therefore the invocation of an indigenous deity is
patently insincere. If you choose to write Christian religious
propaganda, do so, but leave our gods alone! It is bad
enough for Christianity to have displaced our gods from the
consciousness of our elite. It is worse for a seeming revivalist
to address our gods as if they were Christian gods or in the
Christian manner. The net effect would be to absorb our
pantheon into the assembly of lesser Christian godlings, and
this is cultural suicide. It should be the other way around—
Christianity should be domesticated and absorbed into our
existing indigenous religious systems—and it is being domesticated among the Cherubim and Seraphim sect and other
such non-elite adapters of Christianity.

The Ibadan-Nsukka Poets:
An Assessment

In conclusion, of the Ibadan-Nsukka group, J. P. Clark,
Wole Soyinka and Christopher Okigbo clearly deserve the
most attention. The early works of Okigbo give the impression of tossed salad, an unassimilated juxtaposition of religious and secular imagery from Europe and Africa and
elsewhere. But unlike some other African poets who seem
to have neither the humility to serve an apprenticeship nor

the strength to move on to their own authentic voice, Okigbo does grow to final strength. He moves from the stilted rhythms of "Heavensgate" (1960–61) to the incantatory, trancelike flow of "Distances" (1964). Although the obscurity is present all the way, the mannered archaisms have finally been dropped.

Through most of his career Okigbo indulged himself in writing captivating nonsense, developing his voice. But luckily for him, just before his death, events gave him public occasion to use that voice. This obscurantist "poets' poet" was jolted off his elitist clouds. He found matter for his manner, and became a candidate for greatness. In "Path of Thunder" (1965–66), a sequence of six poems, he not only sustains and develops the incantatory style, but he also employs African forms for the first time in an authentic manner. His invocations are in marked contrast to the awkward attempts in "Heavensgate."

> out of the depths my cry:
> give ear and hearken . . .
> ("Heavensgate")

Now contrast that with

> O mother mother Earth, unbind me; let this be
> my last testament; let this be
> The ram's hidden wish to the sword the sword's
> secret prayer to the scabbard—
> ("Path of Thunder")

"Path of Thunder" is resplendent with proverbs, dirges and elegies, praise names and praise songs, leader/choral antiphonies in traditional voices:

> CONDOLENCES . . . from our swollen lips laden
> with condolences:

The mythmaker accompanies us
The rattles are here with us

condolences from our split-tongue of the slit drum
condolences . . .

        . . . .

        . . . .

THUNDER that has struck the elephant
the same thunder can make a bruise—condolences:

we should forget the names
we should bury the date
the dead should bury the dead—condolences

from our bruised lips of the drum empty of condolences:

trunk of the iron tree we cry *condolences* when we
break,

shells of the open sea we cry *condolences* when we
shake . . .
                    ("Path of Thunder")

"Path of Thunder" is a supreme example of what we
mean by a healthy traditionalism. The trajectory Okigbo was
blazing might have launched him into the orbit of the great
poets of the world. But he died too soon—just as he had
jettisoned the retarding euromodernist baggage. Therefore he
remains in our memories only as a candidate for greatness.

J. P. Clark has fewest of the glaring faults of the Ibadan-
Nsukka group; but he attains no great heights either. His
"Streamside Exchange" and "Ibadan" are brilliant flashes.
But on the whole his poetry suffers from a blameless
blandness. His voice is not jarring, but is like faint back-

ground music amidst the clatter of raucous voices in the foreground. And whereas Soyinka begins with the brilliance of "Telephone Conversation" and descends to the contorted opacity of "Idanre," for Okigbo the journey is from the first foundering steps of "Heavensgate" to the assured stride and sweep of "Path of Thunder."

The high peak attained by Okigbo in "Path of Thunder" towers above the low irregular landscape of Nigerian poetry in English. So far, the only other peak that rivals it in African poetry in English is Okot p'Bitek's *Song of Lawino*, which is possibly the best rounded single work of African poetry in English today. Like "Path of Thunder," Okot's Songs—*Song of Lawino, Song of Ocol, Song of a Prisoner*—deal illuminatingly and well with matters of central importance for contemporary Africa. And they do so using authentic African imagery, proverbs, laments, invocations and curses, thereby successfully rooting the modern in the traditional.

On the whole, then, in evaluating the poetry of these euromodernists, with their elaborate techniques of ineloquence, the impression is hard to escape that their slim and overrated output is apprentice work stunted by early and too much praise. They are at best middle-mettle poets who package their mediocrity in mannerisms which they assume are sufficient to turn the prosaic into poetry.

In fact, to the unjaundiced eye, the much vaunted Nigerian euromodernists are not nearly as good poets as the best of the traditionalist and middle-ground voices from all over Africa. Soyinka, Clark, Echeruo and even the early Okigbo (who shows powerful promise rather than accomplishment) are no match for a Lenrie Peters or an Okot p'Bitek. And when they are viewed in the context of 20th-century literature of the entire black world, they disappear from view between the toes of giants like Hughes, Guillen, Senghor, Césaire, and Damas.

THE INCULCATION OF EUROMODERNISM
IN NIGERIAN POETRY:
THE SCANDALOUS LEEDS-IBADAN CONNECTION

Having observed the obscurantism prevalent in Nigeria's euromodernist poetry, its curious severance from the African tradition, and its phony version of an alienating syncretism whereby African elements are inducted into the service of a euromodernist sensibility in Africa instead of euromodernist elements being absorbed into the African tradition to serve it, one is led to wonder about the ways and means whereby this wrongheaded and blighting tendency was imported and entrenched. A search for the fountainhead of this poison leads to an examination of the Leeds-Ibadan connection, personified in the roles of Martin Banham and Wole Soyinka.

In 1954 Soyinka left Ibadan and proceeded to the University of Leeds to complete his undergraduate studies. There he was a contemporary of Martin Banham who was then working for his M.A. In October, 1956, Martin Banham joined the English Department faculty at the University of Ibadan, and during the following school year he, in his own words, "persuaded [the undergraduates] to start a small cyclostyled verse magazine," *The Horn,* under the founding editorship of J. P. Clark. (See Banham 1962: 96.)

For the next several years, the pages of *The Horn* would serve as the weaning ground for the most prominent members of the Ibadan-Nsukka school of poetry. Soyinka on his return from Leeds in 1960 used the pages of *The Horn* to publish both poetry and assorted pieces of cultural propaganda. Several lesser members of the Ibadan-Nsukka school would make their appearance in *The Horn* and also make their indoctrinating pilgrimages to Leeds at various points in their careers. Thus, both the Leeds-Ibadan conduit of ideas, and the magazine through which its influence was most sharply brought to bear upon a coterie of nascent poets and critics, deserve serious examination.

The two principal impacts of tutelage on *The Horn* are easily traced in the records. They are: (1) the dominant cultivation of England's poetic tradition, especially the anglomodernist sensibility and mannerism; (2) a determined fight to wean the poets away from any stirrings of African nationalist consciousness and to indoctrinate them with a universalist-individualist outlook.

On the cultivation of England's poetic tradition, the evidence is there right from the first issue of *The Horn*. Some of the poetry affects the anglomodernist mannerism and sensibility, and others imitate English romantic poetry. The anglomodernist sensibility exhibits alienation from the Nigerian condition past and present, rural and urban, and often exhibits attitudes which would be more appropriate to such colonialists as Joyce Cary and Joseph Conrad. Consider Frank Aig-Imoukhuede's "Life in the Country . . . Life in the Town":

> Night-birds (or witches!) cawing
> To beats of tom-toms,
> Half-clothed virgins with rhythmic buttocks
> Daring the lads to beat 'that' . . .
> And on the morrow
> Almost beating the cock to its crow
> Work!
> Work again in the blistering sun? . . .
>
> Respectability shamelessly rubbing buttocks with harlots
> To immoral tunes by depraved band-boys;
> The usual flight of guided chairs and missiles . . .
>
> The arrival of authority and law and order;
> The slinking off of the delinquent father
> To the respectability of his home and his wife;

Or of the hardened 'regular' with a daughter of Eve.
Aw! I don't like this life either
It is filled with constant fear of the law
And the thought of next meals.

(Quoted in Stevenson 1976: 224)

The attitude exhibited towards rural traditional Africa in this poem is not one of acceptance or nostalgia but of ironic mockery. An African can only talk like that about his women, his sisters and female cousins after he has thoroughly imbibed imperialist prejudices against rural, "half-naked African savages." The view of urban Africa in the same poem is one of disdain and contempt for musicians and the "low life" of night spots in which respectable people would not indulge except in moments of delinquency. Notice the use of the prejoratives "depraved band-boys" and "delinquent father." The poem also shows disdain and contempt for wage-earning life struggles and work.

In this Joyce Caryan portrait of urban and rural Africa, the sensibility at work is that of an alienated African. Not surprisingly, it reflects the view from the secluded elitist comforts of the Ibadan University campus. The enormity of the alienation and the wrongheadedness of the elitism becomes clear when it is realized that these elitist comforts have been provided by the taxes and labor of those portrayed as "half-clothed virgins with rhythmic buttocks" and as "depraved band-boys," and by other producers who must manage along on tidbit wages.

The treatment of the African fauna is equally colonialist. Note the use of "night-birds (or witches!)." Clearly, somebody has succeeded in planting in Frank Aig-Imoukhuede's head the eyes and ears and fears of a Joseph Conrad. And rather than contest this alienation and transmutation of their sensibility, rather than contest the Joyce Caryan view the way Achebe did while he was still an undergraduate at Ibadan, these adolescent poets had internalized it, imbibed its imperialist sensibility, and were gladly mocking their rural and urban compatriots with self-satisfied Anglo-Saxon relish.

This alienated tendency was probably reinforced, if not also provoked, by the erroneous notion that "alienation" was the distinguishing disease of the modern world which any "sensitive" "modern" artist must exhibit by deprecating traditional ways and by showing himself to be at odds with his contemporary surroundings. It is not inconceivable that what began as an affectation of "modern" poetic sensibility quickly turned into a diseased habit.

The anglo-romantic sensibility derived in part from the literary fare of the primary and secondary schools from which the students came to Ibadan. There it was reinforced by the use of such texts as Robert Conquest's anthology *New Lines* as required reading by all students of English. This romantic sensibility encouraged a respectful and obser-vant attitude towards the environment; and since this was in Africa, it resulted in a respectful and observant treatment of the African environment in poetry. It thereby encouraged an observation and rediscovery of the African setting from which the colonial education was weaning them away.

Of these two sensibilities, the alienated anglo-modernist one posed far less of a danger, if any at all, to British cultural hegemony in Nigeria. The anglo-romantic sensibility, however, carried in it seeds of revolt against British cultural imperialism, seeds that were likely to sprout in the intensely nationalist environment of the late 1950s. A close and respectful regard for one's environment in a Nigerian nation-alist setting was far more likely than the alienated attitude to trigger off political consciousness in the poet. If this happened, this consciousness would be Nigerian-nationalist and anti-British.

Such an occurrence, of course, was unacceptable to the British and had to be prevented. Since an explosion of nationalist consciousness seemed likely to be sparked off by echoes of the overtly political and nationalist poetry from the surrounding French African territories, something had to be done, from the British point of view, to stuff the ears of Nigerian poets against the "subversive" echoes of francophone negritude poetry. It is in this context of British defensive measures against a Nigerian nationalist consciousness of an anti-colonialist character that the story of the brief rise and quick suppression of the negritude tendency in *The Horn* can best be appreciated. Let it be emphatically noted that the measures were taken against negritude only insofar as it was a "subversive" example that might incite into being a Nigerian nationalist and anti-British literature. The particular merits or demerits of negritude poetry and esthetic pronouncements were hardly the central issue.

The story of this diversionary coup is told in the following excerpt:

> In the 1950s, students keen on independence, both political and cultural, might have been expected to catch hold of the Negritude of Césaire and Senghor. And in fact *The Horn* gives us a picture of the rise and fall of Negritude in Nigeria. There are only a few references to the word and the concept, but they are adequate to show how the students felt about it. The editorial in the very first issue, presumably written by J. P. Clark, declared, "We venture to submit 'Negritude' as a most compendious word! . . . it stands for . . . that new burning consciousness of a common race and culture that black men in America, the West Indies, and Africa are beginning to feel towards one another." Later he says, "It is to arrest such subtle imperialism [i.e., by Westernized education] that we join those already fighting to preserve our heritage by launching this magazine." John Ramsaran, in Vol. I, No. 3, put in a warning against this sentiment, saying that it "is a negative view of things, a passive acceptance without the inner conviction which comes with the glimmering of truth." In Vol. I, No. 5, the editorial, "Looking Back," accepted this, pointing out, "Of

course, we have flown with the harmattan, swum with mermaids in the creeks and besides being caught in a tornado, have won fame for even the blind beggar. The point however is that we also met Oxford punters, uncanny robots, and Russian sputniks and satellites— all fellow-passengers . . . And here lies the great realisation; human contact with men everywhere. For what is poetry that lacks that?"

The note of Negritude, as distinct from this note of universal humanity, was occasionally struck again. In the introduction to Clark's "Ivbie" (II, 2, p.2), Abiola Irele said he hoped the poem "will contribute to that spirit of 'Negritude' which he [Clark] so ably championed as the first editor of this paper." And again, in the closing editorial of the volume, "Bend in the River" (II, 6, pp. 15-16), Irele wrote that the famous black authors are like a river "flowing towards the great ocean—the great ocean of *Negritude.*"

Many of the poems in *The Horn* can be seen as supporting the concept—the poems that consciously recall cultural heritage of the writers. But Negritude was an idea that took only shallow root in Nigeria, and it soon withered. When Wole Soyinka, coming to fame as Nigeria's first internationally-known play-wright, attacked it (Vol. IV, No. 1) in his essay "The Future of West African Writing," its doom was sealed. "The significance of Chinua Achebe is the evolvement, in West African writing, of the seemingly indifferent acceptance" of the "West African subject-character." There follows what is, I believe, the first appearance in print of a famous saying: "The duiker will not paint 'duiker' on his beautiful back to proclaim his duiker-itude; you'll know him by his elegant leap." The less self-conscious the African is, and the more innately his individual qualities appear in his writing, the more seriously he will be taken as an artist of exciting dignity. But Senghor seems to be so artistically expa-triate that his romanticism of the negro becomes suspect and quite boring sometimes.

After this, the word is, I think, never again used in *The Horn,* except once, and poetry clearly dependent on the concept almost disappears. The "once" is a satiric poem by Frank Aig-Imoukhuede in Vol. IV, No. 2, "The Poor Black Muse" (which was reprinted in *Black Orpheus,* No. 10, under the title "Negritude"):

I cannot continue in a strain that's both forced and
    unnatural.
The sounds, if you think they're 'negritudine,' make
    the 'idiot boy' of me.
O Ne—negri—gri, gri—tud—thud! (does that sound
    well?)—tudes!
Why can't you leave the black Muse alone?

The common feeling among Nigerian writers and critics has always been that they can do without the "self-consciousness" of Negritude, which has always seemed to them a foreign concept. But in one poem towards the end of the magazine's life ("Insomnia," VI, p. 1), Irele brings Negritude briefly back. Sent in from Paris, where Irele was carrying on his postgraduate studies, it reads almost like a translation from the French:

A single persistence in the abyss of my white nights
Harassed by the nightmares of my feebleness
Coughed upon the gulf of my dilemma profound tena-
    cious . . .

* * *

The light snore of my dark brother in the heaviness
    of his African sleep . . .
And here I am rocked on white sheets of punished
    innocence . . .

These phrases show the influence of Negritude, but Irele was in Paris.

(Stevenson 1976: 227–29)

Thus, the rise and fall of negritude and, with it, of African nationalist consciousness in the Ibadan-Nsukka school of "African" poetry! A classically simple case of the derailment of African cultural nationalism, and the substitution in its place of "universalism" in Nigerian poetry. That such a maneuver was possible should surprise no one who is familiar with the repertory of British stratagems for keeping control of the economy, politics or culture of other lands and peoples. Just consider the recent British ploy for withholding from FESTAC the Benin bronze mask which British soldiers had looted in 1897. Their final excuse for not loaning it to Nigeria was that Nigeria did not have the facilities for preventing the deterioration of the mask during the one month of FESTAC. But the mask had been made and preserved in Nigeria for several centuries before 1897! (For other examples of British trickery, see Chinweizu 1975: 270–75, 323–35.) At any rate, the particular logistics in the case of circumscribing the concerns and themes of Nigerian literature is worthy of some brief expository comments.

J. P. Clark, in the editorial of the first issue of *The Horn,* sounds a positive and welcoming note on negritude and on black cultural consciousness. Two issues later, John Ramsaran (the British "house nigger" from another part of the Third World) promptly weighs in with all his professional authority and issues an encyclical, warning the restive undergraduates against this "heresy." Then, two issues later, properly chastened, J. P. Clark surrenders before the authority of the encyclical and publishes his recantation. However, a few others, notably Abiola Irele, persist as dissenters before foreign professional pressure, and proceed to state and restate the "heretical" position.

Then Wole Soyinka, with his brand-new reputation, is parachuted in (1960) from Leeds and the Royal Court Theatre, and lands amidst much fanfare blown by such colonialist propaganda organs as *Encounter* magazine, and goes into action to flush out and swat the remnants of the native resistance to Anglo-Saxon pseudo-universalism. This Marshall Ky of African culture (remember Vietnam?) rehearses in the pages of *The Horn* an early draft of his tigritude counterinsurgency slogan bomb. The local opposition melts before the gun of his "duikeritude." British imperialist triumph over a nascent Nigerian cultural nationalism is complete! Ridicule by voices like Aig-Imoukhuede's merely cry "Amen," and bring laughter to the teeth of the triumphant Britishers and their fellow travellers!

Soyinka, having succeeded so well against the local opposition of his Nigerian peers, prepares his cowboy sheriff act for grander scenes. Two years later, at the Kampala Conference of African writers, *duikeritude* is transformed into a more menacing *tigritude!* And on the continental scene, the spread of negritude into the British colonies and neo-colonies is contained, and whatever variants of active African nationalist consciousness its example might have triggered off is defused, and British cultural imperialism can reign secure a little longer over the minds in its African "commonwealth" possessions.

To appreciate the consequences of this British maneuver, it is useful to note the subsequent entrenchment and enormous influence of various members and disciples of *The Horn* coterie in the present-day literary establishment in Nigeria. Wole Soyinka has shuttled between Ibadan, Ife and Lagos universities, setting up or heading Drama Departments, and is currently Head of the Department of Comparative Literature at Ife, as well as the editor of the influential journal *Transition/ Ch'indaba*. J. P. Clark is Head of the English Department at the University of Lagos and he was for many years the editor of another influential journal, *Black Orpheus*. Michael Echeruo was for several years Head of the English Department at Ibadan, and is now Dean of the Post-Graduate School at Ibadan. Several other of their students and proteges are entrenched in various English Departments in Nigeria.

Thus, the British cultural coup of 1960 (the year of Nigeria's political independence!) has guaranteed that England's literary tradition continues to hold sway in Nigeria today. If these men had acquired a strong African nationalist consciousness, and an active one, during their university days, what great things might they not now be doing with the Departments they have inherited? Might they not be accelerating the decolonization of African literary culture? Might they not, for instance, have dis-established these English Departments and, as Ngugi and his colleagues have done in Kenya, replaced them with afrocentric Departments of Literature? Instead of holing themselves up in the institutional pits the British prepared and handed over to them, the following is an example of what our situation requires that they should have done in order to prepare for that day when the colonial languages we have inherited shall be retired from their role as the official languages of African countries:

The departments of European languages and literatures in African universities need to have been, and still should be, abolished and replaced by three others: (a) a Department of African Languages, Oratures and Literatures; (b) a Department of Comparative Literatures; and (c) a Department of Colonial Languages. We shall elaborate on this project in the concluding section of Chapter 4. Suffice it now to say that one central premise of such a project is that though, as a temporary necessity, we have to learn to read, speak and write the colonial languages bequeathed to Africa as official languages, it should be recognized that these languages can be learned without the encumberance of the national literatures of the European imperial nations. If it is argued, for instance, that the study of English language literature is indispensable to the learning of the English language, then, instead of being made to imbibe the imperialist and anti-African prejudices of England's literature, English should be taught to Nigerians through the English language literatures of Africa, Afro-America, and the Afro-Caribbean; that is, through that current of the English language into which African peoples have poured their experiences of the world.

Another central premise is that only by the intensive and extensive nurturing of African languages, oratures and literatures will the ground be prepared for the emergence of a pan-African language and literature. And a third central premise is that all non-African literatures should be treated as equals, and should be studied for whatever contribution they might be able to make to the fashioning of a modern African literature. For we have much to learn from the literatures of the peoples of the non-Western world.

These considerations prompt a fourth central premise: that center place in the Faculties of Arts and Letters of African universities ought, by right, to be given to the Department of African Languages, Oratures and Literatures, and certainly *not* to the Department of any European or colonial language. And while the Department of Comparative Literatures would need to be permanent but ancillary, the Department of Colonial Languages would have to be ancillary and transient, and would be abolished when the European languages are dis-established as the official languages of African countries.

Now, a generation after independence, when such measures should long have come into effect, we are only beginning to grope our way to see and consider them! And what did we waste that time doing on the cultural front? Quarrelling over negritude; denouncing it with empty slogans like tigritude, when we should, instead, have studied it, understood it, and extracted, corrected and improved upon the usable parts of its impulses and its purposes. Having allowed ourselves to be browbeaten, by "duikeritude" and "tigritude," into the erroneous and self-crippling opinion that we did not need any active African nationalist consciousness; having allowed ourselves to be drugged with the view that a silent unremonstrative and "indifferent acceptance" of ourselves is the brave and mature thing to do—and all this in the face of snide and virulent imperialist propaganda against our humanity!—we acquiesced in the self-hobbling Soyinkaesque proposition that "the less self-conscious the African is, and the more innately his individual qualities appear in his writing, the more seriously he will be taken as an artist of exciting dignity." But Soyinka's audience appears to have never bothered to ask him a crucial question: taken seriously by whom? By Soyinka's British manipulators and promoters? If them, why should their opinion matter in Africa?

And while doing those individualistic, silent and tigritudinous leaps of indifferent self-acceptance which Soyinka had prescribed, many of his generation have been too busy burying their group nationalist consciousness to do much about rooting out the disorienting cultural apparatus which the departing British left among us. They have been too busy celebrating their individualist selves to join their voices together in a concerted nationalist roar to scare off further Western cultural intrusions.

What Soyinka and his tigritude pack conveniently chose to forget is that it takes an active collective consciousness for even a group of real tigers to know when they must roar together, announcing their tigritude in unmistakable terms and thereby scaring off hunters. Even tigers must know when to put themselves in a fighting mood and pounce together to prevent their being ambushed and shot down. There are indeed situations when silent and indifferent self-acceptance, even by fierce tigers and other powerful beasts, is not enough; times and circumstances when such an attitude plays into the hands of those who would destroy them. But Soyinka, with all his trumpeted "vision," fails to see that.

Let us all bear actively in mind that the British, in their imperialist guile, will slow down what they cannot prevent; and will guide astray any movement which they cannot block, and which they deem dangerous to their hegemony. And in their campaign to slow down and guide astray any active nationalist consciousness in the literature of their African colonies and neo-colonies, Soyinka served them as pointman and demolition expert. Soyinka's success has wasted for us a generation of opportunities for our cultural liberation. This lamentable waste should indicate the enormity of our loss from that British cultural coup in which Wole Soyinka, who delights in masquerading as the authentic and quintessential African literary force, played so quisling a role.

THE FOSTERING OF EUROMODERNISM IN NIGERIAN POETRY

Once euromodernism was implanted in a strategic group of Nigerian poets and critics, they began themselves to foster it through example and precept. The main part of this task has been shouldered by the critics, and they have carried it out primarily (1) by cultivating the Hopkins Disease and its allied obscurantisms, and (2) by strenuously promoting an anti-African outlook in Nigerian literary culture. How have they gone about doing these things?

The Cultivation of Obscurantism

In an article published in *Nigeria Magazine,* No. 89, Michael Echeruo, a representative voice of the Ibadan-Nsukka school of euromodernist critics, claimed that

> one of the problems facing the Nigerian writer today in transferring from indigenous to modern poetry is that of suppressing the over-explicit nature of traditional reflective poetry and of encouraging a more subtle complicating of narration, reflection and resolution.
>
> (Echeruo 1966: 150)

First of all, the problem facing the Nigerian writer is not in transferring from "indigenous" to "modern" poetry, but in transferring from the "modern," in which he has been educated and which he practices, to the traditional modes of African poetic expression. Secondly, if anything, the "subtle complicating of narration, reflection and resolution" has to be discouraged. The devotion to artificial complexity and gratuitous obscurity is a legacy of the modernist poetry of the West and goes against the grain of African poetic tradition.

Echeruo's wrongheaded dictum is an item in a program whose overall goal is to shepherd Nigerian poetry onto a euromodernist wilderness pasture, covered with an imported, attenuated and mutilated version of Western modernism, and there to graze it full of the Hopkins Disease. Critics who dissent from their program are denounced as "neo-Tarzanists" and "pretenders to the crown of Pontifex Maximus of African poetics," an undesirable crown which some euromodernist critic presumably already wears.

If the euromodernist critics should have their way, our poets will be coached in the Hopkinsian recipe for writing "serious" poetry, and the poetry reading public will be browbeaten into a taste for the vile products of the Hopkins Disease. The critics appear to have no problem in imposing their views on the poets since they have them as captive apprentices in their classrooms. The poetry reading public, however, is not entirely captive, and has from time to time tried to resist shepherding from such critics. When this has happened, the critics have tried to intimidate them by blaming them for an alleged lack of sophistication or "vision." For example, in a series of radio lectures broadcast in Nigeria in 1973 and later printed as "Two Decades of Modern Nigerian Literature" (part of which was quoted earlier), Theo Vincent had this to say:

> The hue and cry against the incomprehensible nature
> of the poetry of some of our poets must be re-examined
> and part of the blame put on our own insensibility

and slavish inability to adjust to novel creations that
immensely enrich a universal store of vision.

(Vincent 1975: 59)

Other critics attempt to persuade the reading public that
it is not the poet's responsibility to be clear and understandable but rather the responsibility and, indeed, the privilege
of the reader to puzzle out the obscurantist crudities of the
euromodernist Nigerian poets. Some of them go to great
lengths to invent fanciful justifications for the glaring faults
of craft. Some even go as far as to try to persuade their
audience that these blemishes are in fact perfections. Their
arguments for obscurity contain a network of prejudices
against simplicity and lucidity, and embody the view that
for African poetry to acquire the obscurantist aims and
deracinated habits of the Hopkinsian strand of euromodernist
poetry, constitutes progress, the only form of progress appropriate to these times.

It is useful to examine the catalog of excuses which these
critics have offered in support of obscurantism in the poets.
Donatus Nwoga, in a spirited defence of obscurity in his
essay, "Obscurity and Commitment in Modern African Poetry,"
serves up an engaging variety of excuses:

> Finally, I think it needs to be pointed out that
> there are degrees and variations of obscurity in modern
> African poetry. As we have seen, there is a large
> body of poetry which is direct and simple in the
> expression of idea or feeling. Other poems have the
> semblance of obscurity because of their complicated
> syntax, and the reader needs only to restore the words
> to their normal order or supply the missing links to
> come to a position to appreciate the poems. Some
> other poems are found difficult because they are involved
> in the exploration of ideas which, in the first place,
> are difficult of comprehension to many, or describing
> a situation with which the reader may be unfamiliar.

In this case, glossaries and explanations will open the way to appreciation. In other poems the vastness of the poet's field of reference is the source of obscurity. The poet takes his images and figures from areas ranging from distant civilizations through a variety of literary sources to local myths, legends, and rituals, and it would require the same breadth of reference for the reader to come to grips with his work.

Two sources of obscurity remain, and these offer more problems to the conscientious reader. The first arises from the tendency of the poet to give unusual and private symbolic meaning to his images. This is where the break with African tradition is most pronounced. And this is where the experimental nature of modern poetry can lead the unwary or unconscientious poet astray. I suggest however that the successful creative poet, through a continuous and sincere usage, finally clarifies the meaning of his symbols which then pass into the tradition.

The second of the causes of complexity is that which belongs as much to the 'modern' as to the traditional approach to poetic creation and presents a nearly insurmountable problem to a mind restricted to the logical mode of poetic creation. It operates on the level of continuity of symbolic meaning, using images which on their literal level either make no meaning or even appear to conflict. Passages are constructed with the metaphors as their semantic constituents. This approach produced for example Awoonor-Williams' *Songs of Sorrow* and Christopher Okigbo's *Path of Thunder*. It demands that the reader escape from the clutches of logical mental sequence and release the mind and imagination to reach out and acquire the impact of images which accumulate to drum in their meaning.

(Nwoga 1974: 36–37)

In other words, Nwoga attributes obscurity to one or more of the following six sources:

1. allusiveness ("vastness of the poet's field of reference")
2. non-logical v. logical modes of presentation
3. privateness of the theme and symbolism being treated in the poem
4. complicated syntax
5. exploration of unfamiliar and difficult ideas
6. one source of obscurity named earlier in his essay is the influence of foreign literary traditions and models, in particular, Hopkins, Pound and Eliot.

A handbook on the myriad sources of obscurity would be very useful if it aimed at helping the writers to avoid those sources of obscurity. But such a purpose seems very far from Nwoga's intentions. That obscurity has such a variety of sources would seem to be, for him, something to know in order to perpetrate more and more obscurities. As it were, why limit yourself to one or two kinds of obscurity when you can have more? But his encouraging rationalizations won't do, and deserve to be exploded.

On the question of obscurity allegedly due to the influence of Pound, etc., we ask: are there no Poundian poets whose language is not obscure? What about Ifeanyi Menkiti who apprenticed himself on Pound and whom no one in his right mind could accuse of linguistic obscurity? It should perhaps be emphasized that the issue is not mimesis but *botched mimesis*. As Satchmo once said, it doesn't matter who you blow like so long as you blow good.

Above all, we should add, you should not blame that which you imitate for your own failure in imitating it well. For those who choose to imitate the obscurantist manner of Hopkins, we would like to point out that *botched mimesis* extends to wrong headedness in the very choice of what to imitate. This responsibility cannot be escaped by any writer. Though Shakespeare is a great writer by general consent, this does not license one to copy and repeat his failings; in particular, one should not feel licensed to repeat what for Shakespeare might have been virtues but in our times would be literary vices. So you've got to blow it good *for your times.*

Moreover, to the unwary who try to use Pound to rationalize their stupidities, it should be pointed out that Pound himself disclaimed responsibility, and rightly so, for the botches of his imitators and pretenders to his legacy. In "Ezra Pound's Voice of Silence," an article in the *New York Times Magazine* of January 9, 1972, Alan Levy reports the following portion of an interview with Pound:

> I quote from the next generation of poets: W. H. Auden's assertion that "there are few living poets . . . who could say, 'My work would be exactly the same if Mr. Pound had never lived.' " Then I quote from yet another generation of poets, Harvey Shapiro, who told me: "Ezra Pound remains very much alive in the States as a strong, maybe the strongest, influence on young poets today." And I ask Pound: "Have you any reaction to this?"
>
> Silence.
>
> "How closely do you follow the American literary scene today?"
>
> Silence.
>
> "Are there any younger writers you particularly admire or detest?"
>
> Silence again, but the eyes flash, so I wait. And then it comes like an angry thunderclap: *"Disorder! Disorder! I can't be blamed for all this damned disorder."*
>
> (Levy 1972: 59)

Pound's retort, we believe, would be applicable to any other allegations of deleterious influence. Our artists have to learn to be responsible for their own products. No matter who influenced them, their work is their own, and the praise or blame for it is entirely theirs. Critics who do not hold them to this code of responsibility are doing a disservice to both the artists and their audience.

By the way, to a question so inane as whether Pound admires or detests any younger poets three or four generations down the drain from his fountainhead, Pound might, if he had chosen, have replied as Yeats did to a similar question: "Was there ever a dog that praised his fleas"? What the questioner forgot was that admiration or detestation has to be merited. You do not ask a king whether he admires or detests a laborer, for it is hard to see that a laborer belongs to the category of persons whom a king might possibly admire or detest without lowering his dignity and belittling himself. But of course, an interviewer has to ask questions, however ludicrous, or there will be no interview.

On the excuse of complicated syntax, and Nwoga's misplaced request to the reader to "restore the words to their normal order or supply the missing links to come to a position to appreciate the poems," we ask: Why should the poet mangle the syntax and scramble the words in the first place? It is surely an excess of poetic license for the poet to mutilate the very medium of his communication only to force the reader to repair it in order to understand him. As we said earlier, poetry is not a jigsaw puzzle or any other kind of puzzle. We would also like to point out that the reader is neither the writer's editor nor his grammar teacher. Besides, why should the reader be asked to do the writer's work for him? Is there any good reason why the writer should ignore or unilaterally abjure the rudiments of his medium? Who but an irresponsible critic would encourage a writer to do so?

On obscurities arising from the poet's exploration of unfamiliar and difficult ideas, it should be pointed out that a writer who has any modicum of respect for his audience and who values their time and attention, would not force his unfinished explorations upon them. He would rather wait until he has worked his ideas through and found a way of presenting them so that they would be comprehensible to many. An audience is entirely within its rights to boo off the stage and walk out on an ill-rehearsed play—which is what an unfinished exploration is—especially if they've paid to come and see it. And a critic is inviting to have his head bashed in if he stands at the door and tries to constrain the audience to sit it through. The critic might brandish all manner of glossaries and explanations and rave reviews, but to no avail, after the audience has tasted the porridge and found it stale and mouldy. Such a critic would have no defense if he should be hauled off and charged with inciting the public to riot.

The attempt to use the vastness of the poet's field of reference to justify some types of obscurity does not stand up under examination. Allusions are a permissible literary device, but they demand to be used well and judiciously, with an eye to what the primary audience can be expected to have access to. As is the case with the introduction of expository material of any kind, the issue is to recognize what the primary audience can be presumed to know or have ready access to, and find a proper vehicle for introducing into the work in hand, in a manner comprehensible to them, those other things which they cannot be presumed to know.

One must know one's primary audience well in order to handle the allusive technique properly. A certain homogeneity in the audience, in terms of a shared culture, history, and pool of facts, is essential in determining what would be a permissible range of allusions for it. This consideration rules out, as a matter of general practice, idiosyncratic and private allusions, and those in-jokes to which the primary audience is not privy. Thus, the writer has a grave responsibility in employing this literary technique. Of course a lack of judiciousness could be compounded by a writer's willful use of allusions to show up the ignorance of his own audience.

Such contemptuous one-up-manship is a decadent mannerism which no self-respecting audience will put up with.

In the African situation, given the diversity of oral traditions, languages, geographic localities, histories, cultures and the funds of reference, the need for expository care is great. If a writer has to allude at all, he should do so with African materials rather than with non-African materials, but always with the necessary care in light of the issues raised above. For what the Ewe man knows or can properly be presumed to know, the Igbo man or the Xhosa man may not. A safe rule would be to consider whether a particular allusion is such as would normally be recognized in all parts of Africa, and if not, to so introduce it that any African reader would become sufficiently acquainted with the matter from entirely within the work.

Similarly, when one is writing for a sub-region of Africa, for the members of a given country, province, or town, or for one's co-workers in an office, the particular audience in mind will determine the range of permissible allusion. When material that was written with a particular primary audience in mind is made available to a larger secondary audience, there may be a need to either alter the allusions or supply glossaries and footnotes for that larger audience. This of course might be done by the writer or by an editor who knows the permissible range of allusions for this larger secondary audience.

Nwoga can take no comfort from these considerations by claiming that Okigbo, for instance, was writing for a small educated elite, for it is from this same small educated elite that complaints about Okigbo's obscure allusions have come. Thus, for his supposed primary audience, his allusions did not work when, for instance, they were either to esoterica from ancient Sumerian tablets or totally idiosyncratic and buried in his personal history. In short, vastness of the poets field of reference cannot be used to excuse obscurity.

216

On the matter of unusual and private symbolism, we must draw attention to the primary need in publicly communicated material for a publicly available symbolic meaning. If a passage has this public symbolic meaning and you later discover that it also has a private one, you can feel enriched by the discovery; but if it has no public one, you feel poorer from the outset, and would be within your rights to consider the passage problematic and obscure, especially if the ambiguity or obscurity is of the sort that is intrinsically non-resolvable.

Nwoga appears to be confused in his comments regarding obscurity that allegedly could arise from a non-logical mode of organizing images. Contrary to his insinuations, a demand for clarity is not a call to restrict poetry to the logical and discursive mode, for the non-logical, symbolic or surrealistic organization of images is an old and tried technique of poetry in many cultures, the African included. The demand for clarity applies to both modes of organization. The issue is that of taking care to do it well, given that when it is done without appropriate care, it leads to confusion and obscurity. One image misplaced in its sequence can obscure a whole poem, whereas an appropriate and strategically placed image can clarify and lend force to the entire sequence. Contrary to Nwoga's argument, the point is not that this technique can sometimes work without producing obscurity, but that it should be so handled as not to produce obscurity. Experience can be communicated in many ways; the inescapable requirement is that it be communicated.

Whereas Nwoga's defense of Okigbo's obscurities are of the rather standard type, Stanley Macebuh has invented some quite curious explanations and justifications for Soyinka's obscurities. In his essay "Poetics and the Mythic Imagination," he tells us:

> Part, at least, of our impression of the harsh inscru-
> tableness of Soyinka's language may be seen as an

exact equivalent in words of that unease of the mind that is the lot of all those who have suffered a modification of vision through colonialism.

(Macebuh 1975–76: 80)

Well, well, well! If Macebuh is right, what else is there to do but send condolences to Wole Soyinka! It is indeed a loss to all Africa is one of our sharper minds has suffered at the hands of colonialism so severe a modification of vision that it is now impossible for him to communicate his vision in accents we can understand!

Macebuh goes on to suggest other ancillary explanations for the obscurity of Soyinka's English. He says:

The roots of Soyinka's English are uncompromisingly Anglo-Saxon rather than Hellenic or Latinate because they represent for him the closest proximation to the primal roots of Yoruba cultic diction. But the virtue of 'originality' lies not merely in its freshness or quaintness but indeed in its vitality, in its ability to evoke in the mind a memory of the dynamism of the original Yoruba. For Soyinka, particularly in those poems in which legend, tradition and ancestral custom constitute the internal structure of his poetry, is in fact a *translator*. . . . And if it is true, as we have suggested, that Soyinka is a 'translator,' we may then raise the question whether effective translation is a matter of equating that which is to be translated as closely as possible to the verbose sensibility of con- temporary times, or of seeking to convey the vast ambience of meaning implicit in the original.

(Macebuh 1975–76: 82)

This is a most tendentious defense. First of all, if one does not translate for one's times, whatever one's feelings may be about the supposed verbosity of its sensibility, who does one translate for? For the dead? Though we doubt it, it may well be true that Soyinka in his poetry is a translator rather than an original poet. And if it is true that what he has translated in his poems is cultic Yoruba material, it may very well be that they are best rendered using English words of Anglo-Saxon origin. But still, we see no reason why Anglo-Saxon-derived diction has to be obscure, contorted, and syntactically mangled. If we are being told that fidelity to Yoruba cultic diction compels such obscurantist distortions in the English into which they are rendered, then we must resort to comparing Soyinka's performance as a translator with the performance of others who have translated Yoruba mythic or cultic material into English. For example, what about the translations of Ifa divination poetry by Bakare Gbadamosi and Ulli Beier in their book, *Yoruba Poetry*? If it is objected that the co-translator, Ulli Beier, is not a native speaker of Yoruba, what about Wande Abimbola's translations of poems from that same Ifa divination corpus, as in the following sample:

Títítí lorí ogbó;
Bììrìpé bììrìpé lomi ọkọ̀ọ́ dà

Dídà lomi ọkọ̀ọ́ dà,
Omi ọkọ̀ kìí yí;
A díá fún Oòduà atẹ̀wọ̀nrọ̀.

Nwón ní bó rúbọ,
Lọ́dún yìí ní ó goróyèe baba ẹ̀;

Bì ó rúbọ,
Lọ́dún yìí ní ó goróyèe baba ẹ̀.

Sàbẹ̀ẹ́ lóró,
Tògún lọ́fà.
Nwọn ò jẹ́ ṣígun ìlóbìnrin
Kí mbà wọn lọ:
Mbá mú pa,
Mà mú tá;
Mbá mú relé lọ ṣobìnrin.

Ọràn bí òyí bí òyí;
A díá fún itú,
Ọkọ ewúrẹ́
Ọràn bí òyí bí òyí;
A díá fún àgbò,
Ọkọ ìlagùtàn.
Ọràn bí òyí bí òyí;
A díá fún àparò yẹyẹ̀,
Omọ olúoko.
Ọràn bí òyí bí òyí;
A díá fún akérépọ́njú. . . . .

The-soul-of-elders-is-everlasting;
The-water-inside-a-canoe-moves-backwards-and-
    forwards;
The-water-inside-a-canoe-only-splashes-about
It-does-not-spill-away;
Cast Ifa for Oodua, he who has enough powers to
    soften an iron chain;
They said if he made sacrifice,
It was in that year that he would ascend the throne of
    his fathers.
And, if he did not make sacrifice,
It was in that year that he would ascend the throne of
    his fathers.
The people of Sabẹẹ have poison.
The people of Togun have arrows.
They dare not open up the siege of the city women,
I would have gone with them.
I would have killed some,
I would have sold into slavery,
And I would have taken some home as wives.

Matters-that-seem-always-unstable;
Cast Ifa for He-goat,
The husband of all goats.
Matters-that-seem-always-unstable;
Cast Ifa for Ram,
The husband of all sheep.

Matters-that-seem-always-unstable;
Cast Ifa for the greatly-feathered-bushfowl,
Son of the King of farmland.
Matters-that-seem-always-unstable;
Cast Ifa for akereponju. . . . .

(Abimbola 1968: 7)

Is the English diction in Wande Abimbola's rendition unfaithful to the "primal roots" of the Yoruba original? Or would Macebuh argue that Ifa divination poetry is not cultic? If so, he would do well to tell us what would qualify as Yoruba cultic diction, and in any case he would have to show where whatever he considers Yoruba cultic material and diction is present in Soyinka's poems.

Ultimately, it is up to native-speaking Yoruba scholars to determine whether Abimbola or Soyinka is being faithful to Yoruba cultic diction in their translations. Whatever their answer, we must point out that translations are judged by the standards of the language in which they exist and not by those of the language out of which they were made. Thus Soyinka's translations, if that is what his poems are, must be judged by the standards of contemporary English expression. Soyinka's translations have to be judged in the same manner as those by Okot p'Bitek out of the Acholi, Kunene out of the Zulu, Hampate-Ba out of the Bambara, D. T. Niane out of the Mandinka, Birago Diop out of the Wolof, etc.

Indeed, quite contrary to Macebuh's speculations, there is evidence that when Soyinka is undeniably translating from the Yoruba, he is able to restrain his obscurantist proclivities and produce poems in English which have surface clarity. For instance, in his essay "Salutations to the Gut" Soyinka translates several Yoruba *oriki* into clear, contemporary English. Here is a typical example:

Og'aja f'owo m'eke
Ebi Opapala

221

O sun sile ro dun-dun
O sun sile ka gi aja
Ebi o pa mole o ni oun je aya
Ebi pa Sule o j'obo
Iwo ko jeun sun
O ji, o ni o la alakala
Ki o to sun ki o ti ri irikuri
Ebi lo pa orisa oko
To fi ti ina bo ogbo isu kan
Ebi npa mi ko se fi ife wi.

Bends you double belly clutching
Hunger the All-powerful
Try to sleep the big drum rumbles
Try to sleep your eyes rove round rafters
Full-bellied the Moslem swears he will break no taboo
When Hunger seized Sule he wolfed a monkey
Supperless to bed, you woke
Complained of horrors and night fantasies
Did not your tribulations dear friend
Begin right from your waking hours
It was Hunger that maddened the Farm Deity
Goaded him to set fire to the yam plot
'I am famished' is said with a bellow
Not piped with a thin whistle.

(Soyinka 1969: 359–60)

From the foregoing it would appear that when Soyinka has a known Yoruba original to guide and restrain him, he can indeed manage to avoid the tortured, obscurantist language which characterizes his own poems. If he could do so with non-cultic material, we see no reason why he could not do so with cultic material. Unlike Macebuh, we find no grounds whatsoever to appeal to Yoruba diction, cultic or not, or to any other "ethnocentric compulsions," to explain away what Macebuh himself has listed in his essay as the characteristics of Soyinka's poetry—namely, its difficult, harsh, tortured language, archaic syntax, impenetrable verbal structures, cacophony, disruptiveness and archaism (Macebuh 1975–76: 80, 83). Soyinka's poems, botches and all, are Soyinka's, and he is entirely responsible for them. Why Macebuh should choose to blame the Yoruba language for Soyinka's idiosyncratic linguistic misdemeanors in English escapes us. But just as we have done in the case of those who tried to blame the African oral tradition for real or imagined shortcomings in the African novel, we would like to urge Macebuh and critics of his kind to cease and desist from such abuse of African oral tradition.

Nigeria's euromodernist poets and critics who defend obscurantism appear to have sandbagged themselves behind a complex of prejudices and attitudes against simplicity and clarity due to several mistaken notions of what these are. When you tell them to be simple, they react as if you were telling them to be simpleminded. When you ask them to be clear, they react as if you were asking them to be superficial. When you talk to them of vividness, they restrict the term to the vividness of an epiphany or a mystic flash. When you question the surface complexity of their diction, they react as if you were questioning the sophistication of their language. When you question their wilful obscurity or private esoterism, they react as if their status as profound and imaginative thinkers were under attack. Nwoga, for instance, prefers to see simplicity as a manifestation of artistic incompetence. He finds it

> necessary to conclude that simplicity is a factor of artistic incompetence. There is a simplicity of language which is a result not of artistic control but of failure of knowledge; a simplicity of perception resulting from an inability to reach out to any subtle connotations from a setting, event, or situation; a naivety of thought which sees none of the varied implications, the subtleties and deeper reflections, attaching to a projected notion. These might be 'versified intelligibilities' but they do not make exciting poetry.
> (Nwoga 1974: 29)

223

We would merely like to reassure Nwoga that in specific cases, complexity as well as simplicity can be a consequence of artistic incompetence. Neither simplicity nor complexity by itself is a sufficient condition for excellence. To complicate the simple is as much a violation of fidelity to reality as it is to simplify the complex. For poetry involves a certain congruence of the manner of presentation and the matter being treated. And as for "versified intelligibilities" not making exciting poetry, it may be useful to point out that *unintelligibilities,* versified or not, do not make poetry at all.

In his essay "Neo-Tarzanism: The Poetics of Pseudo-Tradition," Soyinka disagrees with our appraisal of Matei Markwei's poem "Life in Our Village." In the original version of this essay, we had observed that Markwei's poem is "simple and vivid," and that it "conveys the experience of moonlight play." Here is the poem once again:

> In our little village
> When elders are around
> Boys must not look at girls
> And girls must not look at boys
> Because the elders say
> That is not good.
>
> Even when night comes
> Boys must play separately,
> Girls must play separately.
> But humanity is weak
> So boys and girls meet.
>
> The boys play hide and seek
> And the girls play hide and seek.
> The boys know where the girls hide
> And the girls know where the boys hide—
> So in their hide and seek,
> Boys seek girls,
> Girls seek boys,
> And each to each sing
> Songs of love.

Soyinka's reaction is as follows:

> This trite, prosaic, coy, kindergarten drivel which my
> seven-year old daughter would be ashamed to write is
> extolled by the troika critics. ... In what line do
> Markwei's verses achieve a moment of "vividness"?
> Do Messrs Chinweizu and Co., understand the word?
>
> (Soyinka 1975: 40)

A naive question. For the vividness is not embodied in
a single line but in the totality of the experience as rendered
in the poem. That Soyinka should demand that "vividness"
be contained in a single identifiable line is absurd, for, surely,
it is the vividness of a scene presented, rather than that of
any single verbal line in its presentation, that ought to count
here. The mistake in Soyinka's notion of the kind of vividness
required here is revealed by his demand for a *moment* of
vividness. Is he perhaps looking for a sudden vividness of
an epiphany or mystic flash of the kind that comes to a
Zen-Buddhist monk walking through a Bush of Revelations,
or the kind that comes to a desert hermit, who prepares for
it by contorting his body into a knotted rope, on the 99th
day of his terminal fast? It should be clear that a "moment
of vividness" which suddenly clarifies all is the wrong kind
to expect in a depiction of a dramatic scene. Each item or
event which goes to build up the picture of moonlight play
needs to be vividly presented; and the totality of the portrait
needs to be vivid. But there need not be one line in which
all the vividness is concentrated. A presentation which meets
these requirements cannot be condemned for lacking what it
does not need.

These prejudices and attitudes all come out of the euromodernist basket, as we shall see below. And as is normal
for euromodernists, attempts are made to shift the responsibility for clarification of a work to the readers and critics.
For instance, Nwoga, at the end of his essay rationalizing

and justifying obscurity, tries to mollify the reader's resistance by assuring him that

> time, study, and critical commentary, will continue to reduce genuine obscurity and dismiss the polemics about presumed obscurity.

> (Nwoga 1974: 37)

This of course reiterates his long-standing view that

> it would be naive, however, to think that because the poems are written by fellow Africans, they should be understood, appreciated and enjoyed immediately and without any effort by the African reader. No writing of any value can yield its beauties so easily to any reader. We know, for example, that the English have been writing books upon books to help themselves understand their own poets. We must be ready to work for our enjoyment and our mental and emotional development.

> (Nwoga 1967: preface)

Quite the contrary! Many English writers can be "understood, appreciated and enjoyed immediately," not "without *any* effort" but surely without undue effort by the English and even by the African reader. They yield their beauties readily: you don't have to be an erudite scholar to understand and appreciate them. Many Nigerian poets do not yield their beauties readily to anyone, *solely* because they are syntactically eccentric. Whatever deeper meanings they may have are barricaded behind their surface obscurities.

But let us, for the sake of argument, assume that many English writers are syntactically difficult. Are they usually the best? We would like to urge that, insofar as we must keep touch with the native practitioners of the foreign language in which we presently write, we should keep touch with the vigorous and vivid among them. Though we doubt it, it may well be true that "no writing of any value can yield its beauties so easily to any reader." But that is no excuse for promoting a cult of syntactic obfuscation, for cluttering the surface of our writing with assorted linguistic impedimenta whose only end is to make our scholars write tedious books of gossip and explication to help us understand what our poets are said to be saying.

Nwoga's approach, besides being elitist, makes for waste work. What one person, the writer, could very adequately do, that is, taking care of allusions, grammar and syntax, honing his images and organizing them well, etc., should not be dumped upon the vaster number of readers. Just consider the economics of it all: if it takes ten minutes for a person working under the best circumstances, where the right books and the proper explanations are at hand, to uncover one allusion or straighten out the mangled syntax of a phrase, that would mean that for a national readership of one million, this author will have wasted ten million minutes of national time, wasted incalculable calories of energy, whereas the whole waste could have been avoided by ten minutes of the writer's time!

As if this wasn't bad enough, these elitist critics and writers expect to be praised for such conduct. We should bear in mind that we in Africa are engaged in various tasks of national development and are suffering from manpower shortages. An awareness of this fact enables us to appreciate the full enormity of this kind of thoughtless demand upon our time. Some critics might claim that such exercise in hunting down allusions and puzzling out obscurities is good training for the mind; but we submit that it should be seen rather as an intellectual species of unproductive waste work where a student under punishment is asked by a prefect to dig a ditch and then fill it right back up. If he had instead been sent to clear an overgrown path, or to sweep a room, his work would have been useful.

An interesting implication of Nwoga's prescription would be that our judgment of a text should depend not upon a direct confrontation with the text but upon an accumulation of critical commentaries and explications upon the text over an extended period of time. It is as if we should base our estimate of Shakespeare not on the direct impact of his work upon us but rather on the accumulation of commentaries upon it over the centuries! Such a view, of course, is more likely to come from a professional commentator than from the creative writers themselves.

We must emphasize that working to extract depths of rich meaning in a poem is one thing: toiling to make elementary sense out of a rubble of jargon is useless work. No one needs that. We have better uses for our time and energies. Rather than urge the reader to suffer through unnecessary difficulties, Nwoga would do well to demand from our writers that they work at writing vigorously and lucidly. We should never forget that easy writing makes for hard reading, and hard writing makes for easy reading. If writers do not strive to be discourteous to their readers, they should make their reading as easy as possible. If they don't they can't complain if they are neglected. It should be pointed out that if in the African situation there were many more poets available, and many more works from the oral tradition in print, few would bother with these obscurantist euromodernist poets who now clutter up the landscape.

The critics who have helped to lead our poets astray have a responsibility to now help those poets to understand that depth of meaning is not a matter of syntactic jugglery; that profundity is not a matter of wilful obscurity and private esoterism; that vividness and imaginative challenge are not exclusively a matter of epiphanies and mystic flash; that simplicity is not synonymous with simple-mindedness, nor complexity with genius; that clarity is not synonymous with superficiality, nor surface complexity of language an index of artistic dexterity; and that, above all, simplicity should not automatically be regarded as evidence of artistic incompetence. In their search for models, our writers and critics would do well to look at the best of Afro-American writing. Langston Hughes, for instance. His is writing that attains surface lucidity, yet can carry an abundance of rich meaning. Consider the rich historical overtones of "The Negro Speaks of Rivers":

> I've known rivers!
> I've known rivers ancient as the world and older than
> the flow of human blood in human veins.
>
> My soul has grown deep like the rivers.
>
> I bathed in the Euphrates when dawns were young.
> I built my hut near the Congo and it lulled me to
> sleep.
> I looked upon the Nile and raised the pyramids above
> it.
> I heard the singing of the Mississippi when Abe Lincoln
> went down to New Orleans, and I've seen its
> muddy bosom turn all golden in the sunset.
>
> I've known rivers!
> Ancient, dusky rivers.
>
> My soul has grown deep like the rivers.

Or the stark potency of "Suicide's Note":

> The calm,
> Cool face of the river
> Asked me for a kiss.

Our insistence on clarity may be taking the yam out of the mouths of a certain breed of scholars. But then, poetry is not for scholarly explication but for understanding by the people. Poetry should speak directly to the reader, not through the elaborate footnotes of scholars.

229

The Anti-African Outlook and How It Is Promoted

The *tigritude* outcry, as we have already shown, succeeded in driving out of Nigerian poetry the issue of a nationalist outlook; it also drove sympathizers with such an outlook off center stage and underground, as it were. In this atmosphere, arguments about the necessity for a nationalist outlook degenerated and retreated into debates about which language, European or African, African writers should employ. Other aspects of literary craft such as techniques, forms, treatments and attitudes were left, for the most part, unexamined. Even the argument over which language to use practically petered out soon after the famous 1962 Kampala Conference. Obiajunwa Wali fired a salvo called "The Dead End of African Literature?" in *Transition*, No. 10 in 1963, provoked a flurry of responses (No. 11), briefly replied to them (No. 12), and quit the arena of controversy, and in support of his convictions went off and wrote his 346-page novel *Ngozi Dili Chukwu,* in Igbo. Thereafter, an Anglo-Saxon peace reigned in the polemical pages of African literature on this matter.

When the nationalist issue was resurrected in a form in which it could neither be quietly ignored nor quickly scotched, defensive outcries arose from the tigritude camp of African soldiers for British cultural imperialism. Some cried out against commitment, others cried out against what they fancied as "neo-Tarzanism." And what was the provocation? It was a little essay entitled "Towards the Decolonization of African Literature," written by us, which circulated in manuscript, starting in 1972, in the English Department of the University of Nigeria at Nsukka, and finally was published in 1974–75 (*Okike* 6 and 7; *Transition* 48). The two principal responses from the eurocentric camp were the essay "Obscurity and Commitment in African Literature" by Donatus Nwoga of the English Department, Nsukka (*African Literature Today* 6, 1974), offering up assorted apologies for

obscurantism and for lack of pro-African commitment, and
Wole Soyinka's "Neo-Tarzanism: The Poetics of Pseudo-
Tradition" (*Transition* 48, 1975). We shall examine the defenses
for universalism against African nationalism in poetry that
were put up by Nwoga and Soyinka.

For the purposes of his apologia, Nwoga interprets commitment as requiring that poets write on public themes and
especially on political matters. Based on this narrow interpretation of the term, he tries to explain away the absence
of political poetry and the prevalence of the privatist mode
of treating public themes, and he also attempts to show that
the privatist, "internal orientation of awareness" is also a
kind of commitment, albeit an unconscious one.

In 1962 Lewis Nkosi had criticised Nigerian writers in
the following words:

> The young writers of Nigeria can also be charged with
> a local form of romanticism; too often they regard
> their writing as a private human activity. The sym-
> bolism of their soliloquies becomes convoluted, private
> and obscure. . . . This sharp separation between lit-
> erature as an art form and its content has resulted in
> a kind of poetry and drama which seems to shy away
> from social criticism.
>
> (Quoted in Nwoga 1974: 39)

In reply to this criticism, which Nwoga himself admits
to be valid and pointed in the right direction, Nwoga proffers
the following apologia:

> Differences exist between the lives and social con-
> texts of the past and present. Where the pioneers were
> members of a new educated *élite* involved, by the
> circumstances of their prominence, in the political
> struggle for independence, the later poets belong to a
> more diffuse community of educated people with only
> a peripheral influence on the course of events. And

> the issues are less clear. The large public events of
> colonialism, setting up a dichotomy of indigenous ruled
> and foreign rulers, therefore calling for large and
> flamboyant public gestures, have given way to an
> internal situation of nagging minor issues. These issues
> are minor not in terms of their social consequences
> but because they break up into many facets that cannot
> easily be visualized in one big apocalyptic concept.
> Introspection becomes an understandable reaction in
> such a situation.
>
> (Nwoga 1974: 39)

This of course is a long-winded way of just saying:
colonialism is over, and therefore the themes found in the
poetry of Osadebay, Dei-Anang, Hayford, Senghor, and Diop
are no longer appropriate. Nwoga's position is indeed news,
and strange news at that. He probably had never understood
either neo-colonialism or cultural imperialism. If he had, he
would not claim or imply that with the ceremonial transfer
of colonial power from a white elite to a black elite, with
flag raising and anthem singing, colonialism and foreign rule
became a matter of the past, leaving only "nagging minor
issues." Direct rule might have ended, but what of indirect
rule? What of African political elites managing their independent nations for Europe's economic benefit? Or of intellectual elites managing Africa's minds for the benefit of
Western cultural imperialism? What of grand atrocities taking
place all over the continent—genocide, massacres, disappearance of political opponents, failures in food production
and distribution, the circus of all manner of self-seeking
leaders, political disintegrations, erosion of traditional mores,
destruction of self-respect, the swamping of our markets and
lives with Western junk, the waste and under-utilization of
our resources, the cheap and wholesale export of our irre-
placeable minerals, the intervention of troops and munitions
merchants from outside Africa in African affairs? And so on.

Would Nwoga consider these to be "nagging minor issues?" Are these not fit material for our poets? Perhaps by "nagging minor issues" Nwoga has in mind such things as whether one should drive a white Mercedes-Benz or a Silver Cloud Rolls Royce; or whether one should have 12 agbadas instead of 11, or 10 three-piece suits instead of 9, or 5 trunks-full of lace and gold instead of 4, or whether one should pay his houseboy the approved Udoji-scale salary or less.

On this matter of an alleged disappearance of colonialism, Nigeria's crop of poets and critics, who routinely parade their claims to "vision" and perceptiveness, must be a dull-sighted lot indeed if they do not see what a lot of ordinary Nigerians see and decry. Such self-parading but dull-sighted "legislators" ought perhaps to remain permanently unacknowledged.

While Nwoga points out correctly that an assortment of public themes have entered into the poetry of Nigerian poets, he fails to recognize or explore the consequences of the privatist manner in which they have usually handled these themes. Their privatist manner wraps in dense obscurities whatever they have to say that might be of public importance. If in doubt consult Soyinka's treatment of consequences of irresponsible fucking in "In Paths of Rain." How does such privatist treatment of a public theme contribute to public understanding? How can it "have the effect of changing men's consciousness and making them aware of what previously they had not even guessed?" (Nwoga 1974: 39–40). As regards such privatist treatments of public themes, Ama Ata Aidoo's outcry is still germane:

> We are waiting around for answers and praying that those who can see things will sometimes speak in accents which the few of us who read English can understand. For we are tired of betrayals, broken promises and forever remaining in the dark.
>
> (Aidoo 1968: 41)

233

Further, Nwoga would have us believe of our poets that:

> Their specifically African commitment is in their cir-
> cumstances—their historical, social, and spiritual, envi-
> ronment. That they are African men, reacting to a set
> of African circumstances from a sensibility developed
> from an African upbringing, and the unconscious con-
> ception of art influenced by their exposure to traditional
> oral literature, should have inferential significance to
> the African reader.
>
> (Nwoga 1974: 41)

As we pointed out earlier, this kind of unconscious
approach is not enough. The performance of our poets,
which we have analyzed, and especially their botched mimesis of African traditional poetry, shows that they need more
than a haphazard and unconscious exposure to the African
tradition in order to develop the proper sensibility and skill
for working in it. They need *conscious, determined, metic-
ulous* and *thorough study*. They need extended *immersion*
in the traditional mode and *apprenticeship* in its methods.
The contrast between the early and later Okigbo should
make this quite clear. So also should the examples of
Senghor, Kunene, Okot and Awoonor, when contrasted to
Soyinka's unstudied absorption of incoherent bits and pieces
of African tradition.

In fact, the prescription that the poet should not consciously study the African tradition while he is diligently
studying the European is the bedrock of the *tigritude* attitude.
It is a ruse for inducting the African poet into the euromodernist camp. The poet's sensibility becomes overwhelmed
by and saturated with the foreign euromodernist sensibility
which he has intensively studied in school, but becomes
resistant to the random and unsystematic influences from the
African tradition which he has not consciously and assiduously studied. The champion of this tigritude approach which
Nwoga espouses is of course Wole Soyinka. We shall now

turn our attention to some of the anti-African and pro-European implications of his esthetics.

With his tigritude tirade against an active pro-African consciousness in our literature, Soyinka cleared space for the promotion of a universalist-individualist approach as the "mature" one in African literature. As a practitioner of what he advocates, Soyinka treats public issues in the privatist mode and from the universalist-individualist outlook. He is much concerned with man's inhumanity to man, but shows practically no interest in Europe's historical and systematic inhumanity to Africans. When such issues interest him, he exhibits a deep commitment to the imperialist European view of Africa. We shall examine Soyinka's affliction by considering the implications of his slogan, "neo-Tarzanism."

Soyinka regards the employment in African poetry of elements from Africa's flora and fauna, and devices from traditional African imaging devices, as "neo-Tarzanist." He does not welcome the appearance of elephants, beggars, calabashes, serpents, pumpkins, baskets, town criers, iron bells, slit drums, iron masks, hares, squirrels, iron birds, etc., in contemporary African poetry. He would rather have African poetry deal preferentially with precision machinery, oil rigs, hydro-electricity, typewriters, railway trains, machine guns and other European imports. (See Soyinka 1975: 38.) Note that the former represent items from pre-European Africa, items that are still there as part of the natural geographical and social landscape, and that the latter represent the artificial inputs into that landscape brought in by Europeans. In our view, both belong in African poetry since they are there as part of the African setting. Soyinka also claims that both belong to his conception of Africa.

Granted this agreement, what then is the basic difference between his position and ours? Since he inveighs against us for urging that the African geographical and biological landscape, and the traditional, non-European African society, should be brought to the center of our perception, one must conclude that he would prefer to grant the center to a different class of phenomena. He appears to want to give center stage to the European cultural imports since he insists that to give center stage to traditional African phenomena is to create a neo-Tarzanist Africa.

Now, we ask, is that a possibility at all? In order to answer this, we must ask: What was Tarzanist Africa? Was it the African reality? Did it exist at all outside the European imperialist imagination? If Tarzanist Africa was a figment of the European imagination, then it was not the same as traditional Africa. In that case, giving center stage to traditional Africa cannot be the same as recreating a Tarzanist Africa in our poetry. In particular, granting center stage to traditional African phenomena cannot bring back into concrete existence a Tarzanist fiction which never had concrete existence. African reality and the European idea of it are two radically different things. Employing the former in our poetry is not the same as employing the latter, and Soyinka's fears are clearly unwarranted.

But why does an intelligent and renowned man like him exhibit such unwarranted fears? What complexes is he the victim of? Let us look into this a bit. By screaming neo-Tarzanism at our suggestion, Soyinka is in effect saying: Don't you realize that the Europeans will laugh at you and call you a savage for writing about elephants, squirrels, iron birds, etc.? Don't you realize that such things will make you appear primitive to them, and will confirm in their minds their view that we are all primitives under our modern, detribalized clothes and advanced degrees, primitives incapable of uttering anything besides such mumbo-jumbo as "Bwana, bwana, me see big iron bird"?

Soyinka's inferiority complex is not difficult to diagnose. European attitudes to Africa have led him to confuse two things—our land and our traditions in all their autonomy, and Europe's contemptuous view of our land and our traditions, especially as that view has been popularized in

Tarzan movies. The "modification of vision" which he has suffered through colonialism (Macebuh 1975–76: 80) seems to be such that he can no longer see the difference between our traditions and the European caricature of them.

Soyinka's basic error has to be made quite clear. He misidentifies the real Africa with the Western Tarzanist caricature of Africa, and he furthermore accepts the caricature as providing the only possibly correct view of the African past. He is therefore compelled to think that the reality that would emerge from our call to give center stage to phenomena traditional to Africa, if our call is heeded, would have to be identical with that Western caricature. In this, this "perceptive" man sadly errs. His vision can't be very clear or sharply focussed.

The real neo-Tarzanists are those who take the Tarzan view of Africa as valid, and who have not repudiated it. The real neo-Tarzanists are those who, instead of laughing the whole caricature out of court, feel put to shame by it and lash out defensively at those who they fear give a bad impression of Africa to the European. They are those who expect us to meet European expectations, who would caution us to "put our best foot forward" and not let the race down before European opinion.

To assist these real neo-Tarzanists in curing themselves of their inferiority complexes, we must point out the absolute irrelevance of European opinion to a liberated African consciousness. Neither European praise nor European blame should matter to a liberated African consciousness. A liberated African consciousness will do and judge things entirely on its own grounds. To adapt a famous declaration by Langston Hughes: If Europeans are pleased, it doesn't matter; if they are not, it doesn't matter. Soyinka's consciousness has not moved this far, and we would like to pray to all our ancestors to help him get rid of his neo-Tarzanist inferiority complexes, his craving for European acclaim, and his terror of European blame. We hope that someday soon he will give up his misguided ambition to be just a writer, and be proud to be an *African* writer.

Thus, the kind of apologetics offered by Nwoga, and the kind of tigritude and neo-Tarzanist slogan-campaigns mounted by Soyinka, attempt to misdirect and misorient African literature and its audience by turning the attention of African writers, critics, and readers from things they ought to be and do, and, instead, focussing their attention on things they ought not to be or do. They attempt to retard the decolonization of African literature by hampering the emergence in it of a conscious and powerful African nationalism, and by coaxing and whipping our writers towards a suicidal eurocentric, individualist, pseudo-universalist consciousness.

CHAPTER 4

Issues and Tasks in the Decolonization of African Literature

▼▼▼▼▼

BASIC ASSUMPTIONS

Our basic assumption in this essay is that contemporary African culture is under foreign domination. Therefore, on the one hand, our culture has to destroy all encrustations of colonial mentality, and on the other hand, has to map out new foundations for an African modernity. This cultural task demands a deliberate and calculated process of syncretism: one which, above all, emphasizes valuable continuities with our pre-colonial culture, welcomes vitalizing contributions from other cultures, and exercises inventive genius in making a healthy and distinguished synthesis from them all.

If decolonization is the aim, such synthesis must be within the parameters of the African tradition rather than outside it. It should expand and renew the tradition through new syntheses and breakthroughs rather than leave it unchanged and in moribund stasis. In order to achieve such synthesis, experimentation is crucial. The kind of experimentation called for may be described as *traditionalist,* that is to say, experimentation for the purpose of modernizing and revitalizing the tradition.

The critical norms currently advocated for African poetry and prose fiction do not encourage such experimentation. If African literature is not to become a transplanted fossil of European literature, it needs to burst out of the straitjacket of anglomodernist poetry and of the "well-made novel" and it needs to find more ways of incorporating forms, treatments and devices taken from the African oral tradition. The demand for such incorporation is not a mere matter of antiquarianism, nor is it a matter of searching for some vague authenticity. It has to do with the function of a literature in its society.

The dictum that art is a simulacrum of life ought to be taken seriously, with its implications effectively realized. An African literature, whose addiction to European techniques of presentation compels it to attenuate or eschew entirely the flavor of African life, cannot sustain its claim to being an African literature, no matter who produces it. And the flavor of African life is a matter of contemporary realities and life tones as well as of the cultural inheritance from the past. For instance, novels about contemporary Africa need to capture the flavor of contemporary African life; similarly, African historical novels need to convey the flavor of African life in the place and period in which their action is set. It is this need, above all else, which makes imperative a grafting of African literary sensibilities and techniques onto their ancient roots. Those approaching the task from a training in the Western narrative tradition, whether of the "well-made" or the modernist tendencies, need an apprenticeship in the African oral tradition before they can succeed in making their art a simulacrum of African life.

The kinds of experimentation required by this apprenticeship are likely to be far different from those encouraged by the modernist revolution in the Western narrative tradition, or the Eliot-Pound-Hopkins school of anglomodernist poetry. Where these have degenerated into a congeries of fads, into a compulsive reaction against anything with a sense of tradition about it, and into an unbridled nouveaumania, the kind of experimentation required by the African situation is one determined by the overall need to capture African realities and the flavor of African life, past and present.

PARAMETERS OF TRADITIONALIST EXPERIMENTATION

The need to capture the flavor of African life, past and present, for an African audience, imposes several constraining parameters upon African traditionalist experimentation. Among these are salutary constraints on the writer's craft and his language by the characteristics of his audience, the writer's commitment to his society and its well-being, and the consequences of such commitment for his treatment of his themes.

Community, Craft, and Language

The following are some of the issues important in the consideration of community, craft and language:

Community and Craft: The artist in the traditional African milieu spoke for and to his community. His imagery, themes, symbolisms and forms were drawn from a communally accessible pool. He was heard. He had sense. But our "moderns"? When you cannot speak to your people there is a burning temptation either to speak to yourself (privatist mysticism), or to speak for them to outside ears (orphic messengers); to pose as ambassadors to foreigners, to pretend to be bearers of self-composed messages from your people to the rest of the world. The outsiders hear and understand you (perhaps), but your own people wonder what's going on, what the jabbering is all about.

The African writer or critic must confront this issue of what community he is writing for. Is he content to scribble marginalia to the literatures of Europe? Is he content to write for an audience whose interest in his work is mostly exotic? Or is he more interested in writing for a community whose members, in reading his works, can confront their own life experiences and find them illuminated? Who will quote him to their children in order to

241

make their lives more intelligible to them? Let us point out that the immortality of a work—something most writers desire—depends on writing for a community for whose situation the work is resonant with meaning, a community which finds itself expressed in the work. Writing for an alien community which takes only exotic delight in your life is probably the surest route to unre-membrance.

Let it also be noted that the demands of an artist's cultural community are the features against which he must sharpen his craft. It should therefore not surprise us that Africa's colonial and neo-colonial poets, for instance, being overly devoted to their European and American audiences and mentors, trim their sails to the modernist squalls from the West. Simplicity of diction is therefore devalued, artificially difficult diction is esteemed, African themes that would make sense in an African cultural matrix are eschewed. The African writer and critic should understand that what makes a good work of art is in large measure defined by the central expectations and concerns of a given culture. They should therefore work from the standpoint of the African community, not the Euro-American, not that of some abstract *Civilisation de l'Universel.*

Language and Community: We would like to call an end to the debate over the use of Western languages by African writers. The use of these languages is a part of the problem of contemporary African culture. Ideally, African literature should be written in African languages. But the same historical circumstances that presently compel African nations to use Western languages as their official languages also compel African writers to write in them. Until those historical circumstances are changed—and we hope they change soon—it is pointless debating whether or not to use these Western languages in our literature.

A more immediate issue is how to write well in those languages. And we have argued all along that to write well in English today it is necessary to write clearly, using contemporary 20th-century diction and idiom, so that anyone literate in the language can make literal sense out of every sentence or line that is written. It's so little to ask! Let the educated elite worry about the many layers of rich meaning that may be buried beneath that surface clarity. This is not to suggest that what is needed is a poetry of nursery rhymes; but even so, some of the great poetry of the world has the linguistic clarity and simplicity of nursery rhymes. Consider "Humpty Dumpty":

> Humpty Dumpty sat on a wall
> Humpty Dumpty had a great fall
> All the king's horses and all the king's men
> Couldn't put Humpty together again.

And Blake's "The Tiger":

> Tiger! Tiger! burning bright
> In the forests of the night,
> What immortal hand or eye
> Could frame thy fearful symmetry?
>
> In what distant deeps or skies
> Burnt the fire of thine eyes?
> On what wings dare he aspire?
> What the hand dare seize the fire?
>
> And what shoulder, and what art,
> Could twist the sinews of thy heart?
> And when thy heart began to beat,
> What dread hand? and what dread feet?
>
> What the hammer? what the chain?
> In what furnace was thy brain?
> What the anvil? what dread grasp
> Dare its deadly terrors clasp?

> When the stars threw down their spears,
> And water'd heaven with their tears,
> Did he smile his work to see?
> Did he who made the Lamb make thee?
>
> Tiger! Tiger! burning bright
> In the forests of the night,
> What immortal hand or eye
> Dare frame thy fearful symmetry?

And Langston Hughes' "Harlem":

> What happens to a dream deferred?
>
> Does it dry up
> like a raisin in the sun?
> Or fester like a sore—
> And then run?
> Does it stink like rotten meat?
> Or crust and sugar over—
> like a syrupy sweet?
>
> Maybe it just sags
> like a heavy load.
>
> *Or does it explode?*

Any literate child can read and understand these poems; and at the same time, any industrious Ph.D. could, if he chooses, spend the rest of his life pondering their metaphysical profundities. By the way, that would be a less unhealthy endeavour, we think, than puzzling out obscure syntax. Similarly, one could spend a lifetime pondering the profundity of social dialectic embodied in the following lines translated from the traditional Yoruba poem, "New Yam":

> You put the yam to bed in the ground
> it will bring you money
> that will plant you on top of a beautiful woman.

Despite their simplicity of diction, it is generally agreed that Blake's "The Tiger" and Hughes' "Harlem" are profound poems. But there appears to be doubt in some minds on whether "Humpty Dumpty" could be included in such company. For instance, in response to the original version of this essay, Soyinka made the following comment:

> What the rightful inheritors of these delightful lines dared not do, our troika have more than dared—raised "Humpty Dumpty" to the level of "great poetry" and equated it not only with William Blake's *Tiger* but with Langston Hughes' "Harlem"! Fools rush in. . . .
>
> (Soyinka 1975: 39)

"Humpty Dumpty" is, in our view, a profound poem, nursery rhyme though it be. Why? First, we see no *a priori* grounds to deny profundity to any children's poem that possesses it, and certainly not on the adult chauvinist ground that a poem written primarily for children cannot *ipso facto* be profound. Second, "Humpty Dumpty" does indeed possess the simplicity and profundity of the best of parables. It is an archetype of things impossible to put back together once broken, not even, or perhaps especially by main force, be they innocence, virginity, trust, friendship, unity or an old order of things. There are processes and changes that are irreversible. And "Humpty Dumpty," though so clear and simple and supposedly written for children, makes that point for even the wisest old persons to grasp. That, we submit, is profundity.

Now, if we find value in what the British, we are told, do not hold in esteem, that is our prerogative. If we choose to tell the British what is valuable or not in their tradition, why not? We have a perfect right to do so. After all, the bloody British have been going around the world for centuries, telling other people what they should find good or shameful in their own traditions. They may be long overdue for a dose of their own medicine. But really, we have no

245

intention of wasting our energy instructing the British. We only insist on evaluating things for ourselves, on our own terms, in the light of our own interests and perceptions, and not, like Soyinka, in dancing after the march of British opinions on things. We do not have to buy the British opinion of anything, not even of themselves and their literature.

Now, as far as the matter of simplicity in African poetry is concerned, anybody who can read what is popularly known as Onitsha Market literature, or Frank Aig-Imoukhuede's poem "One Wife for One Man," or the works of Amos Tutuola, or Okot p'Bitek's *Song of Lawino* or Matei Markwei's "Life in Our Village," should be able to read whatever our other poets write in English. This simple literacy test should define the African writer's primary audience and community. Any African writer who insists on making the West his primary community, on the grounds that he can thereby reach a larger audience, should be told that if he writes with clarity on matters of sufficient general concern to his educated African peers, chances are that most literate Africans will appreciate him, and he will have all the audience he needs. In addition, foreigners will aso appreciate him (as they appreciate Tutuola and Okot p'Bitek), and rather than have less of each audience he will have more. Our artists may have something to learn from one of the greatest Chinese poets, Po Chu-yi, who wrote and rewrote his poems, correcting and simplifying his diction, till, when read, they were intelligible to the random peasant he met in his walks. But that takes humility.

Language and Imagery: One of the most telling qualities of African orature (and one which we believe it shares with other oratures) is its economy of means. This may be seen in the density of meaning compressed into a line of proverb, and in the spare, uncluttered language of our epics, folk tales and court chronicles: their control of their matter displays an almost ruthless exclusion of convoluted, jargon-plated chaff. Orature, being auditory, places high value on lucidity, normal syntax and precise and apt imagery. Language or image that is not vivid, precise, or apt compels the listener to puzzle it out, interrupts his attention, and makes him lose parts of the telling. We see no reason why these virtues of orature should be abandoned in literature. These qualities which are mandatory in the auditory medium should be insisted upon in the written. For even abundant leisure cannot be blamed if it gets impatient with unnecessary puzzles that keep it from the experience it wants to share. Also, whether or not they have precedents in our orature, these qualities must be insisted upon out of sheer courtesy to the reader.

Structure and Logistics: Efficient structure and logistics is valued in orature, for it takes one through to the climax without tedious or unnecessary diversions. Contemporary poetics should make the same demand upon writers.

Poetic License: Where poetic license enriches the devices of the literary language, it is welcome. But it must not be misused. Where it leads to inconsistencies between imagery, tone and mood, it must be curbed. License is laudable when it leads to felicitous, mellifluous, and apt expression.

Other Considerations: While obscurity, sentimentality, clichés of expression and attitude, vague or unrealistic situations, incongruence of thought and feeling, and inadequacy of substance behind an emptily assertive tone can damn a work, what may make a work memorable includes the following: lyricism of speech, musicality of rhythm, mellifluousness (smooth and easy flow), emotional intensity and sweep of vision, evocative power, and concreteness of imagery and persona. As in folk tales, the personification of animals, deities and ghouls evokes them more vividly than an abstract presentation.

Equally important in making a work memorable, and in situating it within a tradition, are its fidelity to traditional forms and themes, the importance of whatever social issues it deals with,

247

and, in the case of an embattled culture such as ours, how *engagé* it is, and what contribution it makes toward raising our consciousness. These considerations, we think, must be made part of any African esthetic.

We should emphasize that our job as writers is to be articulate, and to present to our audiences the stresses and joys of our societies as they take place, not just in the private psychological transformations of individuals, but also in their public manifestations. We must capture and recreate the tone, flavor and texture of life in our society for those who read us. And if many have to do that in borrowed languages, that is not a fault to be interminably lamented, not a fault of the writer alone, but a symptom of the deeper decay within our culture. When the deep diseases of our culture are cured, most writers will write in the indigenous languages. What we write in borrowed Western languages will still be African if it is addressed to Africans and if it captures the qualities of African life. It will be a species of African literature written in English or French or Portuguese, etc.

In conclusion, we would like to emphasize that whatever the language he writes in, a writer is a maker; let him make beautiful and effective things. And a maker needs technique; let him master it to good effect. And lest technique run away with him, let him have a clear purpose before him as he makes. If he would bore us, let him bore us; but he should not bore when he wants to delight or amuse. That would be unpardonable.

Commitment and the Writer's Social Responsibilities

The issues usually argued out in the vocabulary of privatism and commitment are those concerning the responsibility of writers to their society. Before we go into them, there are various matters that need to be clarified concerning the terms "privatism" and "commitment." There is a privatism of *matter* as well as of *manner* which issue forth in obscurantism. Obscurity due to a privatism of matter is that in which allegedly incommunicable experiences, experiences said to be beyond verbal expression, are presented. But, we must ask, why bother writing about such experiences if they are intrinsically incommunicable *in words?*

Obscurity due to privatism of manner is that in which matters that are quite capable of communication in words are so presented as to be incomprehensible to readers. This is a question exclusively of treatment—of *privatist versus public treatment* of any theme whatsoever, *not* a question of whether the themes treated are from public or private life, and not, as is commonly supposed, a question of whether the themes are public or private in nature. Public themes can be treated in a privatist manner, resulting in privatist, obscure work; and private themes can be treated in a public manner, thus avoiding privatist obscurity.

The point is that no matter his topic, the writer's language should not be tuned to some idiosyncratic perceptual matrix which obscures it for the public. Surely, a writer can write about his emotion and perceptions, his self-explorations, his love affairs, the death of his dear ones, his thoughts about suicide, his prospects for promotion in his job, etc., and about all the complex emotions that might accompany these events, but his treatment should not be obscurantist. We do not deny that works on such subjects are "a valid exercise in growth" and that they can "have the effect of changing men's consciousness and making them aware of what previously they had not even guessed." (Nwoga 1974: 39-40) Rather, we would point out that such an exercise would be ineffectual if it failed to communicate its experience. We should re-emphasize that *private* themes do not necessarily result in *privatist* writing, as the poetry of Lenrie Peters, for instance, amply demonstrates.

Discussions of privatism, insofar as the term involves an attitude towards the public, usually lead to questions about the writer's responsibilities to the public and therefore to talk about his social commitment. Misunderstandings about the term "commitment" quickly arise. This is usually because of a confounding of two questions, namely: (1) the social responsibility of the writer *as citizen*, i.e., a citizen who happens to be a writer by trade; and (2) the commitment or *engagement* of the *products* of his trade, i.e., his writings.

Though the public may have become conditioned to the notion that commitment in art demands that the artist carry guns or join protest marches, we should point out that such acts of political or social commitment—which he engages in as a citizen—should properly be kept distinct from the commitment of the literature which he produces. In our view, an artist who chooses to engage in acts of social or political activism (fighting in wars, signing petitions, joining protest marches, etc.) does so only in his capacity as an ordinary citizen. For example, when military service is not required of him, a writer who volunteers does so in his capacity as a citizen. He has no professional obligation to volunteer, nor does he have a professional obligation to not volunteer. It is entirely up to him and his citizen sense of what the occasion calls for. If his sense of citizen responsibility should move him to volunteer, and if he should get killed in battle or be forced to endure imprisonment, he should not be accused of having deserted an alleged responsibility to art. A responsibility to art, whatever that is, cannot take precedence over his responsibility to his society to play his role in it as a citizen. And even his art has social value only insofar as it is a means for serving his society. In that sense, it is on a par with any other means of social service for which he has competence, be it soldiering or administering or doctoring. In this regard, Ali Mazrui's *The Trial of Christopher Okigbo* is predicated upon an error on this point.

On the other hand, when military service *is* required of him, a writer cannot claim exemption on the simple basis of being a writer. The kind of argument which says that writers or any other artists, as an artistic elect, are intrinsically exempt from "carrying guns" (to use their fashionable hyperbole for a broad range of citizen responsibilities) is simply disingenuous. That you are an artist does not exempt you from your citizen responsibilities. The notion of an artistic elect intrinsically exempt from the social responsibilities common to all members of the society is simply fatuous. The arts are merely one group of professions among others. Why an exemption for artists but not for farmers, carpenters, or cooks? There may indeed be other grounds for individual exemptions, e.g., for cripples, cowards, pacifists, or the insane; but such exemptions, surely, must apply to all professions alike.

It needs to be pointed out that when a writer fulfills his citizen responsibilities, even at the price of imprisonment or death, this fact may change our estimate of him as a person. We might choose thereafter to admire him for his courage and heroism as a citizen, but even such heroism is no reason for his literary work to be esteemed more highly than it deserves. These considerations would of course hold true for a cook, carpenter, farmer, gossip columnist, doctor, lawyer, teacher, burglar, hangman, bartender, or any member of any other trade.

This necessary separation of citizen and professional responsibilities does not at all imply that writing and politics are autonomous and must be kept separate and apart. Literature and politics influence each other, and those writers are deluded who, drawing support from the absurd pretensions of art for art's sake, put on the airs of an artistic elect who must keep their works unsullied by the political concerns of their fellow citizens. Their notion is that art should concern itself with "eternal verities" and "universal" themes and must fastidiously shun matters of contemporary concern to their community as topical, journalistic, sociological ephemera. This is all sheer humbug.

251

A writer does have a minimum professional responsibility to make his work relevant and intelligible to his society and its concerns. He may do so by treating the burning issues of the day; or he may do so by treating themes germane to his community's fundamental and long-range interests. There are no intrinsically artistic grounds for avoiding either. Art is not sullied by either. The only plausible grounds for avoiding either are personal lack of interest and personal incompetence in handling that kind of material. If an African writer wishes to avoid both these kinds of issues, either by writing for alien interests and audiences, or by writing in a privatist code, then why should he publish and circulate his works in Africa?

It won't do for him to claim that a writer has no mandate from anyone to write, therefore no one should advise him what to write about or how to write. One may ask such a writer why he bothers to make his writings public, why he uses public resources, lays claim to public attention, yet disdains all responsibility to society. If he insists on the prerogative claimed by some decadent and alienated bourgeois artists of the West, he should move to the West where he can join them in indulging in the social irrelevance of art for art's sake. If he chooses to remain in Africa, he should keep his scribblings to himself. For the function of the artist in Africa, in keeping with our traditions and needs, demands that the writer, as a public voice, assume a responsibility to reflect public concerns in his writings, and not preoccupy himself with his puny ego. Because in Africa we recognize that art is in the public domain, a sense of social commitment is mandatory upon the artist. That commitment demands that the writer pay attention to his craft, that he not burden his public with unfinished or indecipherable works. It also demands that his theme be germane to the concerns of his community.

In focussing on these concerns, the matter for his poetry, novels or other writings may be historical, philosophical, sociological, scientific, fantastic, or topical. He may choose to explore some of the values of his society, or some of the dangers in its path; or he may choose to lampoon its foibles or castigate its wrongdoings. The quarry for themes is as big as all of the society and its history, its imagination and its future. And by the way, it should be pointed out that the distinction between *topical* and *non-topical* matters is not a distinction among literary themes but rather a distinction about the state of social interest in literary themes. For any particular theme, be it love or politics or war, could become of topical interest at any given time, and could drop back into being a matter of fundamental, long-range and unfocussed concern at some other time. It is misleading to talk as if love, private grief, personal ambition, etc., are somehow "eternal" and "universal" themes, and as if such public matters as war, peace, corruption, territorial aggrandizement, and politics somehow are not. The former can be just as topical or non-topical as the latter. A society concerned with its future would be concerned at some point or another, and at one level or another, with every aspect of its affairs, private and public, transient and enduring, past, present and future. Thus, any one of these could supply the writer with issues germane to his community.

But must a writer write about every one of these in order to be considered committed? To say yes would be foolish. Who would have enough time do so even in ten lifetimes? The most that a writer could reasonably be asked to do is to write only about that which he knows well and is skilled enough to handle well. Once he chooses to write about a particular subject and from his particular orientation, his responsibility to his audience is to write it well so they can understand and learn from his presentation.

Artistic commitment, as we see it, is therefore a matter of orientation, a matter of perceiving social realities and of making those perceptions available in works of art in order to help promote understanding and preservation of, or change in, the society's values and norms. Thus, the commitment of a work is a matter of its quality, its orientation, and the perceptions it fosters. Commitment, so understood, requires, in particular, that even moments of private reflection, when treated in works of literature, be so presented as to be accessible to the audience, not coded in cipher meaningful to the author alone. If the reflection is so private that it cannot or should not be made accessible to the public, why present it for public consumption?

Treating the burning issues of the day is what is usually referred to as political *engagement* in literature. Though non-mandatory, the times may well demand that writers, like other citizens, be politically *engagé* through their work. *Engagé,* but to what side of a partisan affray? None can decide for the writer, as none can decide for the cook, the teacher, the soldier, doctor, merchant, lawyer, farmer, musician, athlete, or politician. Each would have to decide which cause to serve by donation of his or her skill. In any case, a writer who chooses to use his writing to serve a given social cause or interest should show his commitment through what matters he treats in his tracts, his propaganda, his satires, his affirming or muckraking works, and his *prima facie* apolitical creations, and by the manner in which he treats them. He can defend or attack the state, if that is where his impulse leads him. He can satirize such individuals or such manners as he disapproves of. He can mourn public losses, or celebrate them.

Engagement or political commitment does not predetermine what a writer's politics should be; it merely demands that the writer write in such ways as might advance the interests and purposes he espouses. For instance—to use an example out of that Greco-Roman world so beloved by some of our writers and critics—in the Athens of their day, Aristophanes was a conservative, Euripides a radical reformer: both were great dramatists, and their works were very *engagé*. With their opposing politics and temperaments, they waded into the social battles of their day, taking sides, representing the views of their factions persuasively, ridiculing those of their opponents, and making their drama vehicles of public education as well as entertainment.

However, writers who, like Aristophanes and Euripides, choose to serve a cause through imaginative works rather than through tracts and propaganda, must be warned against producing literary works which forget that their central concern is to tell their story and tell it well. If a literary work fails in that, it will lose the attention of the public, and the cause to which its author is committed will have been ill served. To drive this warning home we can do no better than to quote what Gabriel Garcia Marquez, the renowned Latin American novelist, once said against Latin American novels

> that are not concerned with telling a story, but rather with overthrowing the government . . . look, after so many years of this literature paved with good intentions, we have not succeeded in overthrowing one simple government with it, and, instead, we have invaded the bookstores with unreadable novels . . . we have lost our public.
>
> (Quoted in Coleman 1977: 21)

Thus, if a writer wants to write a literary work that says, in effect, "Destroy the status quo," let him do so but do it well. If a writer wants to write a literary work that says, in effect, "Preserve the status quo," let him do so but do it well. In either case, he should write clearly so that those who agree or disagree may know what they are agreeing or disagreeing with. Just because a writer is *engagé*, just because he is equipped with the "right" enthusiasms, is no excuse for him to be a hack. We are ultimately, on grounds of an artist's esthetic responsibility to his community, asking that *engagé* art be well executed.

Cultural Continuity:
The African Writer and the African Past

In contemporary African literature and criticism there have been three dominant attitudes towards the African past: shamefaced rejection; romantic embrace; and realistic appraisal. Those who reject the African past and would have as little to do with it as possible are those who, shamed by imperialist propaganda and misrepresentation, would wish to forget it entirely and to hurry off into a euromodernist African future. Prominent among them are those champions of tigritude, those African neo-Tarzanists who dismiss African literature that deals with the African past as a "literature of self-worship," a literature of narcissism. Against this school of thought headed by Wole Soyinka, it must be emphasized that since our past has been vilified by imperialism, and since an imperialist education has tried to equip us with all manner of absurd views and reactions to our past, we do need to reclaim and rehabilitate our genuine past, to repossess our true and entire history in order to acquire a secure launching pad into our future. Thus, a concern with our past will never be out of place.

Those African writers and critics who understand the need for us to repossess and rehabilitate our past have approached it with either romanticism or critical realism. In our view, there are excellent grounds for avoiding a romanticization of our past and for according it a critical and realistic appraisal. Most important is the fact that we cannot afford to build on misinformation, and romanticism has a tendency to put misleading glosses upon whatever it gazes upon. In this regard, the romanticism of the negritude school is notorious. But before proceeding to examine this, we should first disentangle three important aspects of negritude and state our attitudes about them.

First, there is its African nationalist consciousness which revolts against European cultural imperialism. As we argued earlier, an active African nationalist consciousness is indispensable to the task of African liberation. For its stand and contributions in this department, African nationalism is indebted to negritude. To its champions we offer our salute!

The second important aspect of negritude is its concern with recapturing for modern literature the technical repertory of traditional African orature. This again is a crucial project in cultural retrieval. Without it, the task of ensuring continuity between traditional and modern African culture would be practically impossible. For its pioneering efforts in this department, African nationalism is again indebted to negritude. To its champions, we also offer our salute!

The third important aspect of negritude is the image of traditional Africa which it has held up to view. This is highly questionable. In reaction to colonial insults the negritude poets generally salve their wounds with extravagant nostalgia for a vaguely conceived past. But ought we to persist in this disservice to our past, and even to our present? Was our past one uninterrupted orgy or sensuality? One boring canvas of idyllic goodness, fraternity and harmony? Were our ancestors a parade of plaster saints who never, among themselves, struck a blow, or hurt a fly, and who suffered at all?

No doubt, at its inception, even this romanticism filled a historic need. It was an understandably extreme reaction, offering blanket praise in retort to Europe's blanket condemnation of Africa. But that mythical portrait of traditional Africa can prove to be a new prison. In the task of decolonization we cannot afford an uncritical glorification of the past. We may brandish our memories of empires of ages ago as shields against Western disparagement but we also know that before colonialism came there was slavery. Who hunted the slaves? And who sold them for guns, trinkets and gin? And the African attitudes and roles which made that slave trade possible, are they not part of that nostalgic past? Are those attitudes not still with us, poisoning our

257

present? How much of this illusion of purity and sanctity can survive the events of the past decade? After all, "When a nigger kicks a nigger/Where is the negritude?" (Madubuike). Even though other parts of the blame belong elsewhere, we cannot deny our own share of the responsibility.

As regards the arts, romanticism of the negritude kind, because it venerates what it considers a golden past, could discourage our use of exemplars from that past as points of contemporary departure. By encouraging the minting of facsimiles, it could imprison the contemporary imagination in a bygone era. As has happened in the plastic arts, especially in the lamentable case of airport art, the romantic minting of facsimiles from a golden past could saddle us with anachronistic imagery, and prevent the evolution of new literary forms out of the old, resulting in a fossilization of forms and a literary stasis.

In contrast, critical realism, because it does not spread a gloss of sanctity on the past, does not extol every aspect of it. It is content to praise what it sees as praiseworthy, and to dispraise what it sees as not praiseworthy. It thereby treats our past like any other valid era of culture. This enables us to see welcome as well as objectionable similarities between our present and our past, and such discrimination and selectivity enables us to adopt desirable features from the arts of our past as we endeavor to anchor our modern culture in our tradition. Because critical realism prevents us from treating exemplars as sacrosanct, it allows for the evolution of new forms through adaptations from the old. When, as in Okigbo's "Path of Thunder," contemporary events and objects are put into the traditional image matrix and described with traditional terms of rhetoric, the effect is refreshing. We thereby obtain a modernism that has emerged from a clearly African poetic tradition.

Other examples in which aspects of our modern literature have been successfully grafted onto traditional trunks include the following: Tutuola's *Palm-Wine Drinkard, My Life in the*

Bush of Ghosts and other novels, which are embedded in the Yoruba mythic imagination; Achebe's *Things Fall Apart* and *Arrow of God* which capture, in English, Igbo speech patterns, proverbs and idiom; and Okot p'Bitek's *Song of Lawino, Song of Ocol, Song of a Prisoner* and *Song of Malaya,* each of which uses authentic African imagery and Acholi rhetorical devices to examine an aspect of the contemporary African condition.

THE DECOLONIZATION OF AFRICAN LITERARY FORMS, THEMES AND TECHNIQUES

Deficiencies in Poetry and Prose

Understandably, much of contemporary African poetry has so far been protest poetry. The other large category has been privatist and mystical poetry. A general survey compels us to ask: Where are the narrative poems? Where are the parables, fables, paradoxes, myths, legends and proverbs in the poetry? Our forebears were minters of proverbs; we are their heirs, are we not? Where is the poetry of tenderness that conveys the tenderness and does not merely refer to it? Where are celebrations of laughter and joy? In spite of our oppressive reality we still laugh, do we not? Where is the poetry of wit, where is the humor? Where is the poetry that realizes these emotions and affects, the poetry that does not merely celebrate them in the abstract? Where is the choral poetry, or don't our women sing together as they circle their dances at naming ceremonies, puberty rites? Where are the love songs, the songs of courtship, wedding songs, farm songs of planting and harvesting, funeral dirges, hunting songs, drinking songs, epics, boasts, satire, songs of praise and of abuse, the songs that celebrate absences, deaths and other varied aspects and transitions of a regular full life? Our forebears were entertainers; we are their heirs, are we not?

259

These forms, themes and treatments are overshadowed in the corpus by privatist and protest poetry. The present preponderance of poems of privatist mysticism and of protest (in particular, of grim-faced protest—protest does not have to be grim-faced to be effective!) should be redressed. We are not, in principle, against either mystical or protest poetry; we merely wish to stress the need for a flowering of works of other kinds so as to balance out the corpus of modern African poetry and make it reflect the diversity of African interests and activities.

And we ask, in addition, that poetry on private themes be made lucid and accessible, and that our protest voices should not be turned exclusively outward to Europe, to America, to audiences of white faces, to the supposedly exclusive foreign sources of our hurts, but should turn homewards, to an African audience, against African wrongs. Especially after the 1960s and 1970s there is plenty to protest in African life. Our poets should stop regarding themselves as primarily orphic messengers to the West. If we are serious about reconnecting our poetry with our past, with our present for that matter, with life as we live it in our society, our poets must begin to include these themes and forms in their works.

In our narrative prose, there has been an emphasis on novels and short stories to the neglect of such traditional forms as tales, legends, allegories, parables and fables. These traditional forms should not only be incorporated into novels and short stories but should also be continued in their own right. It should also be possible to utilize in these narrative forms, and in novels and stories as well, the traditional style of oral rendition where the audience is assumed to be, not a reader or readers, but a group of participant-listeners. Such a rendition would mean that the written story would have as narrator a master story-teller, a spell-binding raconteur whose delivery will conform to the styles of traditional story telling, utilizing its familiar techniques and rhetorical devices, with the audience chiming in with questions, comments and laughter, interrupting the narrative from time to time, and taking part in those segments of the narrative which call for group singing or dramatization. Such a rendition would, in other words, incorporate some of the dramatic performance dimensions of traditional African narrative.

In addition to the above deficiencies of form and technique there appears to be a dearth of themes from African mythology and history, and of materials treated allegorically, with hugh doses of fantasy, to transform and illuminate a tale. The corpus of comic, humorous and satiric stories does not reflect its proportion in the oral tradition, or in daily life for that matter, as reflected in African journalism, for instance. Sad to say, the notion that equates the serious with the pompous has not removed its shadow from African prose fiction.

The incorporation and development of traditional techniques of orature should go a long way towards infusing eloquence into our poetry, improving the narrative style of our prose, and imparting a genuinely African flavor to both. Thus, some central concern of experimentation for the decolonization of our prose and poetic techniques would be the continuation of traditional forms with a pouring of new wine into old bottles, as it were; the incorporation of these forms as elements in novels, poems and short stories; the employment of traditional devices in saturating quantities that will impart an African tone to the product; and the development out of all these of new forms and techniques suitable for rendering new aspects of the contemporary African reality.

Narrative Rhetoric and Its Devices

The three aspects of narrative rhetoric which we shall here consider are: (1) narrative language; (2) the handling of expository material that might be unfamiliar to some part of the African audience; (3) the utilization of descriptive devices and techniques of characterization derived from African orature.

(1) A necessity for linguistic experimentation lies in the fact that Africans do not use English the way the English do, and in the fact that the rhetorical devices of each African language and community are peculiar to it and are a legacy of its cultural inheritance. If a flavor of African life is therefore to be captured in novels written in English, the English language has to be flexed and bent to allow these idiomatic and rhetorical usages to be presented. Several African writers have experimented to this end. Some have been more successful than others.

To date, Achebe is perhaps the best conscious experimenter in this matter in English, and Ahmadou Kourouma in his *Les Soleils Des Independences* in French. In contrast to Gabriel Okara, whose experiments in *The Voice* have not been successful, Achebe's and Kourouma's experiments have been acclaimed for their success. A crucial difference in their approaches is that whereas Achebe tries to convey the idiom and tone of Igbo rhetoric, and Kourouma of the rhetoric of his mother tongue, Okara focusses more on arranging his English words according to Ijaw syntax. To those familiar with the problems of translation it might not come as a surprise that Okara's results do not work. For the strategy of translation is not to reproduce word for word with the aid of a dictionary, but rather to discover and use *idiomatic equivalents* between two languages, and to invent equivalents where none are available.

If the stylistic features of African oral narrative are to be captured in the African novel in English, it is necessary that the full range of linguistic resources of African prose traditions be rendered in English. Proverbs, legends, fables, puns, jokes, similes, metaphors, allusions, hyperboles, declamatory speech, rhetorical devices of conversation and public oratory—these are just some of the resources that need to be marshalled and so rendered that their flavor comes out in English. As Achebe has pointed out:

> The prose tradition of non-literate peoples is often presumed to consist of folk-tales, legends, proverbs, and riddles. Dr. Whiteley reminds us that these categories represent only a part of the tradition. I would go so far as to say that they represent the least important part. If one takes the Igbo society, which I know best, it seems quite clear that the finest examples of prose occur not in those forms but in oratory and even in the art of good conversation. . . . Serious conversation and oratory . . . call for an original and individual talent and at their best belong to a higher order. Unfortunately there is no way of preserving them in a non-literate society. One catches glimpses of the glory of Igbo oratory by listening to the few people remaining in the villages who can deploy the full resources of the language. . . . The good orator calls to his aid the legends, folk-lore, proverbs . . . of his people; they are some of the raw material with which he works. . . . One hopes that African writers will make use of them [proverbs] in dialogue, for which they were originally intended.
>
> (Achebe 1964: vii-viii)

In addition to capturing in the African novel the narrative devices of African languages, there is the task of appropriately employing the various types of English that are spoken by Africans, e.g., pidgin, creole, the English of secondary school leavers, the English of university graduates, officialese, etc. The task of capturing the flavor of African life in the African novel would be sadly incomplete if these were left out and if the King's or Queen's English were insisted upon in all contexts.

Here we should mention the successes of Tutuola and the Onitsha Market writers in producing their works in the variants of English used in their respective milieux. Instead of applauding them and administering sympathetic criticism that is compatible with these writers' aims, some African critics have expressed embarrassment and hostility at Tutuola's "bad English" (or "young English," as Dylan Thomas called it), and would on that account prefer to see such works excluded from the body of "serious" African literature.

We would like to point out that the King's English, or the English of schoolmen, is not the only kind of English. Writing in an English different from standard English should not be construed as "letting Africa down." Africans have no business speaking the King's English indistinguishably from an English don; and they have no business trying to prove to Europeans that Africans can speak or write European languages indistinguishably from Europeans. Therefore, no sense of embarrassment is warranted when an African deviates from standard English by speaking or writing an African variant of it. These observations would apply equally to African writing in any non-African languages.

(2) The question of introducing "anthropological" or "sociological" material into fiction is really only a special case of introducing expository material which the reader is likely to need in order to follow the narrative. In deciding what should be given expository treatment, it is important to bear in mind that the proper primary audience is the African audience. While some things about Kikuyu culture or history might need to be presented for the conveniece of non-Kikuyu African readers, features common to or understandable by most African cultures, e.g., polygamy, extended family, libation pouring, sacrifice to ancestors, and reincarnation, would not need to be so introduced. Only if the writer has in mind as his primary audience a non-African readership would it be necessary to explain matters of the latter type. For the African novel, as we have repeatedly urged, the proper audience is the African. Therefore, expositions required solely by the deficiencies of non-African audiences ought not to be encouraged. The job of making

African features understandable to non-Africans properly belongs to translators and to those who introduce appropriate editions of African works to non-African audiences. It is for them to supply appropriate glossaries, explanations, footnotes, etc., useful to their specific audiences.

When some information important for the narrative must be presented, care needs to be taken to do so in a manner that enhances rather than detracts from the narrative. Digressionary treatises which interrupt the narrative flow are probably the least desirable. While footnotes and glossaries might have their place, it seems preferable by far to so integrate the information into the treatment of the story that it does not obtrude, so that it is acquired, as it were, in the normal flow of the story. In this matter, Onuora Nzekwu and Chinua Achebe might be taken as examples of failure and success respectively. Whereas Nzekwu introduces such material by long passages that read like sociological treatises, or by conversations that provide information without advancing the story, Achebe proceeds in such a way that from the context a reader has little need to puzzle out the text or to pause for some elaborate treatise before he can continue.

(3) In the matter of descriptive devices and characterization techniques, there is much to be learned from African orature. More use can be made in the African novel of ideophones, descriptive names, praise names, metaphorical descriptions, germane and recognizable allusions, onomatopoeic imagery and other resources derived from the oral tradition. An exemplary use of many of such devices occurs in René Maran's *Batouala,* a novel with an African setting written, not by an African, but by an Afro-Caribbean who had spent a good part of his career in Central Africa. Chapter 11 of *Batouala* opens as follows:

> Brush roads, so wet in the morning, and so fresh.
> Damp perfumes, soft scents, shuddering grass, mur-

murs and rustlings caused by the breeze among the leaves; drizzling fogs, vapors—hills and valleys rising toward the pale sun; smoke, sounds of man, tom-toms, calls, cries, wake up! get ready! Ah! too high the birds sing in the trees! Too high the flight of the buzzards turns and turns! Too high is the sky whose blue seems pale in so much light!

A beautiful day! "Goussou" the brush, all the brush is going to burn! léhé, the m'balas, elephants with bowels always full of flatulence, there is no more time to trumpet! You, wart hogs, you, wild boars, you would do well to stop scooping out your dens with ravenous snouts! To us, antelopes! To us, cibissi and "to'ndorrotos"! Roll yourselves into balls and bristle your quills, to'ndorrotos! The fire will do what it will. Gogouas, run away bellowing your most beautiful wildbull songs. Flee in disorganized groups, tails straight out, kicking and jumping, belly to the earth, fear infusing your intestines with diarrhea, faster than the arrow, faster than the wind, as if, behind you, all of a sudden, you had heard Bamara the lion roar.

Depart also Oualas, you rabbits who are still called Darra'mbas! Frightened of the shadow of your long ears and of everything, now having confidence only in the rapidity of the zig-zags of your course, flee, flee! Fear the ferocious people of all the brothers of Djouma. Don't lie any longer in the folds of the land as brown as your body. Down with subterfuge! Even your burrows aren't secure. Go straight ahead, far from these blackish plumes of smoke announcing that fire is devouring the brush. You must flee, flee, flee! . . .

A beautiful day! A beautiful day! The flushing out by fire cannot help being full of game! Certainly, at the tally, one will not see Kolos or giraffes. These animals with very long legs and very long necks dominate the highest grasses. They usually live over there, very far away, between the Ouahm and Kabo, between Kabo and N'Délé, among the expanses rich in spiny plants on which they seem to feed.

Aha! the Kolos, with their tall spotted bodies. Another animal which will not be seen is the Bassaragba or rhinoceros, the massive Bassaragba, his muzzle burdened with two disproportionate horns.

The Bassaragba, his cruel little red eyes which see so poorly, the ugliness of his muscular and thick-set neck and shoulders, his formidable build, ayayai! . . .

As soon as he sees you, roou!—he charges straight for you, straight. Nothing deters his course. Through thickets, swamps, trees, and vines he breaks, crushing and ripping up everything in his path. Misfortune to the one who chases him! Misfortune to the one who wanders in the places where he grazes and chews his cud! May he keep on his guard, that one! May he invoke the all-powerful protection of N'Gakoura! And if by chance he should happen to come upon the still-steaming dung piles of Bassaragba, at the sight of their enormity, oh! above all, don't let him go away screaming, "Iche! how big it is!" For then, panting, heavy, grunting, moaning, angry, belly distended and retaining the perpetual storms which his digestion produces, Bassaragba arrives, jostles him, knocks him over, and by lying down on him makes him snap like dry bamboo, gets up, tramples him and finally goes away—patala-patala—only when the shapeless corpse is no more than bloody pulp, whose remains the jackals will share when night falls.

The best thing to do in such an event is to pinch one's nose, spit with disgust, and say: "Uffe! how that stinks!" For once these disrespectful words are uttered, Bassaragba the rhinoceros is shamed and takes off as rapidly as possible. . . .

No giraffes, no rhinoceroses, what matter! One hunts what one finds. The hunt is the game of the strong, the fight of man against beast, of skill against brute strength. It prepares for war. Prove who can his ability, his courage, his vigor, his endurance. When chasing the beast one has wounded, it is necessary to be able to run a long time without tiring or getting winded, and to be sure of eye, agile of foot, and lithe.

It is easy, with the help of the dogs, to snatch the rabbits, the cibissis and the hedgehogs in the snares of the stretched-out "banda." The mesh of the strings are irresistible traps for them.

But if one can, with force, trap certain kinds of small antelope this way, it is impossible to do the same in the case of the bozabo or horse-antelope, of the wart hog, of the wild boar, and of the elephants.

It is necessary to tire the first, harass them, wear them out, corner them, try to make them fall in specially prepared ditches. Now, indeed, when cornered, the wild bull becomes more than dangerous. Sensing death as little by little the blood drips from his wound, he faces the assailant and charges at him, head lowered. . . .

Chatting in this manner, Bissibi'ngui and Batouola, the former behind the latter, strolled along peacefully. Djouma followed them with lowered ears.

(Maran 1973: 127-30)

This presentation of country scene, with two persons talking along their way to the hunt, is done through a bardic voice as if conjuring up a picture before an audience. It employs direct physical description, as in the opening paragraph; it makes a roll call of the animals, some that will be seen in this hunt, some that will not, invoking them, summoning them by direct address:

You, wart hogs, you, wild boars, you would do well to stop scooping out your dens with ravenous snouts! To us, antelopes! To us, cibissis. . . .

It incorporates praise names and praise poems:

Nothing deters his course. . . . Misfortune to the one who chases him! Misfortune to the one who wanders in the places where he grazes and chews his cud! May he keep on his guard. . . .

It employs hunters' boasts:

> The hunt is the game of the strong, the fight of man
> against beast, of skill against brute strength. It prepares
> for war. Prove who can his ability, his courage, his
> vigor, his endurance. . . .

There are ideophones and onomatopoeia:

> Roou! . . . Patala-patala. . . . Uffe! . . . Iche! . . .

These are just some of the traditional narrative devices
which Maran uses to describe a scene and report a conversation. Innovative African writers should find study of Maran's work extremely rewarding. They should find equally
rewarding the works of others who have reworked African
traditional materials, and those who have modelled aspects
of their narrative styles upon that tradition. The following is
a partial list of such writers and their principal works: Birago
Diop, *Tales of Amadou Koumba;* Sol Plaatje, *Mhudi;* J.
Luke Creel, *Folk Tales of Liberia;* Zora Neale Hurston,
Their Eyes Were Watching God and *Mules and Men.*

Other works that would be invaluable for their study
would be the writings of Tutuola and those of D. O.
Fagunwa—the latter especially, if and when competent English translations become available. Innovative African writers
who can read Yoruba could of course go directly to Fagunwa.
The importance of Fagunwa for the African novel lies in the
fact that Tutuola, though writing in English, is regarded as
belonging to the Fagunwa tradition. Ayo Bamgbose in his
illuminating study, *The Novels of D. O. Fagunwa,* tells us
that

> Fagunwa . . . was quite familiar with certain works in
> English literature, including translations of stories from
> Greek mythology. Two possibilities were open to him.

269

> He could use his knowledge of English literature to
> produce a European type of novel . . . or he could
> create something of his own, drawing his inspiration
> from traditional material. It was the latter course that
> Fagunwa chose. Fagunwa based his novels on the
> tradition of the Yoruba folk-tale
>
> (Bamgbose 1974: 15)

And of Tutuola, Ayo Bamgbose informs us:

> Of all the writers in the Fagunwa tradition, the one
> writer who has been most successful to date is Amos
> Tutuola. Although his novels are written in English, it
> is quite clear that his brand of English is little more
> than a literal translation of Yoruba into English. So
> he may rightly be regarded as being in direct succession
> to Fagunwa. Tutuola's debt to Fagunwa is consider-
> able. Like the other writers in the tradition, he has
> borrowed the framework of Fagunwa's novels, partic-
> ularly in *The Brave African Huntress* and *Feather
> Woman of the Jungle*. . . . Apart from the framework,
> several incidents and characters are taken directly from
> Fagunwa. (p. 6)

Thus, Tutuola, whether by directly working from the Yoruba
folktale and narrative tradition or by borrowings or adaptations from Fagunwa, is in his English-language novels an
extension of an African tradition.

Bamgbose in his study reports several traditional narrative
devices employed by Fagunwa. These include: physical
description of characters, often in great detail for the unusual
or for fantasy persons or creatures, and hardly any at all
for normal human beings—a procedure which makes eminent
sense, for it can be taken for granted that a normal human
being has a neck or a belly, whereas it is the unusual which
most needs to be graphically brought to the reader's attention.
When descriptions of normal human beings occur, they tend
to be stylized, often using a mixture of negative descriptions
and positive descriptions of their persons and of their effects

on their surroundings. For example, according to Bamgbose, Fagunwa describes Adiitu as a handsome man. The reader is told that

> His head is not excessively big, his back is not thick and enormous like that of a tortoise, his neck is not longer than it should be; it is not like the neck of an ostrich, yet it is not too short, it is not like the neck of a cat.
>
> (Quoted in Bamgbose 1974: 128)

And part of the description of Iyunade, another character in *Adiitu,* is as follows:

> She is not unnecessarily and excessively fat, yet she is not lean like rake . . . her eyeballs are clear like the day, they are not bloodshot like those of a snake; her lips are not too thin, yet they are not very thick; the teeth are white like the clear sky; her legs are not skinny like the legs of chameleon, yet they are not thick and heavy like those of an elephant; the head is not big, it is not flat, it is not long—the Creator made it proportionately.
>
> (Quoted in Bamgbose 1974: 129)

Commenting on Fagunwa's use of negative descriptions, Bamgbose says:

> Another possible explanation of the negative description is that for Fagunwa, as indeed it is for the Yoruba in general, the most desirable state is 'a mean between extremes.' One of the highest compliments that can be paid to a girl is that she is physically 'moderate' and well-proportioned. This attribute is summed up in the word 'iwontunwonsi' (moderation) which is used quite often by Fagunwa in these descriptions. As shown in the above passages, the beautiful girl is one that is not too thin and not too fat, whose legs are not too short and not too long, whose head is not too big nor too small, whose lips are not too thick nor too thin, etc. By denying the extremes as he does in the

271

descriptions, Fagunwa is emphasizing this desirable mean. The description itself must of course be seen for what it is—a fanciful, stylized generalization which does not in any way convey any picture of the person being described. (p. 130)

We seem here to have a case of a narrative device that is rooted in traditional values. Usage of such techniques by Tutuola would be an instance of debts owed by the African novel to traditional African narratives and values.

Other techniques employed by Fagunwa include character depiction by use of symbols, by use of appropriate names that sum up a character or give a clue to his behavior, and by use of historical sketches that give either the genealogy of the character or an account of his past deeds, or of significant incidents in his life.

Tutuola, like Fagunwa, gives physical descriptions, often in great detail, for fantastic characters and unusual persons and places, but scant descriptions or none at all for normal human beings. For instance, in *The Palm-Wine Drinkard,* whereas the Tapster, an ordinary human being, is hardly described at all, the Complete Gentlemen is presented in terms of his physical appearance, his dress, his impact on onlookers, and even his potential worth were he up for sale. Likewise, in *Feather Woman of the Jungle,* Famine Town and its inhabitants are presented as follows:

> This town was very big and famous. It was near a very wide and deep river. Immediately I entered the town, I was greatly shocked first with fear when I saw the terrible appearances of the people or the inhabitants. Every one of them was so leaned that he had no more muscle on his body. Every one of them was as thin as a dried stick. The legs and arms were just like sticks. The eyes were seeing faintly in the skull except the head which was so big that the thin neck could not even carry it. Both upper and lower jaws had already dried up like a roasted meat. The

stomach was no more seen except the breast and exposed ribs.

(Tutuola 1962: 68)

Also the nymph is presented as follows:

> As far as I saw her, she was about thirty years old. Her eyes were very clear and the face was very fresh as the face of a fifteen-year-old girl. There were no scars or pimples on her cheeks or face and the hair of her head was not so much dark but of course, probably the climate of that town had turned the hair to be like that. Her teeth were very white and very closely to each other. Her nose was quite pointed like that of an image, the slippers on her feet were made from the soft leather of crocodile. She had clear and lovely voice and her face always seemed as if she was kind and merciful.

(Tutuola 1962: 74)

In Tutuola, some examples of character presentation of persons and places by appropriate naming are: The Complete Gentleman, the Faithful-Mother, the Television-handed Ghostess, Death, Feather Woman of the Jungle, Drum, Song, Dance, Laugh, Wraith-Island, Town of Famine, Town of the Water People, Red-People, Red-Bush, Red-Town, Red Lady, Bush of Ghosts, Give and Take, Invisible-Pawn, etc.

Character presentation by use of historical sketches, whether by reciting a character's genealogy or recounting his past deeds and important incidents of his life, can readily be seen as an adaptation from the widespread African practice of greeting or introducing persons by reciting their praise names. Praise names often include references to the deeds of one's ancestors as well as one's own deeds. An exemplary modern use of this device in the novel is in the opening paragraph of Chinua Achebe's *Things Fall Apart* where Okonkwo is introduced to the reader through his reputation as a wrestler, highlighted in the second paragraph by a description of his exploit in the particular wrestling match that established his reputation.

In addition to the examples of technical achievement in Achebe, Tutuola and Maran, we would like to call attention to the achievements of those writers who have resuscitated in modern form various genres of African narrative. Among them are Yambo Ouologuem with his historical epic, *Bound to Violence;* Tutuola with his heroic epics, *The Palm-Wine Drinkard* and *My Life in the Bush of Ghosts;* Ferdinand Oyono with his social satires, *Boy* and *The Old Man and the Medal;* and Mongo Beti with his social satires, *Mission to Kala, The Poor Christ of Bomba,* and *King Lazarus.*

Ousmane Sembene's works, especially *God's Bits of Wood* and *The Money Order,* deserve special mention as the most successful to date in the group of African novels devoted to exploring the African experience in the late colonial and post-colonial eras. He is to be commended for an uncompromising realism and for a thorough critical eye which both enable him to avoid the sentimentality and vagueness present in the works of some other African writers dealing with the same experience. Also exemplary is his adoption of the point of view of the ordinary people in treating his material. In this respect, he can be said to continue the tradition of *the people's griot.*

Poetic Eloquence and Its Devices

What has been said for narrative rhetoric naturally applies also to the matter of poetic eloquence. But in addition, we shall now consider other matters which are specific to poetic diction.

As we said earlier, the three tendencies current in African poetry are the euromodernist, the African traditionalist, and the middle-ground miscellany of individual voices. Having already shown that the stock in trade of the euromodernists is obscurantist ineloquence rather than eloquence, we shall concentrate here on the traditionalist and middle-ground poets and see what we can discover from their practice about poetic eloquence and its devices.

The middle-ground poets, such as Gabriel Okara and Lenrie Peters, have over the euromodernists the virtues of clarity and simplicity of diction. However, lacking the strengths which the traditionalists are exploring and absorbing, they run a great danger of being prosaic. Basically, they have no powerful ideas to explore or moving stories to tell, and when they do, their lack of the devices of eloquence is a source of the discursive and prosaic quality of their product. For instance, they exhibit a sparseness of metaphoric language; they are not rich in powerful and compelling imagery; their voice lacks assurance, lacks sustained lyrical sweep, and they tend to be low-keyed, intellectual, and distant in their stance. Passion, energy, and cutting irony are not the hallmarks of their poetry. When they approach eloquence here and there, it is rarely sustained.

With all these limitations, however, the middle-grounders are still better poets than the euromodernists. Their prosaicness is at least honest, whereas that of the euromodernists is disguised by obscurantism and syntactic jugglery. But in all, it is the traditionalists who are pointing the way to eloquence in modern African poetry, and to them we shall now turn.

An inescapable condition for a poet's eloquence is that he should have something fully formed and clear to say. No amount of girdles can mold pap into a pillar. But given that basic element, poetic eloquence becomes a matter of various devices—of diction, of imaging techniques, of logistics or the strategies of organization and development, and of tone and style of utterance. We shall examine these devices very concretely by looking at the works of the later Okigbo, of Awoonor, Kunene, Okot, and Senghor.

In the early Okigbo we find a developing persona, not yet fully formed, struggling for expression through a motley of fragmentary and half-formed thoughts, unfinished images, with a brilliant flash here and there. In his "Heavensgate" and "Limits" the plot of the story is not worked out, and this contributes to a fragmentary and half-cooked quality which even his notes (in *Labyrinths*) do not remedy. Though these works occasionally flash with considerable power, their lack of coherent plot, finished story and well formed thoughts makes them rather sorry imitations of Okigbo's anglomodernist masters.

In contrast, the later Okigbo of "Path of Thunder" emerges with a fully-formed persona of town-crier speaking in confident tones of prophetic utterance, advising, describing, warning, denouncing, protesting, chiding:

> AND THE HORN may now paw the air howling
> goodbye . . .
>
> For the Eagles are now in sight:
> Shadows in the horizon—
>
> THE ROBBERS are here in black sudden steps of
> showers, of caterpillars—
>
> THE EAGLES have come again,
> The eagles rain down on us—
>
> POLITICIANS are back in giant hidden steps of
> howitzers, of detonators—
>
> THE EAGLES descend on us,
> Bayonets and cannons—
>
> THE ROBBERS descend on us to strip us of our
> laughter, of our thunder—

THE EAGLES have chosen their game,
Taken our concubines—

POLITICIANS are here in this iron dance of mortars,
    of generators—

THE EAGLES are suddenly there,
New stars of iron dawn;

So let the horn paw the air howling goodbye . . .

O mother mother Earth, unbind me; let this be my
    last testament; let this be
The ram's hidden wish to the sword the sword's secret
    prayer to the scabbard—
                    (Okigbo, "Elegy for Alto")

Among the devices of his new but sadly brief and final eloquence are his incorporation into his poetic oratory of proverbs, fables, praise chants, parabolic and gnomic sayings. Equally important is the maturation of his musicality and of his previous experiments upon strategies for developing and organizing his material. He now speaks in an alternation of long cadenced lines and abrupt declaratives organized for cumulative impact, reinforcing one another and strongly and clearly delineating the precise things which Okigbo wishes to convey. The confidence in his new tone and the power of his style come in part from the maturation of his persona and craft, and from the fact that he has something to say and with great urgency.

In Kofi Awoonor we find a sage voice employing devices of effective eloquence. His stance is one of public utterance. His poetic strategy is one of an educational encounter with his audience. The observant sage, reflecting on communal memories, pleads, cautions, questions, tells and points things out to his audience. He is sometimes mocking, sometimes contemplative, using illustrations and admonitions from the communal repertory:

What has not happened before?
Though they said
The prince should not hasten for the stool
and the young leopard
Should not be in haste to walk
There are noises in the air.
The young leopard should stand up against
the tree.
And the prince should run for his father's stool.
The turbulent river becomes calm again
The desert river was dry
Before the harmattan came
And the storm wind does not
Frighten the eagle.

My people, where have you been
And there are tears in your eyes?
Your eyes are red like chewed kola
And you limp towards the fetish hut.
My people, what has happened
And you bear many cudgel wounds
and rope marks cover your naked bodies?
Wipe away your tears
And knock the door of the sacred hut
The gone-befores are waiting for you.
                    (Awoonor, "I Heard a Bird Cry,"
                         Night of My Blood, p. 44)

With Mazisi Kunene we find an elegiac voice with a sensibility grounded in the natural and perceived world of a South African homeland, drawing extensively from a world outlook little touched by European influences:

I who have sung you songs over the years
I depart.
The staff is broken
The young ebony plant sinks in the mud.
These winds are wailing with seeds.
They will scatter them on the open space

Where rains will give birth to jungles.
I believe in the great day
Which will make our paths meet:
I shall wake then from the desert
Seeing you approach with pots filled with water.
We shall sit at the place of the old man
Untying the knots in the expanse of the afternoon,
In the fertility of the fig tree
In the vastness of the willow tree
In the savannahs of the fleeting antelope.
        (Kunene, "A Farewell," *Zulu Poems,* p. 38)

Was I wrong to laugh asphyxiated ecstasy
When the sea rose like quicklime
When the ashes on ashes were blown by the wind
When the infant sword was left alone on the hill top?
Was I wrong to erect monuments of blood?
Was I wrong to avenge the pillage of Caesar?
Was I wrong? Was I wrong?
Was I wrong to ignite the earth
And dance above the stars
Watching Europe burn with its civilisation of fire,
Watching America disintegrate with its gods of steel,
Watching the persecutors of mankind turn into dust
Was I wrong? Was I wrong?
        (Kunene, "Thought on June 26,"
        Zulu Poems, p. 41)

Kunene deploys metaphors of elemental grandeur; his images are primal, not artificial or technologized. He employs cumulative repetitions and parallel phrasing to draw out and build up the power of his precise metaphors and his elegiac understatements.

In Okot we find an informal, humorous, witty, unvarnished style of great vigor. The utterance is tuned for public outcry by the power of direct address and dramatic evocation. After all, you don't cover your mouth or speak with your mouth full of water when you want to be heard and

understood. One with something to praise, lament or denounce
has no difficulty understanding the need for clarity:

> He says
> They are fighting for Uhuru
> He says
> They want Independence and Peace
> And when they meet
> They shout "Uhuru! Uhuru!"
> But what is the meaning
> of Uhuru!
>
> He says
> They want to unite the Acoli and Lango
> And the Madi and Lugbara
> Should live together in peace!
> He says
> The Alur and Iteso and Baganda
> And the Banyankole and Banyoro
> Should be united together
> With the Jo-pa-Dhola and the Toro
> And all the tribes
> Should become one people.
>
> He says
> White men must return
> To their own homes,
> Because they have brought
> Slave conditions in the country.
> He says
> White people tell lies,
> That they are good
> At telling lies,
> Like men wooing women.
> Ocol says,
> They reject the famine relief granaries
> And the forced-labour system.
> > (Okot p'Bitek, *Song of Lawino,* pp. 180–181)

And while the pythons of sickness
Swallow the children
And the buffalos of poverty
Knock the people down
And ignorance stands there
Like an elephant,
The war leaders
Are tightly locked in bloody feuds,
Eating each other's liver
As if the D.P. was leprosy
And the Congress yaws

(Lawino, p. 196)

Okot abundantly dips into the traditional repertory of images and metaphors based on the flora and fauna of his native East Africa. His technique includes the use of multiple metaphors, repetitions, and parallel phrasings to give cumulative power. Songs and lullabies are freely incorporated into his texts:

Or when your daughter
Sings a lovely lullaby
To her baby brother
Strapped on her back,
And she sways forwards and backwards
As she sings

> *O baby*
> *Why do you cry*
> *Are you ill?*
> *O baby stop crying*
> *Your mother has fried the aluru birds*
> *In ghee!*

(Lawino, p. 203)

Here is my bow-harp
let me sing greetings to you,
Let me play for you one song only
Let me play and sing
The song of my youth:

She has taken the road to Nimule
She will come back tomorrow
His eyes are fixed on the road
Saying, Bring Alyeka to me
That I may see her
The daughter of the Bull
Has stayed away too long
His eyes are fixed on the road

All I ask
Is that you give me one chance.
Let me praise you
Son of the chief!

(*Lawino*, pp. 215–16)

In Senghor we find the elevated, polished formal style of a court griot, a praise-singer, recounter of communal history, treasurer of the communal memory who must evoke things past and half-forgotten through a verbal embroidery of vivid scenes:

Femme, pose sur mon front tes mains balsamiques,
tes mains douces plus que fourrure.
Là-haut les palmes balancées qui bruissent dans le
haute brise nocturne
A peine. Pas même la chanson de nourrice.
Qu'il nous berce, le silence rythmé.
Écoutons son chant, écoutons battre notre sang sombre,
écoutons
Battre le pouls profond de l'Afrique dans la brume
des villages perdus.

Voici que décline la lune lasse vers son lit de mer
étale
Voici que s'assoupissent les éclats de rire, que les
conteurs eux-mêmes
Dodelinent de la tête comme l'enfant sur le dos de sa
mère

Voici que les pieds des danseurs s'alourdissent, que
s'alourdit la langue des choeurs alternés.
(Senghor, "Nuit de Sine," *Chants D'Ombre*)

(Woman, lay upon my forehead your balsam hands,
your hands softer than fur.
Above us, the swaying palm trees but barely rustle,
high up there among the night breezes.
Not even a lullaby is to be heard.
It is only the rhythmic silence that cradles us.
Let us listen to its song, let us listen to the beat of
our dark blood,
Let us listen to Africa's deep pulse beating in the mist
of forgotten villages.

Now the weary moon goes down to her bed over the
sluggish sea
Now the peals of laughter grow drowsy, and even the
storytellers
Are nodding their heads like a child on its mother's
back
The dancers' feet grow heavy, and heavy the tongues
of the alternating choirs.)

In this mode of public communication, Senghor employs
a lyrical style marked by the flowing cadences of long lines,
by parallel phrasings, and by the highly evocative device of
comparing a thing to various other things in a sequence of
metaphoric tropes which highlight its various aspects and
attend it as a praise poem attends a ruler or a great man
or woman:

Femme nue, femme noire
Vêtue de ta couleur qui est vie, de ta forme qui est
beauté!
J'ai grandi à ton ombre, la douceur de tes mains
bandait mes yeux.
Et voilà qu'au coeur de l'été et de midi, je te découvre
terre promise du haut d'un haut col calciné

Et ta beauté me foudroie en plein coeur comme l'éclair
d'un aigle.

Femme nue, femme obscure!
Fruit mûr à la chair ferme, sombres extases du vin
noir, bouche qui fais lyrique ma bouche
Savane aux horizons purs, savane qui frémis aux
caresses ferventes du Vent d'est
Tam-tam sculpté, tam-tam tendu qui grondes sous les
doigts du Vainqueur
Ta voix grave de contre-alto est le chant spirituel de
l'Aimée.
(Senghor, "Femme noire," *Chants D'Ombre*)

(Naked woman, black woman
Clothed in your color which is life, in your form which
is beauty!
I grew up in your shadow, and the softness of your
hands was laid over my eyes.
And now, in the heat of summer and of noon, suddenly
I come upon you, my Promised Land, from the
top of a sun-baked hill
And your beauty strikes me to the heart like the flash
of an eagle.

Naked woman, dark woman!
Mellow fruit with firm flesh, sombre ecstasies of black
wine, mouth that makes lyrical my mouth
Savannah of pure horizons, grassland trembling under
the fervent caresses of the east wind
Sculptured tom-tom, tight drum booming under the
fingers of the Vanquisher
Your solemn contralto voice is the spiritual song of
the Beloved.)

What is made clear by the manifest eloquence of these
traditionalist masters of contemporary African poetry is the
need for African poets to study well the spririt, structure,
devices, attitudes, and forms of Africa's orature. They cannot

284

properly utilize in their works the history or mythology of their people, or the flora and fauna and landscape of their locality unless they have studied them with devotion. Nor can they effectively take their images from their immediate environment and their contemporary society unless they have observed them carefully and well. Such study will make it unnecessary for them to borrow seasons of an alien land to mourn their country's loss. They cannot hope to masterfully speak with the styles of eloquence of their own culture until they have mastered the technical devices of their orature. The need for re-immersion in the traditionalist sources, and for sustained apprenticeship in traditionalist attitudes and craft, cannot be underestimated, especially for those nurtured in a disorienting euromodernist sensibility. It is asinine to assume, as many supposedly learned African critics and poets do and urge, that these things can be adequately imbibed from the air, as it were, without conscious and determined study. The masters in the traditional milieu attained their mastery only after intense and prolonged apprenticeship and study; and there is no reason whatsoever to think that persons brought up in a milieu dominated by Western culture can absorb enough from traditional Africa without an at least equally rigorous and deep apprenticeship.

THE ROLE OF AFRICAN CRITICS
IN THE DECOLONIZATION OF AFRICAN LITERATURE

How can our critics support and aid our writers in their efforts to decolonize and Africanize their techniques? In posing this question in this manner, we wish to emphasize that the role of the critics is secondary. Their proper role is that of a helper, not legislator, to writers and audience. Their authority exists only insofar as they remain representative of the society for which the writers produce. They certainly have no independent authority to lord it over either writers or audience. In the ideal state of things, where everybody in the society is sufficiently educated to serve as his or her own critic, the role of the professional critic ought to disappear. That, we believe, would be a very healthy thing. A recognition of this fact should teach professional critics some genuine humility. It is with all this in mind that we now address ourselves to the supportive function that African critics must learn to perform if they are not to be obstacles to Africa's cultural decolonization.

High on the list of what they could supply to both the writers and their audience would be a well researched and well analyzed knowledge of things valued in traditional African orature, and why these are valued. Their top priority should be to investigate Africa's artistic values and to transmit their findings to writers and audience alike.

Secondly, by correctly reflecting and sharpening the community's sense of these values, the critics can help that interplay between writers and audience who work from common assumptions, values and expectations in order to make and enjoy a healthy, confident culture. As helpers and advisers delegated by a community to guide its writers to better accomplishments, it is the critics' responsibility to hold up to the writers' work the mirror of their own community and not a mirror from any alien land. This is a principle which African critics must always bear in mind and consciously apply.

Under this ground rule, the functions of the African critic include the following:

1. Writing advertising jingles for publishers.
2. Exploring themes and ideas, thereby illuminating the layers of meaning beneath the surface of a given work; evaluating the work and situating it within the African literary tradition.
3. Exploring the relationships between African art, the African artist, and African society.

4. Criticism of craft for the purpose of:
   (a) nurturing talent by encouraging and discouraging tendencies among African artists;
   (b) educating the taste of the African public.

The economics of literature makes function 1 necessary. Among our critics of poetry, function 2 has largely been neglected. Misled by euromodernist example and precept, they have been preoccupied with what should be the unnecessary preliminary of prospecting for the surface meaning of texts. Such a diversion and waste of critical effort would, of course, be uncalled for if our poets took the trouble to be clear. When well done, function 2 aids the reader in his efforts to get the most out of a given work. Function 3 is always important to the sociologists and historians of literature, but secondary to the concerns of craftsman and audience, the producers and consumers of art.

But it is function 4 that should be at the core of the critic's concern, for if good works are to be produced and enjoyed, skill and virtuosity have to be encouraged in the maker, and a sensibility for appreciating what is well made has to be developed in his audience. For this purpose, the ability to judge, and common values upon which to base judgment, must be developed. To do this effectively, African critics must develop an African esthetic, encourage an awareness of African tradition, and play the role of critical intelligence guiding the transmission of African cultural values. Whereas the artist creates cultural artifacts, the critic evaluates them. Where the artist is a maker of well-made things, the critic is a maker of judgments.

How well do our critics carry out these functions? Not very well. The active ones among them, as we have seen, appear determined to forget the fundamental ground rule and to hold Europe's mirror to Africa's writers. If they have their way, they will convert African literature into a tributary of European literature. For instance, one common failing is in their habit of attempting to force African works into the procrustean beds of an alien esthetic. This brand of criticism insists on applying Western paradigms or models to African works, predictably concluding that the African work fits the Western model and, by implication, is thereby worthy of recognition by "the world." This is the mentality of cultural inferiority which responds to foreign cultural challenge with "proof": "We've modelled ourselves after you; we've met your standards. Please accept us!"

In their effort to subsume African works under the supposedly legitimizing categories of the Western esthetic, similarities become translated into influences, even in cases where these similarities are clearly fortuitous. For instance, Sunday Anozie imputes the conflicts and supernatural events in Tutuola's *Palm-Wine Drinkard* to biblical influences, even though African folklore and mythology, to which Tutuola is, above all, faithful, is replete with such conflicts and events (Anozie 1970b: 80–88).

Similarly, Charles Nnolim goes to great pains to demonstrate that Achebe's *Things Fall Apart* is an African epic, by which he presumably means an epic written by an African to European specifications. He claims that *Things Fall Apart* is "modelled on" *Beowulf,* and he proffers as proof that "as in *Beowulf* there lurks in *Things Fall Apart* certain persistent elements in Anglo-Saxon thinking like *Wyrd* (Fate) " (Nnolim 1971: 55–60). We suppose that in Nnolim's thinking the Anglo-Saxons not only invented but also hold a world-wide copyright on the concept of Fate.

The truth of the matter is that his use of English apart, Tutuola's mythic imagination is completely within the Yoruba African tradition. For proof, read D. O. Fagunwa who depicts a similar world—but in Yoruba. And Achebe's *Things Fall Apart* was, as he himself has often said, a deliberate (and successful) effort to recreate a pre-Westernized African reality, using authentic Igbo characters, situations, values and religious concepts, and bending the English language to express Igbo proverbs and idioms. That it was written after *Beowulf* and shares some similarities with *Beowulf* does not mean that it was modelled on *Beowulf*. (That I am a man, and older than you are, does not mean I am your father.) Nnolim's *post hoc propter hoc* fallacy (as professional logicians call it) perpetuates the colonial attitudes which seek to deny the originality of our traditions and to deprecate the fidelity of some of our artists, such as Tutuola and Achebe, to those traditions.

These attitudes must be traced to the failure of our learned critics to develop a contemporary African esthetic. To develop a contemporary African esthetic calls for a search into African oral and written traditions—an endeavour which our learned critics tend to disdain.

Unlike the few active and eurocentric ones, others of our critics are content to publish their doctoral dissertations, throw together an anthology of African verse or the like, and then sit down in their three-piece suits, occasionally rousing themselves from sinecured indolence to grind out a paper on Shakespeare or John Donne. In choosing to write on Shakespeare or Donne they are neglecting African needs to cater to European desires. Come to think of it, we can't quite decide whether it is better to do nothing, like most of our learned critics, or to actively do harm, like Mr. Sunday Anozie and his *Conch* coterie.

Anozie claims to be experimenting with critical approaches. Using scraps dredged up from Claude Levi-Strauss, he is engaged in constructing a critical pseudo-system which he calls "structuralism." Issue after issue of his periodical, *The Conch,* is deluged with structuralist paraphernalia; mathematical formulas, circles, squares, triangles, swiggles and other geometric doodles, all encased in opaque scholarly jargon. Simple ideas are elaborately draped in esoteric rags, blocking understanding. From the point of view of central critical concerns, Anozie's structuralist analysis of African literature approaches unedifying irrelevance. Anozie attempts to elucidate both difficult and obscure poetry, such as Okigbo's (Anozie 1969: 19–29; 1970a: 54–65) and simple, unobscure prose, such as Tutuola's (Anozie 1970b: 80–88), with the still more obscure equipment of his structuralist machinery. Whether applied to African poetry, prose or folklore, the result has been equally disastrous. It is like alchemical experiments trying to turn gold into ash. A critical approach to African literature based on structuralism may yet prove to be of value. But Anozie's present effort, insofar as it attempts to explain the obscure by the more obscure, is a useless endeavour.

Now, rather than a disorientive eurocentrism or a disorientive irrelevance, the task of our African critics is to formulate an African esthetic—which in the field of literature would include a poetics, a narrative rhetoric, and a dramaturgy—adapted to the needs of contemporary Africa. This may well be the centerpiece of their function as nurturers of artistic sensibility.

Artistic sensibility usually determines a writer's characteristic emotional and intellectual responses to literature. It determines what experiences he converts into literature, and how he treats them. It also sets up standards of valuation which determine what is valued, what is held in low esteem, and what is ignored. An African esthetic must be grounded in an African sensibility, and the incontestably uncontaminated reservoir of African sensibility is the African oral tradition. It is from there, therefore, that we must extract the foundation elements of a modern African esthetic.

Usually an esthetic is an after-the-fact codification of exemplary devices and characteristics extracted from an already established and acclaimed body of masterpieces—the classics of a given culture. Some might say that there is at present not a sufficient body of contemporary African writing, and that much of the oral tradition has not been recorded and made available; and therefore that we do not have as large a body of masterpieces as is desirable for that analysis that must precede the formulation of an esthetic. This may be true. However, because contemporary African culture is embattled and, in addition, is patently being led astray by apers of alien traditions, African writers and critics can no longer postpone the investigation necessary for the formulation of an esthetic. Otherwise the field will, before long, be preempted by an alien and deleterious one.

Therefore African critics should begin now to record, assemble and analyze the vast store of traditional material in African languages, materials both written and oral; must begin to study and analyze them in order to extract guidance towards the formulation of a contemporary African poetics, narrative rhetoric, and dramaturgy. The paucity of available material surely should not be turned into an excuse for not doing the job. Since there is a vast uncollected treasure of materials, the smallness of the material already collected should indeed goad the critics to intense research activity. Given our circumstances, this task cannot be postponed.

THE ROLE OF AFRICAN DISSEMINATORS AND CONSUMERS IN THE DECOLONIZATION OF AFRICAN LITERATURE

We have so far discussed the writers and critics of African literature. They are culture workers. They are, as it were, the producers and foremen of Africa's literary industry. Now we shall turn our attention to the distribution and consumption of literary artifacts by the society, and the relationship this bears to the mentality of the producers and foremen.

The African literary industry has been quite responsive to the demands of its consumers. The most important among these consumers have so far, and lamentably, been the eurocentric critics and the European as well as Europeanized readership for whom these critics serve as connoisseurs. It is therefore not surprising that our poets especially have been trying very hard to produce artifacts that would be liked by their primary Western audience.

Given this responsivness on our writers' part, the most effective way to cure them of their europhilia, and to wean them from the neo-colonialist hegemony of European culture, would be to generate an extensive African audience, a nationalist, right-minded one that would displace the Western audience from its insidious position as the primary audience of African writers. It is our belief that the esthetic and thematic demands from such an audience would be heeded by our writers, and that their attention and adulation would be an offer which our writers couldn't possibly refuse.

The situation up to now in Africa is that literacy is a very scarce cultural item. But with the spread of universal primary education and adult literacy, it should not remain scarce for long. Thus, a huge audience equipped to participate in a continental literary culture can be foreseen. If the ongoing criticism of neocolonialism should simultaneously continue, an audience will come into begin that is sufficiently large and right-minded. The process of producing such a large, literate, afrocentric audience, we believe, can no longer be reversed. It is part of the inescapable dynamic of our times. Like most things, it may not be easily achieved, but it will be done in another generation or two. The tide of African history is flowing strongly in its favor. When such an audience finally emerges in sufficient strength, it shall give short shrift to such misguided African writers who might still insist on taking their cues from Europe or anywhere else outside Africa, i.e., from any audience but itself.

In the meantime, while such an audience grows, there is much it could do to cure the writers we now have of their eurocentrism and of their perfunctoriness about craft, and to wean them to the literary equivalents of the high and afrocentric standards of the African oral tradition. This growing audience can make its demands felt by exercising the power of its patronage upon Africa's artistic media. As part of its motivation for consciously doing so, it should realize that African development is not merely a matter of growth in GNP statistics; more importantly, it is a matter of shaping the right cultural institutions, of creating the right consciousness in the African population, so that this consciousness can properly guide the production, distribution and consumption of the items usually reflected in GNPs.

Among the cultural media upon which the growing afro-centric audience would have to exert its influence would be the schools and universities, the newspapers and magazines, libraries, radio and TV stations and cinemas of the continent. They would have to insist not only that these media be widely established, but also that they, the public, shall control what cultural fare they disseminate. We are entirely aware that these media, as they have so far evolved, serve as conduits into African consciousness and culture for the worst elements from both the "high" and "popular" cultures of the West. Such pernicious influence cannot be sloughed off without control of these media being first withdrawn from the West and from its agents, African and Western, in Africa.

The complementary job of changing and improving the contents and standards of these media will require the release of the vast creative potentials of the African population—potentials that have been sat upon, mutilated, or burnt away under colonial and neo-colonial control of Africa. The growing African cultural public, in its campaign to free Africa from the shackles of imperialism, can expect collaboration from the genuinely nationalist elements among the elite; they can also expect to win more of the elite to their side in their endeavours, till the recalcitrant dregs of the elite either take themselves out of the siutation or are forcibly reformed.

True, the entire African population has been tainted by Western debasement, but the taint is not as deep and thorough upon the non-elite majority as it is upon the members of an elite who have been systematically trained and inducted into eurocentrism, and whose thoughts and habits have been so re-formed in the process that, in some cases, it is hard to see any remnant of any drop of African nationalism they might have imbibed during the anti-colonialist movement of the 1940s, 50s and 60s.

There is much ground, therefore, for the view that the general African population remains the reservoir of that African nationalism which shall bring about the end of alien cultural hegemony over Africa. What they have lacked so far have been the right opportunities for ending such hegemony; but the ongoing changes taking place throughout the world shall, we believe, supply them with all the opportunities they need in order to succeed.

Those who presently manage Africa's media, especially the Africans among them, should, as members of the *African* elite, shape up and carry out their responsibilities to the developing African literary audience and, through them, to African culture and its decolonization. They should throughly reexamine the aims, contents, and built-in biases of whatever cultural institutions they manage. They should realize that these institutions exist to serve the interest of the African public and not the interests of Western culture. They should therefore use these schools, libraries, newspapers, magazines, radio and TV stations, cinema theatres, etc. to launch programs which serve to raise African nationalist consciousness and African literary standards. They should resist all efforts that would continue to make them conduits for foisting European values and standards upon Africa. As part of their contribution to this fight against alien cultural hegemony, they could commission books, phonodiscs, films and movies which will help the development of Africa's nationalist consciousness. By commissioning our writers to supply them with the right kind of materials, they would be helping in the task of curing our writers of eurocentrism.

They can begin right now by commissioning these elite *litterateurs* to write for the popular daily, weekly and monthly press. Writing stories, articles and reviews for the popular press, instead of for the elitist intellectual journals, could change the attitudes of these writers by making them use materials from the lives and experiences of the African community. Such writing on their part would be a most needed antidote to the "arty," precious, vanity writing they now do for the elitist intellectual journals. Responding to the audience of the popular press should make them produce well-crafted written equivalents of the traditional master-works of African verbal art. Our writers clearly do need to be given a chance to save themselves from the inbred tastes cultivated within the parochial coteries of elite literary magazines.

Those who control the media, being among the factory managers of our cultural industry, and being disseminators who are in touch with the African public, could become the transmitters who convey to African writers and critics, and in no uncertain terms, the expectations and commands of the African public. The instructions of an African nationalist audience, if effectively conveyed, would provide the best motivation for our writers and critics to cease being university-bound and eurocentric, to break out of the confining habits of their training, to snap out of that meningitis in their intellectual spines which so far has kept their cultural necks twisted away facing their present primary audience far away in the West and its academies. They will help bring these cultural prodigals home in the most important sense, that is, in their consciousness and their cultural loyalties.

THE ROLE OF THE AFRICAN EDUCATIONAL SYSTEM IN THE DECOLONIZATION OF AFRICAN LITERATURE

In preparing the grounds for the germination of a liberated African literature, a central project is the creation of a unified community of writers, critics, disseminators and consumers of African literature, a community unified in their experience of the African tradition of orature and literature, unified in their fundamental expectations of African literature, and unified in the values by which they produce, judge and consume that literature. For the creating of such a unified community, Africa's educational institutions and educational processes need to be modified in the following minimum respects:

The European language and literature departments need to be abolished and replaced by three others: (1) a department of African languages, literatures and oratures; (2) a department of comparative literatures; and (3) a department of colonial languages which would teach the reading and writing of the official languages of African countries but without the disorienting encumberance of the national literatures of the European colonizers who imposed these official languages. For example, for as long as English remains the official language of Nigeria, it will be necessary to teach Nigerians how to read, write and speak English. But it must be emphasized that for the learning of these skills, it is not necessary for Nigerians to study England's literature.

We shall now examine some of the justifications for and aims of this project.

The Department of African Languages, Literatures and Oratures

There is a need for each African to be exposed in thorough depth to at least one African culture and its orature and literature. With such an in-depth exposure, an African would be in a better position than now to understand other African cultures. He would then have a solid experiential and intellectual base for comparing notes with Africans who speak other languages. He would also be in a better position to avoid or stop wild speculations and outright lies regarding the relationship between African orature and African literature in non-African languages. He would have firm experiential roots upon which he could resist Western blandishments and disorienting dicta about esthetic matters. And, perhaps most important, his consciousness would have a firm grounding in one branch of that African orature whose values must be at the center of the process of synthesizing a modern African literature, one branch of that traditional element which must control contributions from outside Africa.

In order to meet this goal, it would be necessary for each university to require each of its students to demonstrate proficiency in the language, literature and orature of one African culture before he may be allowed to graduate. Such a demonstration should involve an ability to think, talk, read and write in the student's chosen language, and an ability to translate material from that language into the national language of his country, and vice versa. Thus, a student must be able to pass an oral as well as a written exam in the African language of his choice. A mandatory part of his training for this exam should include the collecting, writing down and translating of pieces of African orature. A student before graduation would be required to have collected, written down and translated material of whatever genre—oratory, drama, poetry, narrative, etc.—not excluding medicinal and culinary recipes and technical instructions for doing or making things in some traditional way. It would be the responsibility of the departments of African languages, literatures and oratures to (1) collect and compile such transcripts of orature and supervise their translation from the original African language into the national-official language so others could share it; (2) translate African works written in European languages into African languages; (3) translate works from one African language into other African languages. As the products of this kind of preliminary work are disseminated, they would pave the way so that, some day, a continental African language could emerge—one which would have absorbed inputs from various national experiences, one whose speakers would then share a common body of references, experiences, values, etc.

It should be emphasized that a given department of African languages, literatures and oratures does not have to be comprehensive or polyglot. All that is necessary is that each such department should study and teach the languages, literatures and oratures of the area in which it is located. A cardinal principle to be upheld is the *equality* of all African languages, with each developing and flourishing in its locality.

Though the researching and developing of this particular project is a matter for the universities, such requirements would have to be extended throughout the educational system. At each level—elementary school, secondary school or university—an appropriate and demonstrated degree of proficiency in an African language, literature and orature would be mandatory.

This project is, in our view, the cornerstone of any effort to root out the eurocentric preoccupations of our literature. The more we know about ourselves, the more difficult will it be for anyone to disorient us, for we can challenge their aspersions and put-downs out of our own lived experiences and our studies. Wild and glib disorienting dicta will not take root in African minds which are properly prepared.

The Department of Comparative Literatures

A department of comparative literatures would have the responsibility of exposing students to a wider breadth of literatures than those of France, England, Portugal or other West European countries. It would be its responsibility to expose them to the literatures of other parts of the world— South American, Chinese, Indian, North American, Russian, South Asian, etc.—as well as the literatures of Europe and, of course, of Africa. Such exposure would give African students of literature the proper breadth of perspective from which to see through the parochialisms and ethnocentrisms of the pseudo-universalist literatures and criticism that reach them from the West. By being enabled to compare African literatures with the literatures of the world, they would be put in a position to acquire a proper respect for the African achievement in literature and orature.

The Department of Colonial Languages

For as long as the colonial languages remain the official languages of African countries, it would be necessary for Africans to learn to read and write and speak them. Thus a department of colonial languages would be necessary so that, for instance, Nigerians could conduct their official business in English and also conduct their inter-African business in French, Portuguese, etc. When the departments of African languages, literatures and oratures have done their work and Africa has evolved a continental official language to replace the colonial ones, then the department of colonial languages would have to be abolished.

It is important to emphasize that the department of colonial languages should not be permitted to teach the national literatures of England, France, Portugal, etc. We do not need to study England's literature in order to learn English. Ditto for French, Portuguese, etc. Whatever exposure to English language literature one needs in order to learn the English language should be acquired by studying African literature in English, Afro-Caribbean literature in English, and Afro-American literature. If this is judged insufficient, it could be supplemented with good English-language literary texts, both those originally written in English and excellent translations into English from the literatures of the various peoples of the world. What one wishes to learn about the English language must be done without having to imbibe *England's* national prejudices, values and outlook.

CHAPTER 5
Conclusion
▼▼▼▼▼

In our introduction we contended that African culture is under attack. As examples in support of that contention, we have examined some of the charges levied against African fiction by eurocentric critics from premises based on the 19th-century European concept of the well-made novel; we have considered the pseudo-problem whether there is such a thing as the African novel, what it is, and what should belong to it; we have outlined some of the malicious motivations for generating those pseudo-problems which seem designed to divert African creative and critical energies into waste-work in intellectual cul de sacs, and thereby keep them from solving other real and pressing problems; we have also examined the perhaps unconscious importation into the African literary scene of problems that arose in European criticism of European literature, importations done without any attempt being made to question their relevance or applicability to the African setting.

We have examined the hegemonic intentions of eurocentric criticism of African literature and how it has led African poetry astray, how it has attempted to scotch African nationalist consciousness in African literature and attempted to replace it with a pro-European pseudo-universalist, individualist consciousness and values. This foreign domination of African culture is long overdue for overthrow.

We have also examined the quality of the criticism itself, its sloppiness, flabbiness of thought, confusions, somnambulism, imprecision, gerrymandering of evidence, employment of invented "facts" and other *larsonies*. The motivating malice behind this awful performance is that many of these eurocentric critics insist either that Africans are completely different from Europeans, or completely alike but of lower status; consequently, they seem uncomfortable with the notion that in some respects Africans and Europeans are similar, and that they are different in other respects, and that there are, in addition, gray areas of overlapping characteristics and attributes. They also choose to forget habitually that the mere fact of difference does not imply superiority, or even any ranking at all. Their racist and imperialist prejudices would seem to account for much of their exercise in perjorative ranking of African materials—an exercise in which pseudo-problems are constructed and elaborately debated to help imperialist scholars and their African wards to publish lest they perish in their academic rat-race. It was probably the worst thing that happened to the quality of intellectual life when the livelihood of academics was made dependent on the tonnage of paper they cart to editors and publishers. Much that should have gone into wastepaper baskets has found its way into print. Thus, a remedy devised for unproductivity has turned into a cancerous growth that threatens the health of the African literary landscape.

To Western critics we say: take your hegemonic hands off African literature! It is within their rights to interpret to their Western audience whatever literature they please. But it is not within their rights to tell Africans how to receive and what to think about African literature. In their comments on African literature they should show the proper respect for the autonomy of that literature. It is neither their stepchild nor whipping boy.

To African critics we must point out the need for them to liberate themselves from their mesmerization with Europe and its critical canons. They also need to raise the quality of their criticism. The half-baked ideas, unexamined assertions, wild speculations, mystifications, careless thinking, muddled logic, vague generalities, slippery argumentation and other intellectual misdemeanors to which they are prone, are a gross disservice to their own intelligence and to African literature and its readership. African critics need to acquire the habit of thinking things through thoroughly, checking their facts, analyzing them in detail, disciplining their thinking with the rigors of logic. Our critics should not be afraid of facts, of displaying the factual evidence for whatever position they propound. Ultimately, criticism is a branch of scholarship, not of mysticism.

It also needs to be pointed out to our African critics that *literary criticism* is ultimately a branch of *social criticism*. Social criticism of literature demands that critics evaluate a work not merely on its technical virtuosity but *preeminently* by its contributions to the society's thoughts and understanding, by the probable impact upon the consciousness of the society of what the work has to say, and by showing where the work stands within the society's literary tradition. Textual criticism is a preliminary matter; and it is a society's values that should guide its social criticism, not some other values allegedly universal, timeless, transcendental, etc. Society functions within time, space and the movements of history. It is not a Platonist Ideal Form or Idea *sub specie aeternitatis* in some realm allegedly beyond change and decay. More extensive and thorough contact with non-European literatures and thought would make our critics startlingly aware of how ridiculously parochial they sound when they propound their allegedly universal precepts. It would help cure them of a certain narrowness in their values, expand their understanding of what literature and criticism are all about, and help save them from the asphyxiation of Europe's rarefied Parnassus.

In addition, criticism is a species of the essay, and its quality should be made first rate. Critics should train themselves to be, among other things, prose stylists of first quality.

This book has been concerned with intellectual and cultural bush clearing—a job made necessary so that solid ground can be reached on which foundations may be laid for a genuinely liberated African literature. One would have wished that such bush-clearing work were unnecessary; but given the havoc wrought by imperialist hegemony over our culture, it has been unavoidable. This bush-clearing work, together with this laying of new foundations, constitutes the minimum cultural mission of our generation. It is for us to discover the rest of that mission and to accomplish it.

APPENDIX
What is African Literature?

Before an adequate determination can be made of what body of works we are talking about when we say "African literature," there are a few theoretical matters that need to be disposed of. These concern *concepts* and the *sets* they denote, *evolving* and *non-evolving sets,* and the *intensional* and *extensional definitions* thereof.

The concept of African literature, or the term "African literature," has a connotation and is also used to denote a particular set of objects. A given set of objects can either be displayed (individually named, or denoted), or it can be referred to by a term that connotes it. Any given set of objects is either an *evolving set* or a *non-evolving set,* depending on whether or not new members are added to it from time to time.

In defining any set, there are two known kinds of procedure: an intensional definition, and an extensional definition. An *intensional* definition is one which tells us the sum of the qualities and attributes which must be possessed, and the conditions which must be satisfied by every member of the set. An *extensional* definition, on the other hand, displays or names the individual objects which are members of the set. The crucial point of the distinction is that whereas the *intensional* approach to defining a set proceeds by describing conditions, qualities and attributes, the *extensional* approach to defining the same set proceeds by naming individual objects each of which satisfies the conditions and possesses the qualities and attributes stated in the intensional definition.

For a *non-evolving set,* an *intensional* definition is usually supplied by describing the necessary and sufficient conditions for membership in the set. This means that each and every one of these conditions would have to be met by a candidate before it could qualify for membership in the set. To meet some but not all of the conditions is to be disqualified; and no more need be met to qualify. For a *non-evolving set,* an *extensional* definition, on the other hand, would either name all the individual objects which are members of the set, or it would display (i.e., name) an initial sub-set of the set, and then supply a decision procedure for determining the rest of the members of the set. Such a decision procedure, when it is used, can be of two sorts: an *iterative algorithm* for generating the undisplayed sub-set, or an *intensional definition* of the undisplayed sub-set.

For an *evolving set,* an *intensional* definition is characteristically problematic. Most conditions that are advanced turn out to be neither necessary nor sufficient, precisely because the set that is being defined is unfinished, evolving, and, given the protean nature of evolving things, there are too many exceptions to any criterion that could be named. This is what makes it futile to attempt to give an *intensional* definition of an evolving set. In coming to grips with the membership of an *evolving set,* an *intensional* definition, with its rigid inventory of necessary and sufficient conditions, is therefore far less helpful than some appropriate version of an *extensional definition.*

It should be observed that an *extensional definition* cannot display or name *all* the members of an *evolving set;* it would therefore have to name an initial sub-set and then supply some decision procedure for determining the rest of the members of an evolving set. The required decision procedure cannot be an iterative algorithm precisely because an *iterative algorithm* is a predetermined procedure, whereas an evolving process cannot be. Similarly, the decision procedure cannot be an *intensional definition* precisely because the conditions, qualities and attributes of the end products of an evolving process cannot be predetermined. A decision procedure with an *evolving character* is what would be required. And an example of such a procedure would be a generative principle which operates by *family resemblances*. Family resemblance, as is well known, is not determinable by a set of necessary and sufficient conditions since, for example, two persons who are the spit and image of each other may not be related at all, while a set of twins sometimes look and act quite differently from each other. Set membership by criteria of family resemblance is clearly of the sort where even an object which meets most of the criteria for inclusion could still be excluded by a minority of very weighty counter-considerations. It is a pragmatic rather than a rigid or dogmatic approach.

In the specific case of literatures, a *non-evolving set* would be the literatures of eras dead and gone, e.g., the literatures of Pharaohnic Egypt, classical Greece, ancient Rome, medieval Europe, Tang Dynasty China, Pre-Tokugawa Japan, Inca, Aztec and other Pre-Columbian America, and Pre-Colonial Africa. An *evolving set* would be any ongoing literature of the present day or era, or any literature so defined as to include an ongoing literature of the present day or era. This means, for instance, that whereas Tang Dynasty Chinese literature is by itself a *non-evolving* set, all of Chinese literature, including the literature of the Tang Dynasty and of China today, is an *evolving* set.

To return to the practical matter at hand, that of determining what body of works constitute African literature, it should be clear by now that the concept of African literature, like the concept of other national or regional literatures, is one whose denotation is an *evolving set*. It cannot be defined with a simple, clear-cut, dictionary-like definition, through an enumeration of necessary and sufficient conditions. It is therefore not at all surprising that many conferences on African literature, where the standard approach is to try and

Reference List

ABIMBOLA, WANDE
1968 "The Second Odu of Ifa." *Black Orpheus,* 2, 2: 7–12.

ABRAHAM, Willie
1962 *The Mind of Africa.* London: Weidenfeld & Nicolson.

ACHEBE, CHINUA
1964 Foreword to *A Selection of African Prose,* I: *Traditional Oral Texts,* ed. W. H. Whiteley, vii–x. Oxford: Oxford University Press.
1969 *Things Fall Apart* (1959). Greenwich, Conn.: Fawcett Publications.
1975 *Morning Yet On Creation Day.* London: Heinemann.

AIDOO, AMA ATA
1968 "Poets and Ostriches," *West Africa* 2641, January 13: 40–41.

ANOZIE, SUNDAY O.
1969 "A Structural Approach to Okigbo's *Distances.*" *The Conch* I, 1: 19–29.
1970a "Poetry and Empirical Logic: A Correspondence Theory of Truth in Okigbo's *Laments.*" *The Conch* II, 1: 54–65.
1970b "Structure and Utopia in Tutuola's *Palm-Wine Drinkard.*" *The Conch* II, 2: 80–88.

ARMAH, AYI KWEI
1977 "Larsony: Fiction as Criticism of Fiction," *First World* 1, 2: 50–55.

AWOONOR, KOFI
1971 *Night of My Blood.* New York: Doubleday.

BAMGBOSE, AYO
1974 *The Novels of D. O. Fagunwa.* Benin City, Nigeria: Ethiope Publishing Corp.

BANHAM, MARTIN
1962 "The Beginnings of a Nigerian Literature in English." *Review of English Literature* 3, 2: 88–99.

BEIER, ULLI
1967 *Python: Ibo Poetry*. Port Moresby: Papua Pocket Poets.
1970 *Yoruba Poetry*. Cambridge: Cambridge University Press.

BIEBUYCK, DANIEL
1972 "The Epic as a Genre in Congo Oral Literature." *African Folklore*, ed. Richard M. Dorson, 257–73. New York: Anchor.
1978 *Hero and Chief: Epic Literature from the Banyanga (Zaire Republic)*. Berkeley and Los Angeles, California: University of California Press.

BIEBUYCK, DANIEL AND KOHOMBO C. MATEENE
1969 *The Mwindo Epic, from the Banyanga,* as reprinted in *A Treasury of African Folklore,* ed. Harold Courlander, 322–51. New York: Crown Publishers, 1975.

BIRD, CHARLES S.
1974 *The Songs of Seydou Camara, Vol. I: Kambili*. Bloomington: Indiana University African Studies Center, Occasional Paper in Mande Studies.

BORGES, JORGE LUIS
1968 *Other Inquisitions*. New York: Simon and Schuster.

CASTRO, FIDEL
1962 "The Second Declaration of Havana," quoted in *The Mythology of Imperialism* by Jonah Raskin, epigraph. New York: Delta Books, 1971.

COLEMAN, ALEXANDER
1977 "Beyond One Hundred Years of Solitude." New Boston Review, January 1977: 21–22.

CREEL, J. LUKE
1960 *Folk Tales of Liberia,* Minneapolis: T. S. Denison and Co.

DIOP, BIRAGO
1966 *Tales of Amadou Koumba,* tr. Dorothy S. Blair. London: Oxford University Press.

DIOP, CHEIKH ANTA
1974 *The African Origin of Civilization*. Westport, Connecticut: Lawrence Hill & Company.
1978 *The Cultural Unity of Black Africa* (1959). Chicago: Third World Press.

ECHERUO, MICHAEL
1966 "Traditional and Borrowed Elements in Nigerian Poetry," *Nigeria Magazine* 89: 142–55.
1968 *Mortality*. London: Longmans.

ELIOT, T. S.
1965 "American Literature and the American Language" (1953), in *To Criticize the Critic*, 43–60. New York: Farrar, Straus, and Giroux.

FELDMANN, SUSAN
1963 *African Myths and Tales*. New York, Dell.

FINNEGAN, RUTH
1967 *Limba Stories and Story Telling*. Oxford: Oxford University Press.

FORSTER, E. M.
1927 *Aspects of the Novel*. New York: Harcourt Brace Jovanovich.

HAMPATE-BA, AMADOU
1966 "Monzon and the King of Kore," in *Presence Africaine* 58 (English Edition): 95–124.

HOWARD, W. J.
1973 "Themes and Development in the Novels of Ngugi," in *The Critical Evaluation of African Literature,* ed. Edgar Wright 95–119. London: Heinemann.

HUGHES, LANGSTON
1926 "The Negro Artist and the Racial Mountain," *The Nation,* June 23: 692–94.
1959 *Selected Poems*. New York: Knopf.

IZEVBAYE, D. S.
1975 "The State of Criticism in African Literature," *African Literature Today* 7: 1–19.

JAMES, ADEOLA
1975 Review of *An Introduction to the African Novel* by Eustace Palmer, in *African Literature Today* 7: 147–52.

JAMES, GEORGE G. M.
1976 *Stolen Legacy* (1954). San Francisco: Julian Richardson Associates.

JONES, ELDRED DUROSIMI
1973 *Wole Soyinka*. New York: Twayne.
1975 Editorial, *African Literature Today* 7.

KUNENE, MAZISI
1970 *Zulu Poems*. New York: Africana Publishing Corporation.

LARSON, CHARLES R.
1972 *The Emergence of African Fiction* (revised edition). Bloomington: Indiana University Press.

LESLIE, OMOLARA OGUNDIPE
1973 Review of *The Emergence of African Fiction* by Charles R. Larson, *Okike* 4: 81–89.

LEVY, ALAN
1972 "Ezra Pound's Voice of Silence," *New York Times Magazine*, January 9: 14–15, 59–65, 68.

MACEBUH, STANLEY
1975 Poetics.
1976 "Poetics and the Mythic Imagination." *Transition* 50/*Ch'indaba* 1: 79–84.

MCDERMID, SUSIE
1974 Introduction to *Tales from the Basotho* by Minnie Postma, tr. from Afrikaans by Susie McDermid. Austin: University of Texas Press.

MALCOLM X
1965 *The Autobiography of Malcolm X*. New York: Grove Press.

MARAN, RENÉ
1973 *Batouala* (1921). Rockville, Md.: New Perspectives.

MOORE, GERALD
1962 *Seven African Writers*. London: Oxford University Press.
1965 *African Literature and the Universities*. Ibadan: Ibadan University Press.

NIANE, D. T.
1965 *Sundiata: An Epic of Old Mali,* tr. G. D. Pickett. London: Longmans, Green & Co.

NNOLIM, CHARLES E.
1971 "Achebe's *Things Fall Apart:* An Igbo National Epic." *Black Academy Review* 2, 1 & 2: 55–60.

NOSS, PHILIP A.
1972 "Description in Gbaya Literary Art," *African Folklore,* ed. Richard M. Dorson, 73–101. New York: Anchor.

NWOGA, DONATUS
1967 *West African Verse: An Anthology.* London: Longmans.
1974 "Obscurity and Commitment in Modern African Poetry." *African Literature Today* 6: 26–45.

OBIECHINA, EMMANUEL
1975 *Culture, Tradition and Society in the West African Novel.* Cambridge: Cambridge University Press.

OKIGBO, CHRISTOPHER
1971 *Labyrinths.* New York: Africana Publishing Corporation.

PALMER, EUSTACE
1972 *An Introduction to the African Novel.* New York: Africana Publishing Corporation.
1973 "Vox Populi, Vox Sembene: A Preliminary Look at the Art of Ousmane Sembene." *Ba Shiru* 5, 1: 3–13.
1975 "A Plea for Objectivity: A Reply to Adeola James." *African Literature Today* 7: 123–27.

P'BITEK, OKOT
1966 *Song of Lawino.* Nairobi: East African Publishing House.

POST, K. W. J.
1969 Introduction to *Arrow of God* by Chinua Achebe. New York: Anchor.

POSTMA, MINNIE
1974 *Tales from the Basotho,* tr. from Afrikaans by Susie McDermid. Austin: University of Texas Press.

POVEY, JOHN
1972 "The Novels of Chinua Achebe," in *Introduction to Nigerian Literature,* ed. Bruce King, 97–112. New York: Africana Publishing Corporation.

ROSCOE, ADRIAN A.
1971 *Mother is Gold: A Study in West African Literature.* Cambridge: Cambridge University Press.

SENGHOR, LEOPOLD SEDAR
1974 *Poèms.* Paris: Editions du Seuil.

SOYINKA, WOLE
1966 "And After the Narcissist?" *African Forum* 1, 4, 53–64.
1967 *Idanre and Other Poems.* London: Methuen & Co.

1969 "Salutations to the Gut," in *Africa in Prose,* ed. O. R. Dathorne and W. Feuser, 357–63. Baltimore, Md: Penguin.
1975 "Neo-Tarzanism: The Poetics of Pseudo-Tradition." *Transition* 48: 38–44.

STEVENSON, W. H.
1976 *"The Horn:* What It Was and What It Did," in *Critical Perspectives on Nigerian Literatures,* ed. Bernth Lindfors, 215–41. Washington, D. C.: Three Continents Press.

TIBBLE, ANN
1965 *African English Literature.* New York: October House.

TUTUOLA, AMOS
1953 *The Palm-Wine Drinkard.* New York: Grove Press.
1962 *Feather Woman of the Jungle.* London: Faber & Faber.

VINCENT, THEO
1975 "Two Decades of Modern Nigerian Literature." *Oduma* 2, 2: 57–67.

WILLIAMS, CHANCELLOR
1974 *The Destruction of Black Civilization.* Chicago: Third World Press.

Index